Books of Merit

All the Good Pilgrims

All the Good Pilgrims

TALES OF THE
CAMINO DE SANTIAGO

Robert Ward

Thomas Allen Publishers
Toronto

Library and Archives Canada Cataloguing in Publication

Ward, Robert, 1962–
All the good pilgrims : tales of the Camino de Santiago / Robert Ward.

ISBN 978-0-88762-252-6

1. Santiago de Compostela (Spain)   2. Christian pilgrims and pilgrimages—
Spain—Santiago de Compostela.   I. Title.
DP285.W37   2007   914.6'11   C2006-906994-8

Editor: Janice Zawerbny
Cover images: istockphoto (hiker), Alamy (shell)
Maps: Lightfoot Art and Design

Published by Thomas Allen Publishers,
a division of Thomas Allen & Son Limited,
390 Steelcase Road East,
Markham, Ontario L3R 1G2 Canada
www.thomasallen.ca

  **Canada Council
for the Arts**

The publisher gratefully acknowledges the support of
The Ontario Arts Council for its publishing program.

We acknowledge the support of the Canada Council for the Arts, which last
year invested $20.1 million in writing and publishing throughout Canada.

We acknowledge the Government of Ontario through the Ontario
Media Development Corporation's Ontario Book Initiative.

We acknowledge the financial support of the Government of
Canada through the Canada Book Fund for our publishing activities.

12 13 14 15 16   2 3 4 5 6

Printed and bound in Canada

"A todos los buenos peregrinos. Y a los malos también."
To all the good pilgrims – and the bad ones as well.

– A PILGRIM'S INSCRIPTION IN THE
GUEST BOOK OF ESTELLA

Thank you to my editor, Janice Zawerbny, and my publisher, Patrick Crean, for their help and patience; Dennis for good advices; the Little Company of Pilgrims for moral support; the Ontario Arts Council and Toronto Arts Council for timely financial aid; Mom for being my number one fan; and Michiko for making all things possible.

Thanks to the pilgrims and the people of Spain who have given me leave to tell their stories and to those who have not.

In memoriam, brother Steve. You're coming with me next time.

And Alan Hickey, 1930–2006. See you up ahead.

Contents

ATLANTIC OCEAN

BAY O

GALICIA

Finisterre / Fisterra
Cée
Negreira
Arca Arzúa
Melide
Santiago de
Compostela
Palas
de Rei
Portomarín
Sarria

Montes de Galicia

O Cebreiro
Villafranca
del Bierzo

LEÓN

Montes de León

Ponferrada
Manjarín
EL BIERZO
Astorga
Hospital
de Órbigo
Villar de
Mazarife
El Burgo
Ranero

León Mansil
las Mu

THE

PORTUGAL

N

0 km 20   40   60   80

BISCAY

GOLFE DE GASCOGNE

FRANCE

St-Jean-Pied-de-Port

Pyrenees

Roncesvalles

Pamplona

Puente la Reina

Estella

Los Arcos

Viana

Logroño

Grañon

Nájera

Belorado

San Juan de Ortega

Burgos

Hontanas

Castrojeriz

Carrión de los Condes

CASTILLA

LA RIOJA

NAVARRA

SPAIN

FRANCE

PORTUGAL

SPAIN

MEDITERRANEAN SEA

All the Good Pilgrims

Introduction

How did I ever come to be a pilgrim? For someone with my secular upbringing, it's not what you would have predicted. I guess it all started with my legs. They've always been restless, moving, tapping, bouncing, even when I sit still. They love to climb and scramble and take me places, and once they get up some steam, they want to keep going—just to the top of this hill, just around the next corner, just to the other side of that bridge. I like to think this is some memory-in-the-body passed down from countless generations of wandering ancestors. Who knows. I can only say that my legs always had a long walk in them.

Now, if my heart and mind had been nomads like my legs, I would never have needed the Camino de Santiago. I would simply have stepped out my front door one morning, turned left or right depending on which seemed to hold the most promise, and walked till I got tired, then picked up the next day and walked some more. But I'm not a vagabond. I need some structure and ritual—a coffee in the morning, a bed at night, and people to keep me company in the hours between. I also like the idea of a destination, preferably one that's foreign, exotic and old.

What I wanted was *a journey*. An adventure on foot like the ones in books—watching distant mountains grow closer by the day, knocking apples off the trees of autumn orchards, pausing at village wells, huddling around fires in smoky inns to swap tales with fellow travellers. Of course, the irony of these yearnings was not lost on me. For ages, we humans have done everything in our power to go faster, striving to *be* where we want to be without all the time and bother of *getting* there. And there I was, the thankless inheritor, gazing out the windows of speeding vehicles and dreaming of walking.

I suppose I could have walked if I had wanted to badly enough. It was always just a matter of calling to the driver, "Excuse me, could you let me out here?" (a ploy that works better on a bus than an airplane). But then the walking would have been alone, and much of it on the shoulders of highways. The old paths had been paved over, foot journeys were a thing of the past—or so I thought. But it turned out I was not the only one with restless legs and dreams of wandering. There were many more out there, and an enterprising few were already walking their dreams into life on an ancient pilgrimage road known as the Camino de Santiago.

"You make the road by walking it," wrote the Spanish poet Machado, and the Camino was the road made by millions of pilgrim feet as they walked from the Pyrenees in the east of Spain to Galicia in the far west, where the remains of the Apostle James were said to lie. For more than a millennium, pilgrims journeyed to Santiago as a penance, a prayer, an act of thanksgiving, many travelling hundreds, even thousands of kilometres. Bridges, monasteries, cities and towns sprang up along their path to ease their passage; the Camino was a human landscape shaped by a journey.

Then along came the twentieth century, and with it two world wars, the Spanish Civil War, the long dictatorship of

Franco and, more disruptive than any of these—at least where the Camino was concerned—the proliferation of planes, trains and automobiles. Pilgrims never stopped going to Santiago; they just stopped going on foot. By mid-century, the millennial flow of walkers had dried up, it seemed forever.

But every novelty wears thin with time. Even as European travel reached new levels of speed and comfort, people began to remember that there is more to a journey than the destination, that the getting there can mean as much as the arriving. They grew nostalgic for the old, *un*comfortable ways. With Spain's entry into the European Union and reopening to the world, restless feet found their way back to the Camino. The first pilgrims in the seventies were pioneers cutting the foliage back from an overgrown path. But year by year their numbers grew, so that by 1991, when I first heard of the Camino, the journey I had dreamed of, complete with food, lodging and companionship, was once again "in service." And what a journey it was. Eight hundred kilometres of ancient roads, passing through grand cities and sleepy villages, mountains and vineyards, wheat fields and green, rolling hills, all culminating in a glorious destination, the holy city of Santiago de Compostela.

So did I rush off to Spain and start walking? I did not. Years passed before I took my first step on the Camino. What held me back? Partly fear that the dream which had kept fresh for so long in my imagination would spoil in the open air. But beyond that was the fact that the Camino wasn't just any long walk; it was a pilgrimage, a living expression of Christian (specifically, Catholic) faith—and what right did I have to walk with the pilgrims? I was not Catholic, or Christian, or even particularly what you'd call *spiritual*. The word *pilgrim* summoned images to my mind of penitents slinging rosaries

and chanting psalms. Were these companions I could happily share the road with? Would I even be welcome to tromp
on their holy ground? It took several years for my restless
legs to win over my doubting heart, but at last, in July 1999,
I arrived in St-Jean-Pied-de-Port on the French side of the
Pyrenees to begin my journey to Santiago de Compostela.

The next five weeks passed at the speed of footsteps. I
lived the moments of my dream journey, watching the distant mountains grow closer—and looking back to see them
recede. And it was clear from the start that my fear of not
being welcome among the pilgrims had been groundless.
Everyone was welcome on the Camino. It was understood
that each of us had our reasons for what we were doing, and
those reasons were not questioned. The renewed Camino
was not just a Catholic road; it was the pilgrimage for everyone who wanted to make a pilgrimage. And somewhere along
the way, I realized that included me. I was a pilgrim and had
always been one. It was something that dawned on me day by
day, not a lightning flash on the road to Damascus, but a slow
recognition that "pilgrim" is another way of understanding
who we are, and that to make a pilgrimage is only to formal-
ize that understanding.

My first Camino was over in thirty-seven days, but when
I got home I found it wasn't over at all. I was still walking it
every day. I had brought home a bagful of souvenirs—faces,
questions, laughter, places, clouds, vastnesses, lessons half
learned—like the bag of shells, birds' feathers and driftwood
you bring home from a week by the sea. At any moment of
the day I might catch myself examining them, trying to piece
them together and make sense of them. But they were fragments, intimations. I could no more assemble the Camino
from them than you can reconstruct a beach from shells and
driftwood.

I went back. In June 2000, I walked for ten days, from León to Sarria. Then, in the fall of that year, I again walked the "whole" Camino, from St-Jean to Santiago, with the (ostensible) motive of writing about the miraculous Madonnas of the Way, a task that kept me busy for a couple of years. By 2003, however, my legs were ready for another long walk. I wondered if it was time for a new road. There are pilgrim trails in Japan, Norway, Italy, Ireland . . . Or why not approach Santiago from a different direction? The route I had followed till then, the Camino Francés, or French Camino, was only one of many roads to Santiago, albeit the most celebrated. But then I began to dream, night after night, of a certain hour and place on the road to Santiago . . . And I knew the Camino wasn't finished with me yet.

I returned in the fall of 2003. With only two weeks at my disposal, I thought I would mix walking with bus and train hops, seeing a few favourite places and winding up in Santiago. But once I'd started walking, I found I couldn't stop. So I forgot about the trains and buses and just kept on, step by step, as far as Castrojeriz. There, two weeks from the holy city, I stood on a windy ridge, watching the figure of a friend I had accompanied dwindle in the distance. The *meseta* stretched as far as I could see, a vast promise. All I wanted to do was race down that slope and out across the plain in the direction of Santiago. I knew I had done it all before. That made no difference. I wanted to do it all again to find what the Camino still held in store for me. I promised myself I would come back, to be once more a pilgrim.

PART I

Once More a Pilgrim

First Steps

The day begins early with seeing my wife, Michiko, off at Madrid airport. Then it's a frantic crosstown trip on the metro to the long-distance bus terminal, where I arrive just in time to catch the ten o'clock service to Pamplona. For six hours my attention twitches between the TV at the front of the bus (today's feature: *Lost in Translation*) and the Spanish earth flashing by the window. There's time for a quick coffee in Pamplona before I hop on the local bus to Roncesvalles in the Spanish Pyrenees. And now here I am in a minivan, whistling down the French side of the mountains to the town of St-Jean-Pied-de-Port—from where, tomorrow morning, I will take the first steps of the 780-kilometre walk to Santiago de Compostela.

So much speed in the service of slowness.

We are driving into a dense, drizzling mist. Out the window, I can just make out the coniferous forest on the left. The drop on the right I can only guess at. Probably just as well. Our driver, impatient for his Friday supper, cheerfully accelerates through the switchback turns of the two-lane highway, braking only a smidgen to manoeuvre around a truck that has flipped on its back like a beetle. There are five of us in the back of the van. An hour ago, coming up from Pamplona, the bus was packed to the roof with more than forty pilgrims-to-be, their bags, walking sticks, hopes and dreams. Most of them decided, sensibly, that Roncesvalles was already far enough from Santiago and went no farther. Only we five have been perverse enough to tack one more stage onto our journey.

My fellow travellers are Alejandro, a Spanish university student who should probably be in school; Aaron, a fresh-faced young Australian who waits tables back home; and Inácio and Luis, middle-aged Brazilian professionals. As we wind down the mountain road, we try to explain, in the Camino's usual muddle of languages, our reasons for walking to Santiago de Compostela. Alejandro, before anyone has a chance to ask, assures us that for him it's "not a religious thing." It's a test, a chance to prove that he can tough something out. For Aaron it's a "spiritual journey" (we nod our heads, each of us interpreting "spiritual" in his own way), not to mention an adventure and a chance to appreciate a rich culture from up close. For Luis it's a Catholic pilgrimage plain and simple— or that's what he tells us. But his rugged mountain gear and the glint in his eye suggest he is also relishing the manly physical challenge of it. Inácio, clearly not one to be cornered, shrugs off the whole question. "Religion, spirituality—these are words. What do they mean? I'm doing the Camino because it is there."

A lull falls over the conversation. We peer out at the fog and the drizzle, perhaps entertaining some second thoughts. Early tomorrow, come rain or shine (and it's looking like rain), we'll be out walking, all the way back up the slope we're coasting down now. Then Inácio calls up to the driver.

"Monsieur, I hear there are two ways across the Pyrenees. Which way is this?"

"This is the route of Charlemagne, *le grand Charles*," says the driver. "It follows the valley. On the other way, the route of Napoleon, there is no road. You must walk over the open mountains."

"Tomorrow I plan to follow the route of Napoleon," says Inácio with a hint of grandeur, "but maybe that is not wise in this rain. Which way do you recommend?"

"Which way do I recommend?" The driver laughs. "I recommend driving."

The road levels out, the rain stops and we have reached St-Jean-Pied-de-Port. No cars are allowed in the steep, cobbled main street, which is the medieval *sirga*, the track of the Camino through town, so the driver drops us at the top, by the Porte St-Jacques, the Gate of St. James, or the Jondoni Jakue Atea as they call it here in Basque country. We hitch on our backpacks, thank him for the drive and are about to stroll through St. James's arch when Luis calls us all to attention.

"Whoa!" he says. "Stop and think about what you're doing. These are your first steps on the Camino de Santiago."

Luis is right to alert us to this moment. While we've all heard it said that life is a pilgrimage, it is also true that a pilgrimage is a life. We have left our homes and familiar comforts behind us, and as we pass through this arch, we are being born into our pilgrim selves. From this moment, we are part of a new family, a family of the road on its way to Santiago. In a few weeks, when we reach the gates of the holy city, we will die a little death and catch a glimpse of the life to come—or such is the traditional way of thinking. So the steps we are about to take through the Gate of St. James are our pilgrim baby steps, the first of a life-within-a-life. Let's show them some regard.

A few doors down the rue de la Citadelle, in the office of the Association des Amis du Chemin de Saint Jacques, the face that welcomes me back to the Camino is a familiar one. It's the same elderly volunteer *hospitalero*, sparse-haired and gaunt as a mantis, whom I met last year in the pilgrim refuge of Navarrete in Spain.

"*Mon ami*," he says, grasping my hand.

"I remember you," I say, thinking it best not to say that what I remember chiefly is a Spanish pilgrim in a wheelchair calling him a French son of a whore.

We had all expected to stay in the pilgrim refuge tonight, but the hospitalero has unhappy news. "The refuge is full. Full, full, full. The private hostels also, the hotels, every bed in town is full." He tugs at his wispy hair in despair. "I have never seen such crowds in September. Go knock on doors. Someone will take you in."

We leave the office unnerved. The first private hostel we call at is indeed full. But the second has plenty of beds. The proprietor shows us proudly around her centuries-old stone house, whose upstairs and downstairs bedrooms she has crammed with bunks. When we have staked out our beds, Luis and Inácio crash, Alejandro disappears with some Spanish girls, never to be seen again, and Aaron and I head down the road to a cider house called *Hurrup eta Klik*, Basque onomatopoeia, our hostess informs us, for the merry sounds of guzzling. I've been on the move since seven this morning. A little *hurrup* and *klik* sounds like just what I need.

We apply ourselves to our *steak frites* with diligence. It turns out that one of Aaron's motives for making the extra hop down to St-Jean was to have a meal in France. He is a serious foodie and expects his Camino to be a gastronomical pilgrimage. Right now he's a little shaky, giddy, talking fast as he looks ahead to his first day as a pilgrim. It's something he's been moving towards for years. Back in 2000 he was in England, all ready to come to Spain to do the Camino, when a family emergency called him back to Australia. He had to start all over, saving money from scratch, but now here he is. This infatuation with the Camino comes from deep within. He just knew he had to do it from the first time he heard some-one talk about it.

Same here, I tell him. For me the first time was in a book-store, when a cover illustration of a grizzled medieval pilgrim in a threadbare cloak caught my eye. The book was called *The Pilgrim Route to Compostela*. I had never heard of the Camino before, but as I pored over the black-and-white photos of churches, the hand-drawn maps, the detailed directions (the book dated from the seventies, before there were yellow arrows to point the way for pilgrims), I knew I had found what I was looking for. I bought the book as a string to tie around my finger. I never did read it.

We're well into the second pitcher of cider when Aaron says: "Can I tell you something? I saw you this afternoon in Pamplona when you were waiting for the bus to Roncesvalles. You were all by yourself in the plaza, with your stick and your hat and your backpack. And that's when I thought, 'This isn't a dream. People actually do this.' Before then it wasn't real. I'm going to remember that as the moment when the Camino began for me." Aaron has taken me by surprise. I see myself as a collector of the stories of others; it seldom occurs to me that I am a character in theirs. I am honoured that the Camino has chosen me to stand as "Pilgrim" in the frontispiece of Aaron's album of memories.

Aaron's wide-eyed wonder takes me back to my own first day on the Camino, and the first pilgrim I met. He was the only one left in my compartment when we arrived in St-Jean (that time I came by train from Bayonne), a Spanish man who resembled the medieval pilgrim on the cover of my Camino book. He was clearly a pilgrim, and I wanted to talk to him, but at the same time I was sure his motives for doing the Camino were more exalted than my own. With his leather sandals, raggedy backpack and air of Franciscan poverty, he looked like a penitent sinner, while I was just someone who wanted to take a long walk. So I hung behind him all the way to the pilgrim office, where we finally exchanged a few words. He was staying the night in St-Jean, while I was going on. I was both sorry and relieved that we wouldn't be walking together.

But while I spent two days getting to Roncesvalles, he covered the distance in one. When he saw me again there, he waved and hollered, *"Hola canadiense!"* His name was Manuel, and he always made a point of seeking me out and speaking to me. He didn't care about my motives for doing the Camino. I was the first pilgrim he had met, and that had forged a bond between us. It turned out that Manuel *was* a penitent, only not a willing one. His torments, like those of most pilgrims, were less of the soul than of the soles. With every step he took, the rigid inner frame of his sandals was digging an ugly cross-shaped scar into his flesh. He called it his stigmata—as a joke—and by the fourth day he'd done as much penance as he cared to. He took the bus back to Madrid, vowing to resume the Camino next year with better footwear. Whatever story he tells about the Camino today, I hope the *canadiense* is a part of it.

It's a little before eleven when Aaron and I roll into the dark, empty street, smelling like bushels of fermented apples. The sky above is clear, the stars scintillating. Aaron calls it a night, but nostalgia and a certain romantic craving draws me up the hill and through the Gate of Saint Jacques. Sadly, the area is saturated with light, just in case someone comes by and wants to read the historic plaques. But then the hour of eleven strikes and the floodlights are quenched. Thank you, Saint James. It takes a minute for my eyes to adjust to the country darkness, and then I see what I have come to see: dense and white as a marker streak, the Milky Way flowing across the sky in the general direction of Santiago de Compostela.

He is James to us, Iago to the Spanish, Jacques to the French. To his own people, he was Yakob. He was a fisherman, the son of Mary Salome, some say a cousin of Jesus, whom he laid down his fishing net to follow. He died in Jerusalem in the year CE 44 when, as the Book of Acts tells us, "Herod the king stretched forth his hand . . . And he killed James the brother of John with the sword."

But this was only the first act of James's story. One night in the mid-ninth century, after an intermission of nearly eight hundred years, a hermit named Pelayo saw strange lights on a hillside in the remote Spanish province of Galicia. Bishop Teodomiro sent men to investigate, and an old Roman sarcophagus was uncovered. The bishop spent days in fasting and prayer, then declared that the bones within the tomb were those of the Apostle James, he who had once fished the Sea of Galilee, he who now sat at the right hand of the Lord.

The whole thing was wildly improbable. James had died in Jerusalem. What was his body doing in Spain? But it is in the nature of miracles to be improbable. It was said that in life James had spread the word of Christ in Hispania. Spain's Christians, hungry for a champion in their struggle against the Moors, were delighted to believe that in death he had returned. King Alfonso the Chaste confirmed Saint James—*Sant' Iago*—as the patron of Spain and ordered a church built over his tomb. Soon more churches rose, and monasteries, and around the nucleus—the little cemetery or *compostilla* where James was found—a town named Compostela.

Well, such is the history. But, as usual, a yellow brick road of legend runs parallel to history's earthen paths. In the *Liber Sancti Jacobi*, the great compendium of Jacobean lore, the wondrous tale is told of how Saint James on his white charger appeared in a dream to the emperor Charlemagne, pointed to the Milky Way and said:

"My body lies to the west, in Galicia, in a place called Compostela, from *campus stellae*, which is to say, 'the field of the star.' The road of stars you see in the sky signifies that you must set forth to Galicia with a great army to liberate my road and my country, and to visit my basilica and tomb. After you, people will come from every land on the path of the Milky Way to beg pardon for their sins and praise the Lord, and His wonders."

The emperor was heavy with years and weary of warfare, and the Apostle had to return twice to urge him on, but at last the grand Charles rode forth. He led the great crusade that won the Camino, and was the first pilgrim to the Apostle's tomb.

It's a stirring legend. It just doesn't bear much relation to what we know or have reason to believe—namely, that the emperor Charlemagne was long dead before the discovery of James's tomb; that the more likely source of "Compostela" is the prosaic but descriptive *compostilla*, not the dreamy *campus stellae*; and that a pilgrim who tried to use the Milky Way as a compass could end up just about anywhere. The fact is that the Camino was not made by great heroes but by small ones, and it was not a fabulous vision of stars that drew pilgrims but some dry bones in a stone tomb and the promise that they could work wonders.

I feel like a pedant harping on about these things. The starry roads and fields of the medieval tale-spinners have glimmered down the ages, inspiring countless poets, dreamers, filmmakers, songwriters, tourist boards. Why object to them? Only because I believe the Camino needs no fanciful etymologies or fabricated histories to adorn it. The plain truth of it is rich and strange enough.

And now, having got that off my chest, what's to stop me from tipping my head back, gazing into the vault of the night sky and murmuring: "Tomorrow, pilgrim, once again, you will walk the Milky Way to the field of the star."

Happy Returns

In the street, pilgrims are stirring, their sticks tapping the pavement before the shuttered eyes of the massive beige-stuccoed Basque homes. The houses have names and dates carved over the lintels, and I'd like to jot a few down, but it's a chore extracting my big spiral notebook from my shoulder bag. Two minutes into my Camino, I have already identified a lack. There are no stationery shops till Pamplona, but when I get there I'll find something pocket-sized for lightning-quick note taking. Having run out of food on this road before, I provision myself with a baguette and a tin of foie gras. And then, with a deep breath and a "Here we go," I am back on the road to Santiago.

Just outside St-Jean comes the pilgrim's first decision. The high road or the low road? The high road is the *route de Napoléon* (used, not by Bonaparte himself, but by his armies under Maréchal Harispe), a lonely, sublime path over the imperial mountaintops. The low is the valley of Charlemagne, where, tradition has it, the rearguard of the old emperor's army was annihilated in the ambush immortalized by the *Chanson de Roland*. The route of Charlemagne hugs the winding two-lane highway and is recommended only when snowstorms, rain or wind make the high road impassable. After yesterday's miserable weather, today is shaping up to be glorious, perfect for the route of Napoleon. But this morning I am letting nostalgia be my guide. The first time I walked the Camino, I went by the route of Charlemagne, so the route of Charlemagne it will be today.

An hour out of St-Jean is the village of Arnéguy. There's a little river that runs through the middle of town. Cross it and you're in Spain. Cross back and you're in France. You can cross back and forth all day if you like. Welcome to the pilgrim-friendly new Europe. The two (redundant) guards on the Spanish side of the bridge are smoking and chatting. As I set foot on their soil, one of them calls out a double-barrelled greeting.

"*Hola, peregrino.* Welcome to Spain, welcome to the Basque country." He laughs and then gives me a little of the old between-me-and-you. "Don't worry, I'm not a terrorist or anything. It's something in your heart. People can say, 'This is Spain' or 'That is France,' but for me it's all Basque country."

The Camino's passage through the land of the Basques lasts barely three days, but that's still enough time to pick up a phrase or two. "Tell me, how do you say 'thank you' in Basque?"

The guard's smile is a mile wide. "*Eskerrik asko.*"

Eskerrik asko. I roll that one over my tongue as I walk away. I'll be putting it to use in a minute or two when I make a stop at the very first bar I visited on my first Camino. It's a place I've been hankering to get back to for five years, and not just for the sake of nostalgia. It is a little shrine to the Basque national sport of *jai alai*, with walls plastered in everything from this year's team calendars to black-and-white shots of jauntily bereted sports heroes of the Franco era. I've always regretted that I was in too much of a hurry that first day to coax the bartender into conversation or even take some photos. Life, happily, sometimes offers second chances.

And sometimes not. Here is my bar, all locked up and swept clean. The photos are gone, the calendars, the coffee machine, the taciturn bartender. It's an empty shell, a vacant *jai alai* court. I stand, peering in the windows, feeling just a little down. I hadn't planned for my first day to begin with a memento mori. But maybe that's reading too much into it. I'll just take this as a little reminder that the things of this world don't wait for us. That outside our ambered memories, they follow their own Caminos.

So it's on to Valcarlos. The first time I walked this way was a stunning afternoon in late July. I had started out too late to attempt the twenty-odd kilometres to Roncesvalles on the route of Napoleon, but my map showed a village on the route of Charlemagne, eight kilometres past St-Jean. After so many years of waiting, I hated to cool my heels for even one more night. This looked like a start. I was anxious as I raced through those first kilometres, sweating and panting on the climbs, not convinced yet that I could do what I was doing. Surely my map would turn out to be outdated. Or I would take a wrong turn and end up lost in the mountains. Or my unworthiness to be a pilgrim would be detected, and I would be turned away from the refuge. It was with relief and a certain incredulity, then, that I found myself, three hours after leaving St-Jean, settled for the night in a homey *pensión* in Valcarlos. I had not strayed, erred or faltered, and no meteorite had fallen on me from the clear blue sky. I had set out from one place with a pack on my back and walked to the next. Tomorrow I would do the same. That was really all there was to it. My dream journey was under way.

And here is Valcarlos once more, just as I remember it— the *pensión* where I slept, the tavern where I ate. I sit down on the bench where I sat that night, look out over the mountain valley and hear the faint, lingering echoes of relief and happy triumph. Then I break out my lunch—and look, there's even a welcoming committee for me. A one-eyed cat who's caught a whiff of my foie gras.

"Come here."

I pour some water in the empty tin and we drink to happy returns.

Santiago Peregrino

Today marks the third time I am walking from St-Jean to Roncesvalles on my own. It's become almost a rite of passage, this solitary walk in the Pyrenees before joining the pilgrim masses in Roncesvalles. I don't mind the solitude, because I know by now that you're never really alone on the Camino. Even if you play the hermit, sleeping in the open and shunning other pilgrims, you are still walking a road that was won and made safe for you by fifty generations of pilgrims, warriors, farmers, kings, engineers, rogues and saints. All of them are walking with you, even when you feel most alone, maybe especially then. Never far away, either, is Saint James the Pilgrim, Santiago Peregrino.

There is no other saint quite like James. Where others wait for the faithful to come to them, James goes out to meet his pilgrims. It must have been sometime in the eleventh century, in some sculptor's atelier in France or Spain, that Yakob the fisherman of Galilee traded in his toga for an all-weather cloak, a broad-brimmed hat and a staff, and became Santiago Peregrino. In early portrayals he looks like a humble pilgrim. Later, he is more manly and dashing, though always approachable. He has the air of someone who can sing a good walking song, put back a cup of wine or two, and perform a miracle when needed. The *Liber Sancti Jacobi* retells twenty-two tales of pilgrims miraculously rescued from snowstorms, floods, wolves, bandits, wily innkeepers and the snares of the Evil One by Saint James the Pilgrim. Disbeliever though I am, I must credit these stories, for I have met Santiago Peregrino. It was on my second Camino, on my way from St-Jean to Roncesvalles.

That time I stayed in the clean, cozy refuge of St-Jean. There were only three of us, and when I woke in the morning, the others were gone. The shops on the rue de la Citadelle were not yet open and I had bought no provisions the night before, so the prudent thing would have been to wait a bit to stoke up on caffeine and calories. But I had no use for prudence that day; I was taking the route of Napoleon.

After days of driving rain and lightning storms, it was a splendid morning for walking. I climbed and climbed, looking back often to admire the widening panorama of farms, pastures, green slopes. I felt alive, invigorated, light as air, though part of that was my empty stomach. That was all right. My map showed villages ahead (Othatzenea, Erreculuch, Untto, such gnarled Basque names) where surely I would find a bar or shop. In fact, by my figuring, I should be getting to—what was it?—Othatzenea any minute. I scanned the landscape for the village church spires, but there were only farms and cows. Finally I checked my map. There was no way around it: Othatzenea was the three houses back there on the left.

No worries. I'd be in Erreculuch soon enough. Erreculuch—now there was a name. I tromped along, burbling, *"Erreculuch, Erreculuch,"* like a happy parrot. After half an hour or so I came upon two farms and a barking dog. And that was Erreculuch. My stomach snarled. "Why didn't you buy some bread last night?" "Patience," I told it, "patience."

I had a saving grace: there was a pilgrim refuge in Untto, which surely meant somewhere to eat. I wouldn't be there till past noon, but it would be worth the wait.

In Untto, the cheerful sign on the refuge read *Closed till May*. There were no shops. There would be none now till Roncesvalles. There *were* doors. A pilgrim can knock on doors for help. But I was too timid, or too proud, or maybe I thought it served me right to go hungry. I went on. It was a beautiful day and I was crossing the Pyrenees. In six hours, when I sat down to my first meal of the day, I would truly appreciate it. Till then I was *fasting*. That put a nice spin on it.

The higher I climbed, the wilder and more lonely were the mountainsides. There was no one in sight but the occasional shepherd grazing his flocks below. The sun came out full, transforming the clumps of sheep dung on the grass into glistening clusters of grapes. I sat surrounded by cows, watching jet trails cross the sky. And sometime around three o'clock I drank the last of my water. It ran all the way down to my toes. I had been saving that gulp for the Fountain of Roland at the height of the pass, just after the waymark that says *Santiago 765 kms*. I could see the fountain now just ahead, a little stone cairn with a tap sticking out of it. As I drew closer, I could see the little sign too. It read *Disconnected for the winter*.

By the Fountain of Roland, I sat down and wept. Or nearly. I decided to count my blessings instead. Only four more hours to Roncesvalles. No rain, snow or hail. None of the wolves, bears or bandits that pilgrims of old walked in fear of. Really, I was quite lucky. If only I could convince my stomach. So as I sat by the dry fountain, I told my stomach the old story from the *Liber Sancti Jacobi* of a pilgrim who crossed the Sierra del Perdón in the pounding heat of summer. He'd eaten nothing for days and he could barely set one foot in front of the other. Suddenly there was another at his side, where no one had been before.

"You look thirsty, my friend," said the stranger.

The pilgrim thought his salvation had arrived. "Do you have water?" he gasped.

"I have water for those who can pay," said the stranger with a smile.

Then the pilgrim understood who walked beside him and what price he would ask.

"I will die before I drink your water," he said.

"Well you may," smirked the devil. "If you change your mind, I won't be far off." And in a flash he was gone.

The pilgrim staggered on till at last he fell upon the baked earth. He didn't know how long he had been lying there when he heard the sound of hoofs. Opening his eyes, he saw a brilliance that was not the sun, but a rider cantering down the slope on a white horse. The rider wore a pilgrim's cloak. A broad hat shielded his face. He dismounted, took a scallop shell from his saddlebag and plunged it into the earth beside where the pilgrim lay. There was a sound of rushing water. Then the horseman knelt and offered the shell to the pilgrim's lips.

"Drink."

The pilgrim looked into the rider's eyes. He had seen that honest face before. Where? He fell into a faint, and when he woke, he knew: it was the face he had seen above the altar of every church, the face of Saint James. The stream still gushed from the earth at his side, and it gushes to this day. It is called the Fuente de Reniega—the Well of Renunciation—and every pilgrim should drink of it, for its waters fortify the spirit against the temptation to abandon the Camino.

My stomach had fallen quiet. It was impressed. "And when do we get to this fountain?" it asked.

"In three days. It's after Pamplona."

My stomach went back to growling.

There should have been no one else on the path that day, yet all of a sudden I heard a crunch of boots. A stocky man in his fifties wearing a battered straw hat emerged from the trees. I stood to meet him.

"Henk," he said, shaking my hand firmly. "Just call me Henk." Henk came from Rotterdam. In fact, he had come all the way from Rotterdam on foot.

"How far is that?"

He knit his brow. "I haven't counted lately. Around two thousand kilometres."

"Did you see the sign back there?" I asked.

"Seven hundred and sixty-five kilometres to Santiago? Yes. I'm almost there!"

But where had he come from today?

"I was walking in the rain two days ago and caught a cold, so I stayed an extra night at a guest house in St-Jean. I didn't want to take up a bed in the refuge. This morning I still felt a little sick, but the day looked so fine that I decided to walk."

Henk was brisk—the sort who walks three thousand kilometres briskly, if that makes sense. He sorted out who I was with a few brisk questions, then said, "Well, you're Bob, I'm Henk, we'll see each other tonight in Roncesvalles."

He was about to launch himself up the path when I blurted out: "You don't have any food, do you?"

He stopped. "Food? Have you had no food today? That's not good at all. A pilgrim needs energy. Let me see." He opened up his pack and started tossing out edibles. "I've got these dried fruit bars—they have everything your body needs. And—oh!—here's a can of tuna. From Catalonia. In a tasty tomato sauce. And I still have half a loaf of French bread from yesterday. Not fresh, but I don't think you'll mind. Will you be okay with that?"

I stammered that really I would be very okay, thank you, and then, without benefit of enchanted white steed, my sturdy Dutch benefactor took wing. I watched him vanish briskly up the path, meaning to wave if he looked back. He didn't. I sat down, laid out my meal, said thank you and dived in. The French stick was stale, the tuna swam in a salty, goopy sauce, the energy bars were . . . energy bars. I've never enjoyed a meal more. After, as I sprawled among the rocks and wild-flowers, gazing at the snow-capped mountains to the east, I wondered if the man who had helped me was really just plain Henk, who happened to be in the right place at the right time, or was he the Pilgrim James in the guise of a brisk Dutchman? Did it make any difference? Whoever it is, what-ever it is, that walks with us on the Camino, and cares for us, and saves us from peril when all hope is lost—let that be San-tiago Peregrino.

Eskerrik Asko

The rest of the walk from Valcarlos is silent, solitary and un-eventful. In the late afternoon, I reach Ibañeta, the windy height of the pass, where pilgrims plant a cross in the earth to thank God and Saint James for bringing them safely to Spain, the land of the Apostle. From here it's a downhill, half-hour stroll through a beech forest to the hospital of Roncesvalles—where my day of solitude comes to an end. For here they are at last, the pilgrims! Noisy, excited, bustling around with their alpine sticks and backpacks, acting as if they own the place. Which in effect they do, for Roncesvalles is to pilgrims as an Olympic village is to athletes. It is a "hospital" in the medieval sense of the word: a place of *hospital*ity, where for more than eight hundred years pilgrims have been welcomed, fed, blessed, bathed and, when circumstances dictated, buried.

My first stop is the pilgrim office, in a wing of the old monastery, where a dozen men and women are already seated around the big wooden table, laughing and chatting as they wait to perform the one rite that is required of all pilgrims at the outset of their journey to Santiago: the filling out of the registration form. After a few minutes the volunteer hospitalero, a German this week, bustles in with a box of pencils and passes around the half sheets of foolscap.

We each write our name, passport number, country of origin, then fill in the boxes to indicate our means of travel (foot or bicycle), religion (Catholic, Protestant, Other, None) and motive for doing the Camino. I wonder for this last one what choices the old-time pilgrim might have had. *Fulfill a vow. Do penance. Win indulgences. Fight the infidel.* Today we get to choose from: Religious, Spiritual, Cultural, Sport, and Other. When we are done, the hospitalero collects our forms and hands back our "credentials," the neat little fold-out booklet that is stamped with the *sello* of each refuge where we stay, and which we will present (God willing) at the pilgrim office in Santiago to obtain our Compostela, the Latin diploma that certifies we have completed the Camino. And that's it. We are officially pilgrims.

The hospitalero takes us outside and points us to the "new" refuge. It's a recently restored twelfth-century hall, long and lofty, with unadorned stone walls, bare timber beams, and an austerity worthy of the name of Roncesvalles. It's also close quarters, double bunks with low dividers between them. A restless sleeper could easily wind up in his neighbour's bunk. Most of the beds are already taken. I find one next to a Spanish woman who doesn't look like a snorer—not that you can ever be sure.

I look around for Aaron and the rest from last night, but they haven't arrived or they're already in bed, so I take myself to one of Roncesvalles's two restaurants. The place is packed with pilgrims loading up on the cut-price *menú del peregrino* before the 9:30 p.m. curfew. The mood is boisterous. My table partners are four Spanish boys who plan to cover forty kilometres tomorrow to Pamplona so that one of them can meet his *chica*. Ah, youth. And all too soon it's time to get back to the refuge, where the lights are already dim, the beds full of sleepers.

The Camino is a great leveller. Pilgrims walk the same road, sport the same emblems, cook in the same kitchen . . . and bunk down in the same room. A handful of refuges offer the luxury of two- or four-bunk quarters, but it is more common to find anywhere from a dozen to fifty pilgrims packed in one coed dorm. The great hall here in Roncesvalles sleeps a hundred. For some, this comfortable, informal closeness is a revelation. I remember one pilgrim, a hustling young IT worker, the first pilgrim I ever saw talking on a cellphone as he walked, who spoke about the refuges like an anthropology student discussing his fieldwork: "I spend the whole day hanging out with these old truck drivers, plumbers, mechanics—people I'd never talk to in real life. We walk together, shower together, drink together. And then we go to bed in the same room and I listen to them snore all night. It's like living with thirty of my father."

I shared his enthusiasm for everything but the snoring. For all the nights I have spent cooped up with strangers, and despite experiments with earplugs, visualizing, deep breathing

(Philomena, a philosophical Irish pilgrim, once assured me, "You just have to find the rhythm of the snoring, then slip into the troughs") and plain, old stoicism, I remain acutely sensitive to night sounds. And the splendid refuge of Roncesvalles is an amphitheatre of night sounds. Within minutes of bunking down, the concert begins. Creaks, murmurs, sighs, whispers, coughs. There is a round of giggles when the first snorer starts up (laugh while you can, I say) and, at a lower frequency, a tremor of excitement running through this big room packed with a hundred people who can't wait for tomorrow.

I lie still while the wind rattles the windows and my thoughts swing like a pendulum forward to the weeks to come, then back five years to my first night among pilgrims. Roncesvalles was crowded that time too, even more than tonight, with tents pitched in the fields to handle the overflow, for in 1999, as in 2004, July 25, St. James's Day, fell on a Sunday, making it a *Jacobeo*—a Jamesian Holy Year—and ensuring extra pilgrim multitudes. My timing is flawless.

The snorers are tuning their instruments and it's clear I won't be sleeping any time soon, so finally I slip out of bed and down the stairs. The basement of the refuge is a pilgrim's version of Ali Baba's cave. There are hot showers, a kitchen, a washer and dryer, a comfy nook for sitting and swapping stories. And a "help yourself" shelf that groans with king-size containers of shampoo and shaving cream, Thermos bottles, travel pillows, compasses, cosmetics, sandals, climbing gear, sweaters, caps—a whole travel shop of items jettisoned by overburdened pilgrims. There is a small library too. I pick out Robert Ludlum's thriller *The Prometheus Deception* for bedtime reading, having heard that it is partly set on the Camino.

And then something catches my eye: a small black hardcover notebook. Just the thing I've been wanting. Flipping through, I see that it's travelled some. It was printed in Italy (and comes complete with saints' days), though the few pen-cilled notes are written in French and record the expenses of a trip to the States. It's been waiting for me a long time too; the year of printing is 1991. And it takes to me at once, dis-appearing neatly into my shirt pocket.

This is another of those Camino moments, like the one in the mountains when Henk came out of nowhere to deliver my lunch. A moment when one feels that thanks are due, even if it's not clear to whom. It's a great argument for faith: you always know who your benefactor is. But even if you don't, it still seems only right to show gratitude for the good things life gives. This being Basque country, let me show it in Basque.

Eskerrik asko.

Peregrinus

In the chill early morning, I skulk in the doorway of the refuge. In theory we don't have to be out till eight, but the lights were on at six this morning, and by seven-thirty the hospitalero was bundling the slowpokes out: "Come on, let's go. Long way to Santiago." I don't blame him for wanting us gone. He has a big refuge to clean. A French pilgrim joins me in the door-way long enough to light a cigarette. He was not impressed by the stony hall of Roncesvalles. "Like something from the war of '14," he grumbles. Nineteen-fourteen, I assume.

In olden times, Roncesvalles was a place of pilgrimage in its own right, famous as the site of the last stand of the French hero Roland. In 1670, an Italian monk named Domenico Laffi stopped here on his way to Santiago. Later, he would set down his memories and impressions in what may be the liveliest account of the Camino ever written. Laffi is engaging, chatty and unfailingly credulous, and Roncesvalles offers much to exercise his credulity. He is shown "the very rock" that Roland split with his sword, "the exact spot" where Roland wept for his slain companions, and "the tombs of Roland's knights" (a pilgrim graveyard). Laffi and his companion prayed awhile before the tombs. Then they made, as we all wish to make at times, a mark of their passing: "With the point of a knife, we scratched our names and surnames on one of the stones."

To spend an extra day in Roncesvalles, as Laffi did, has long been on my to-do list. I've always arrived here late, tired and hungry, with barely time to fill my face and grab some sleep before being chased off into the foggy dawn. Wouldn't it be something to take a day to roam the grounds, ply the hospitalero for stories, deface the monuments? I'm writing a book, after all, shouldn't I do some research? But Laffi could justify taking an extra day here; he'd already walked all the way from Bologna. My pilgrimage has barely begun. More importantly, I'm shivering in a doorway while everyone else is out walking. The pull of Santiago's magnet is too strong. Let's go.

So it's out into the dawn, across the highland pastures, where the mountains crowd in like a family leaning over a newborn child and the only sound is the lazy tinkle of cowbells, all the way following the yellow arrows painted on rocks, posts and buildings that point the pilgrim to Santiago. This is a morning to treasure, for there is none more beautiful on the Camino than the descent from the Pyrenees. By tomorrow night the mountains, the forests, the white Basque villages will all be memories. But there are many things to distract us today. A hundred pilgrims have set out within an hour of each other and there is much to talk about. I meet up again with Aaron. He has been busy making friends—with Maribel and Carlos, a mother and son from the States, as well as two French Wives of Bath, who are already tying messages for him to trees and writing his name in pebbles.

Then, a little before noon, when we're far enough down from the misty slopes to feel a little Spanish heat, I see a man in the path ahead walking with a pair of metal hiking poles. On his pack, even from this distance, I can make out the distinctive green and purple crest of the Little Company of Pilgrims, Toronto's own Camino group. He's a big, sturdy fellow, though I see from his ruddy face that he is toiling in the heat.

"Morning. You from Toronto?"

"Oakville," he replies—half an hour from town. He takes off his baseball cap, wipes the sweat from his brow and looks me over. "I know you. What's your last name?"

"Ward."

"You son of a gun, I bought two copies of your book when you did that reading for the Little Company. One for myself, one for my doctor. Remember? Tony Bush." He extends his hand. "Yeah, like the president, but no relation. My grandfather was a Busciatella when he came over from Italy, but he figured he needed a WASP surname to make it in business in Toronto." We slip easily into small talk, as if there were nothing strange about meeting here, thousands of kilometres from home. Incredibly, neither of us says, "Small world."

It turns out I'm the first English speaker that Tony has met here. If he doesn't get his stories off his chest soon, he'll burst. Stories of frustration (missed train connection in France, heavy rain on the way from St-Jean, trouble with pay phones); small triumphs (finding a radiator to dry his socks); divine intervention ("See these walking poles? A friend gave them to me at the last minute, I swear to God, the last minute. There's no way I could have got this far without them"). We stop at a bar in Vizcarret so I can help him call home, but the bar doesn't have the right kind of phone. After the bar there's a variety store, but it doesn't have the right phone either. Tony starts to fret about his glacial pace. He doesn't want to slow me down, and it's true that my legs are aching for a good stretch.

"I'll see you up ahead," he says. "And don't worry about the phone—somebody will show me how to work the darn things."

Poor Tony. He doesn't speak the language. Can't use the phones. Can't read the menus. His family and friends are all back in Canada. He's a stranger here. But that's what a pilgrim is. In the original meaning of the Latin word, a *peregrinus* was precisely "a person from another country; a stranger." You can take the word back even further, to its roots: *per agris*, "through fields." A pilgrim is someone who comes through fields. It's an image at once mysterious and faintly comical: a man with a broad hat, a stick in his hand, a bag on his shoulder, wading through the wheat against a backdrop of sky and mountains on his way from God knows where. What makes someone like Tony do this to himself, make himself a stranger walking through fields far from home? I didn't ask him before, but I do now.

Tony grins. "Do you really want to know? I have Hodgkin's disease. I was diagnosed fourteen years ago. I've had over forty chemo sessions and I'd be having another now if my doctor didn't give me permission to come here. Back when the treatments began, all I hoped was that I'd live long enough to see my kids graduate from high school. Now they've all finished university and started their own lives. I'm doing the Camino to thank God for all he's given me in these years." He gives me a little thump on the shoulder. "Now you get going. Maybe we'll see each other up the road."

As I look back from the top of the next ridge, it's not hard to pick out Tony's big frame. I can almost hear his breathing, and the *chhhk chhhk* of the earth giving way to each thrust of his walking poles. There's something very humble in his premise. He's not angry about his sickness; he's grateful for the remission. God, from his perspective, has been good to him. So he's come here to say thank you. Walking a few hundred kilometres in the punishing heat of God's sun, over his often rough and tilting earth, might seem an odd way to do that. But it's a way pilgrims to Santiago have chosen for a thousand years.

It's a sacrifice; there's suffering involved. But it's also a show of strength, like a child running to make his father proud. And something more: it's an act of faith. Faith that God's world is one, and that when a pilgrim ventures into it he will be welcomed and cared for. It is the paradox of the pilgrim. He goes to a foreign land to find his spirit's home.

A Humble Friend of the Pilgrim

In Larrasoaña, at the foot of the mountains, the main refuge is full, so I find myself in the annex, a refurbished stable. The place stinks of alcohol—the rubbing variety. Aaron is here. He's had a hard day. His backpack is too heavy and it doesn't sit right on him, his ankles are wobbling and he's cultivating blisters. His friend Maribel has a swelling on her shoulder from the pressure of her backpack. I don't really want to touch it, but she insists. "Feel it, it's hard." She's right, it is. It's hard and hot and knobby as a lump of cartilage. How do you grow something like that in one day? Happily, we have a clean, warm place where we can lick our wounds. We have hot showers and wash basins, clotheslines and firm mattresses. We can use the kitchen in the main refuge. And all in exchange for a "suggested donation" of five euros, a pittance.

There are places like this one all along the Camino. Some are sponsored by the locality or the regional Camino association, others run by religious bodies such as the Knights of Roncesvalles or the Benedictines, while others still are backed by foreign Camino organizations and even private benefactors. In recent years, private refuges, which charge a slightly higher rate than the public ones but offer more services and flexibility, have sprung up to accommodate the flood of pilgrims. Every speck of a village today seems to have a refuge. Some have more refuges than inhabitants.

It's hard to imagine that as recently as 1986, when a young Canadian woman named Laurie Dennett walked the Camino to raise money for MS research (a journey recorded with warmth and wit in her book *A Hug for the Apostle*), almost none of this infrastructure existed. Dennett spent her thirty-six nights between St-Jean-Pied-de-Port and Santiago sleeping in *fondas* (small hotels), parish houses, private homes, convents and churches. The only municipal refuge she encountered was in Santo Domingo de la Calzada, while in the forty kilometres between Astorga and Ponferrada—a stretch that now hosts a baker's dozen of refuges, public and private—the only place to bunk down was the sagging, bat-dung-covered floor of the former schoolhouse of Rabanal del Camino. After decades of neglect, the Camino's millennial tradition of hospitality was largely dead or dormant.

So Santiago Zubiri was something of a visionary when, in 1988, as mayor of Larrasoaña, he set aside a room of the town hall as a pilgrim shelter. Since then, the space allocation has reversed; now a room in the refuge is set aside as the town hall. Santiago continues to maintain high standards of cleanliness and welcome. He has himself done the Camino more than once, and his Compostelas are prominently displayed in his office. His was a small, local act of goodness, but it is the multiplication of small, local acts that sustains the Camino. As I settle into the shelter he founded, I intend to recognize his contribution in the pages of my book.

Unfortunately, intentions only carry you so far on the Camino. By the time I've washed and hung my clothes to dry, showered, rested, eaten supper and shared a *patxaran*, the Basque sloe liqueur, with Aaron, it's already 9:45.

Santiago is sitting at his big desk when I come in, fingers laced over his modest paunch. "How can I help you, *peregrino*? Have you eaten? Was there enough hot water?" He's nearing the end of another long day of welcomes and farewells, of answering questions and putting out fires and pointing people in the right direction. In fifteen minutes he will close up for the night and sit down to supper. It's clear that he can hardly wait. I ask about a Japanese book that is on his desk.

"Hmm, yes. A writer. She stayed here three, four years ago." He flips through the book and finds a picture of himself and a Japanese woman standing in his office. I say I'd like to ask a few questions about his life on the Camino. He coughs and looks at his watch. Another writer. "Well, the pilgrims needed somewhere to stay . . . So I started this refuge, yes . . . Sixteen years now, hmm . . . I do my best for the Camino, for the pilgrims, hmm . . ." It's plain that from his point of view he has done nothing remarkable, just what was right. What is there really to say? He invites me to look over the guest books. The first volume covers the first several years of the refuge's existence. The year 2004 already has three volumes all to itself.

Then he shuffles his papers. Supper calls. "If there's anything else I can tell you, I'll be here from seven tomorrow. The earlier you come, the better." I'm halfway out the door when something really important comes to his mind. "*Peregrino*, wait. You are in the annex? When everyone is inside, can you please be sure the door is closed?"

The Gifts of the Camino

In the morning, Maribel is divvying her clothes into two piles. The extra pair of walking shoes, a stack of shirts, the third and fourth pairs of slacks, the grey and the red sweaters (she's hanging on to the blue one), the paperbacks and guidebooks ("I thought I was going to have time to read. Ha!"), along with any number of items that might come in handy for a journey up the Amazon or an audience with the Spanish Royal Family, but are of little use on the Camino de Santiago—all of them are going first into Carlos's bag, to take the strain off her shoulder, and then later, in Pamplona, to the post office to be shipped home.

Maribel overlooked only one thing in her Camino preparations: she isn't a camel. But now she makes the necessary adjustments promptly and without regrets. "It's amazing. In three days I've gone from needing six shirts to needing two. How does that happen?" It happens very easily when those six shirts are weighing on your shoulders. After a few hours in the Spanish sun, you dump your belongings on the bed and ask yourself if you'll ever need that sweater, if you couldn't just buy a raincoat if the need arose. After a few days, it's whether you need that whole tube of toothpaste, or all that shampoo, and if it wouldn't be okay to tear the pages out of your guidebook as you read them. In fact, who needs a guidebook? Just follow the yellow arrows. Pilgrimage strips us down to the essentials. That is why Everyman, at the end of his life's journey, comes naked to the throne of Heaven. He didn't need all that crap.

After Larrasoaña, the Camino criss-crosses the Río Arga on a series of pretty bridges. Horses graze free by the path, and on it. There is something calming about horses in the morning. Slowly the valleys and hills, the wrinkles in the earth at the foot of the Pyrenees, level out. Forests and pastures give way to roads, and just past noon I reach the mighty walls of old Pamplona. When Domenico Laffi arrived here in 1670, he was met by "very tall guards" who grilled him as they pored over his documents. Laffi submitted patiently because "in the end, if they weren't satisfied with your answers, they would throw you in prison or send you to the galleys." I'll bet the Pamplonicos wish they still had some of those tall guards to screen the riff-raff that overrun their city every July during the running of the bulls.

I've stayed in Pamplona every time I've done the Camino— including the first time, when the fiesta was in full swing, and the pilgrims were locked up in a convent with a nine o'clock curfew to keep us from temptation—so today I'm ready for something new. I'm going a few kilometres farther, to Cizur Menor, where the Knights of Malta maintain a rustic refuge in a medieval tower. But just now the sun is high and a grassy riverbank beckons. I'm sweaty and sore-footed. Why not glory in the day? I shuck off my pack, pry my feet out of my shoes, set my glasses on the grass and open myself to the sun.

I have been glorying in the day for all of three minutes when the man on the lawn mower makes his first pass. He cuts across the top of the bank with the roar of an outboard motor, sending a spray of clippings my way and leaving a gas haze in his wake. *Olé!* I ignore him and hope he doesn't come back. A minute later he's back, and two metres closer. I bundle my gear together and head for another patch of lawn. By the Bridge of the Magdalena some pilgrims are looking for someone to take their photo. Could I . . .? Of course I could. That's funny, where are my glasses? I pat down my pockets, shake out my bag. Then the man on the lawn mower roars by. He waves as he passes.

Back at the riverbank, the air smells of diesel and freshly cut grass. I drop to my knees and paw the earth till I find a single metal arm still fixed to its lens. A sweep with my stick stirs up the other twisted arm and some shards of hard plastic.

At first all I do is swear. At myself, my luck, the idiot on the lawn mower, and life in general, then back to the top of the list. After a few minutes, when I'm satisfied that I, my luck, the idiot and life know what I think of them, I check my watch. The shops close for lunch in ten minutes. No time to lose. I pound across the Bridge of the Magdalena, up the hill and through the city gates, down the Calle Carmen, left into the Calle de Estafeta—and there is an optical shop.

"How can I help you, *peregrino*?" The optician shakes his head at the sight of my mangled eyewear, then sits me down for a test. He is honoured to serve a pilgrim. His wife is friends with the president of the Brazilian association. "I will phone the factory before they go for lunch. Your prescription is a common one, perhaps they can fill it today. Ana, please help this *peregrino* choose some frames . . ."

He is kind. The pretty young assistant, too. They fuss over me, lean close to peer into my eyes, balance frames on my nose. I am overwhelmed by their kindness. I am beyond overwhelmed, I am mortified. For against the antiseptic backdrop of the shop I can smell my pilgrim self, and the plain truth is, I stink. I stink with the acrid, goaty stink of a man who has just thrown off his pack after walking all morning in thirty-degree heat. It's worse than that. Running up the hill to the shop has laid a fresh coat of stink on the original one, making my aroma deep, complex, like an aged cheese.

Should I be ashamed? My odour is the product of my labour. I smell as a good pilgrim should. Did not Saint Bernard of Clairvaux once heap praise upon the Templar guardians of the Camino for "never combing their hair, seldom bathing, and reeking of the earth"? But who reads Saint Bernard these days?

I'm relieved when the fitting goes well. The first frames we try are perfect. The girl is being extra selective. While I find a mirror in a distant corner of the shop to admire my new look, the optician gets off the phone. "Good news. We'll have your glasses today at six." I thank him profusely and hurry out of his shop, trailing the odour of sanctity behind me.

In the Plaza del Castillo, I spread last night's laundry over several benches to dry. I will be wearing a fresh shirt when I go back to the optician's. *Vanitas, vanitas.* I go for a beer at the Bar Iruña ("Isn't this where Hemingway used to drink?" I ask the bartender. "This is where Hemingway used to *get drunk*," she clarifies) and by the time I come back, the sun has dried and pressed my clothes. I am packing them when something catches my eye. A euro penny. Well, it's my lucky day.

The Camino has a way of giving us the things we need just when we need them. Every pilgrim has a favourite story of the Camino providing. On my first Camino, I talked to an intense Argentine woman named Gabriela who had a theory that everything, but *everything*, that happened to us on the Camino de Santiago was a Gift. It made no difference whether it was a transparently good thing (a kind word when you felt most alone, a meal when you were hungry, a notebook that fit your pocket perfectly) or an apparent misfortune (a skin rash, a dog bite, broken glasses, blisters); everything that happened was for our benefit. If we didn't see that immediately, it only meant we weren't looking hard enough.

In this way of seeing things, the Camino has taken over the functions of Santiago Peregrino, God and the angels, becoming itself the watcher, the healer, the teacher, the giver of gifts. The Camino discerns our needs and responds to them, tests and rewards us, gives and takes away. It is my reflex to poke fun at ideas like this, rolling my eyes when the rain (or the snoring) starts and saying, "Ah, another gift of the Camino." And yet there's no escaping it. I know that if I want my broken glasses to be a gift, I can make them one. I can say that this episode has given me an insight into myself (my first reaction in adversity is to cast blame). It has provided an example of how kind people can be (even to a smelly pilgrim). It has reminded me how swell it is to have a credit card.

At six o'clock, after a shower at the refuge, I'm back at the shop smelling like roses. The optician smiles proudly. The girl mounts my new eyewear on my nose. And the world is born anew.

"Are they okay?" asks the optician.

"It's a miracle! I can see!"

"When was the last time you got new glasses?"

When *was* the last time I got new glasses? The optician nods his head. He's accustomed to such miracles.

In the street, I have to brace myself against a wall. The world has snapped into high definition, like a photo in the window of a camera shop. How goodly are the faces of the Pamplonicos. I want to kiss them all. In the Plaza del Castillo, I make a 360-degree turn in the centre of the square. Is *this* what it looks like? Stunning.

The trickster Camino has produced a gift from behind its back. Those are often the best ones.

The Invisible Companion

The road out of Pamplona is familiar. It's not just that I've done it before, I did it only ten days ago with my wife, Michiko. We walked together from here to Nájera, six days, just enough for her to get a taste of the Camino. We passed this park, crossed at these lights, stopped for coffee here (the croissants were on the stale side), took a picture at this bridge . . .

It took Michiko some time to get to the Camino. She always told me that she would love to *see* it, but *walking* it, that was something else . . . Then one day she said, "I'm going with you this fall." In the end it wasn't any argument of mine that persuaded her, but a movement in her soul. She was ready. Before we started out, I was all eagerness and nerves. I knew she would love it, and I was afraid she would hate it. But there was nothing to worry about. From the first day, she was hooked.

That she loved the Camino seemed destiny, for the name "Michiko" liberally translates means "Camino girl." *Ko* is "child" in Japanese, while *michi* signifies "road," both in the sense of a physical roadway and a spiritual path. The character for *michi* is also pronounced *do*, and as such it is the final element in words such as *kendo* (the way of the sword) and *budo* (the way of the warrior). In Chinese it is *tao*, the ineffable force that infuses all being. If this is all sounding rather Eastern and inscrutable, consider that *camino* too can mean both the road you walk upon and a spiritual way, as in Christ's "the way, the truth and the life"—*el camino, la verdad y la vida*. And Camino, like Michiko, is a girl's name in Spain, a prayer that the one who bears it will walk through life on the right path.

Michiko practises the Japanese art of shiatsu massage, and she had the tools of her trade with her on the Camino: a supply of long, springy needles; moxa, a slow-burning herb to warm the body's vital points; and two strong hands. On the first morning, I woke to the acrid smell of smouldering moxa. Michiko was giving herself a treatment. "*Ashi no sanri*. This is the point you stimulate when you have to walk a long way. You know Basho, who wrote the haiku about his pilgrimage to the north of Japan. He burnt moxa here before his journey."

It worked for Basho and it worked for Michiko. Over the next six days she covered 120 kilometres without blisters, shin splints, sore joints or inflamed tendons. The walking left her not weary, as she had feared, but strong. She found an explanation for this in Oriental medical theory: walking uphill massages the points on the foot aligned to the heart and lung meridian, while going down stimulates the liver, kidney and spleen points. All those ups and downs between Pamplona and Nájera were doing our innards a world of good.

The path I am walking this morning is among the most memorable of the whole Camino—down from Pamplona's heights, across the plain, then up the bare, steep slope of the Sierra del Perdón, a long, snaking ridge atop which a line of pinwheel-spinning wind turbines stretches to either horizon. It's the same road as two weeks ago, yet different, because this time I'm walking it by myself. Or am I? If you were walking behind me you'd say I was alone, but that's only because you can't see Michiko. She is here with me, walking over this familiar earth. The stick she gave me before she went home is in my hand, and when I say, "Oh, look," it's not only to myself I'm talking.

"Oh, look, remember the turbines? Oh, look, it's that spiral of stones. Oh, look, it's the bench where we sat down last time. And that paper is still hanging from the tree." It is indeed. A single, laminated, typewritten sheet suspended from a branch by a blue and yellow ribbon at just the right height to catch a pilgrim's eye. "Shall I read it again?"

> A human being forms a part of the whole that we call "the universe," a part limited in time and space. We experience our selves, our thoughts, our sentiments as separate from the rest. However, this is a sort of optical illusion of the consciousness, an illusion that acts as a prison, limiting us to our personal desires and to the love we feel for a few people who are close to us. Our task must be to liberate ourselves from this prison by enlarging the circle of our compassion to include all living creatures and nature in all its beauty. If we hope for our species' survival, we must adopt to a substantial degree a new way of thinking.

Last time, as I translated this passage from Spanish for Michiko, I kept wondering all the way to the bottom of the page who this eloquent pilgrim might be. This time I already know it's the one we call Einstein. I thought today I would spend a few quiet minutes at this bench munching an apple, enjoying the view through my new glasses, telling invisible Michiko how things have been going since she went home, and just being a part of the universe, however limited by time and space. But here come Inácio and Carmen.

Inácio is my Brazilian friend from the first day. Carmen is a German pilgrim who started in Roncesvalles. In two days on the Camino, Inácio and Carmen have already "amplified the circle of their compassion." Last night I had supper with them in Pamplona, where they belied their combined century or so of existence with a winning show of adolescent tenderness, brushing hands, giggling, teasing each other in the few words of English they have in common. Today they are strolling hand in hand.

"Good morning, Bob. How are you?"

"Good, very good."

"Do you like to walk with us for a while?"

We talk about the heat and the walking and the walking and the heat, and then Inácio says, "Let me tell you one story very interesting. Is a man from my city, and he write a book about the Camino. And in the book have a story he hear in a . . . how do you say, where live the monks?"

"A monastery?"

"Yes, a monastery. Well, this monastery was a refuge, and in this refuge stayed one woman pilgrim. And in the morning, before everybody leave, they take a picture of all the pilgrims together. Just when they take the picture, suddenly the bells of the church begin to ring. They ring and ring. But nobody rings the bells. Then everybody say, *'Who was?'* But nobody knows. Then after, they go home and they develop the picture. And where was standing the lady pilgrim . . . is only a blank. So then everybody understand, was the Virgin Mary!"

It's curious that Inácio has chosen this of all stories to share with me. He doesn't know that I once walked the Camino collecting tales of its miraculous Virgins. Now he has given me one more. And one more story of the invisible companion. Whether it's Michiko, Saint James, the Virgin Mary or the Camino itself that walks with us, we never walk alone on the road to Santiago. To think that we do is, as Pilgrim Einstein would say, only an optical illusion of the consciousness.

All the Good Pilgrims

Inácio and Carmen are walking at a pace to make this day last forever, so I wish them *buen Camino* and stump ahead. Before long I come upon a fiftyish man flexing his legs by the path. He's John from Ireland, Derry to be exact, and his knee is giving him trouble. We chat about how you can recognize Canadians by their Tilley hats (John has one too, thanks to a sister in Newfoundland), then he waves me on. "I just need to take it slow till the knee loosens up." A little farther on, I find Maribel and Carlos taking a break under a tree.

"The shoulder? Much better, thanks. Would you believe the stuff we sent home from Pamplona weighed seven kilos? My backpack weighs nothing now."

The last bit of the way, the roar of the wind turbines builds and builds till you reach the crest of the sierra and they're towering right over your head. There's always a crowd here, taking pictures and casting last looks back at the Pyrenees. The view is exalting. Did we really walk that far in just two days? Aaron is here, enjoying it with some new female admirers.

"I didn't see you last night," I say.

"I stayed in Cizur Menor. Fantastic hospitalera. She unpacked my bag for me, threw out everything I didn't need and then fitted it to my body. I've got a girl's pack, that's what the problem is. She taped up my ankle and gave me blister pads and a foot massage. I'm a new man." Yes, Aaron's going to be fine.

I love this kind of Camino morning, the brief, friendly encounters, the updates, the sharing of chocolate and dried fruit and nuts. And between the encounters, the time alone, walking. Before this year with Michiko, I have only once had a constant walking companion for more than a day, and that was the very first time, on the way from Roncesvalles to Pamplona.

Loneliness was something I worried about before that first journey. It was not that I feared being by myself in the "lonely" places of the Camino—the mountains, the empty prairies, the ocean shore at Finisterre. On the contrary, that was something I looked forward to. The loneliness I feared was the being alone in a crowd. Would I fit in with the pilgrims? On the first day this was a moot question, as I was the only soul on the road from St-Jean-Pied-de-Port to Roncesvalles. For the next two, I had a walking partner. Ursula was a lively, intelligent Swiss woman. We started talking over supper in Roncesvalles and we never stopped. There was lots to talk about: jobs, families, countries, travels, girlfriends, boyfriends (former and current), books, songs, plans, dreams and why-we-were-doing-the-Camino. (She loved nature, walking, meeting people—and was Catholic.) We climbed over hills and scrambled down ravines and all the while we talked talked talked.

It was great to have such agreeable company. I certainly never felt lonely. For two days we were together from good morning to good night, and ours wasn't the kind of partnership that shut the rest of the world out. Other pilgrims caught onto us like burrs to wool socks, and we talked talked talked to them too. It looked like merry times clear across Spain. But were merry times what I really wanted? It troubled me when I lay down at night and cast my thoughts back over the day to find I had almost no memory of where I had been. My feet were on the Camino, but my thoughts were always somewhere else, in Canada, Switzerland, the future, the past.

On our second afternoon together, Ursula and I passed a

gentle German pilgrim named John. He was standing at the edge of a path above a valley, eyes closed, arms spread wide to catch the racing wind. He looked ready to take off and glide over the treetops. When he heard us coming, he opened his eyes, smiled shyly, then slipped back into the moment. I wanted to do as he was doing, feel what he felt, but that would require explanations and excuses. So I kept on walking. But I had begun to realize that for all I gained from Ursula's company, I was giving up my freedom to be where I was now. It bothered me besides to think that someone I might never see again would forever hold one half of my Camino. And so, when Ursula shook me awake the third day, in Pamplona, and said, "Come on, sleepyhead, time to get moving," I told her, "You go ahead. I'll catch up with you."

I spent that morning in the city getting reacquainted with myself. It felt like a luxury. But soon it was time to set out on my own, to walk the Camino for the first time with no one holding my hand. It was past noon when I started, but I was rejuvenated by my easy morning, and on a day when other pilgrims were crawling along in the heat, I was soon overtaking them. The first I caught up with were an old and a young man crossing the plain together.

"*Buen camino*," I said as I drew level.

"*Bon chemin*," they replied.

For a few minutes we chatted about the heat. They offered me some water, and then the old one said, "Don't wait for us. I need to take it slow."

I felt awkward. Wasn't it rude to run away from someone you'd just met?

"Go on, go on," he said. "This is the Camino. Everyone to his own pace."

So I strode on ahead of the French pilgrims till I saw two girls sitting under a tree and asked to share their shade for a while. Holland and Erika were American college students on a school trip from hell as a fanatical art professor dragged their class over ninety kilometres of Camino in three days. They told some gut-splitting stories about their ordeal, then they both fell asleep. I sat watch over them for a few minutes, until I saw a familiar stick coming up the path. It belonged to Luz, a female life force from Madrid who was walking the Camino as a prayer for her sick mother. Luz had a big laugh, a big heart and a really big stick with a red plastic cross lashed to the top.

"*Ay, peregrino! Qué calor!*" Every one of her joints was bound and trussed, every step she took was a station of the cross. She laughed and moaned and cursed the sun. We were starting our climb to the Sierra del Perdón when she told me, "If you stay with me, you'll be an old man by the time you get to Santiago. Go on. I'll see you tonight in Puente la Reina."

So I hiked on alone, but I didn't stay that way for long. I soon heard a *crunch crunch crunch* coming up the path and it was my turn to be overtaken. Richard from Paris was tall and reedy, his bony white knees on a level with my waist. He walked like a spider and his natural quickness was jet-charged by an urgency to get to Santiago, as if he knew that the woman of his dreams was waiting for him in the cathedral square, glancing at her watch. He decelerated for a few minutes to tell me about his unhappy job, his child out of wedlock, his conviction that this experience was changing his life. But for Richard, walking at my speed was like having his shorts around his ankles.

"You're stopping in Puente la Reina tonight?" I asked him eventually. "I'll see you there. Go ahead."

I paused to catch my breath. Already there was no sign of Richard on the path before me. I looked back but couldn't see Luz. The lonely tree where I had left Erika and Holland snoozing was a speck. And the two Frenchmen? Who knows? I was certain that I wouldn't be seeing any of them again today, maybe ever. But that only showed how much I knew about walking.

In the village of Zariquiegui, pilgrims were gathered around the village fountain like caravans at an oasis. My recent acquaintance Richard was there. He shook my hand as if he hadn't seen me in days. Alicia from Madrid was doling out tomatoes, bread and sweet onions for everyone from her bottomless bag. Montse from Barcelona had apples to share, another pilgrim, chocolate. I plunged my face in the cold water of the fountain, and when I cleared the water from my eyes, Luz's red cross was heaving into sight. I sank my teeth into a tomato, and there were Erika and Holland. I had thought I was miles ahead of them, but it wasn't so. We were only walking, after all.

The day went on at the same gentle rhythm—meeting and being met, slowing down and speeding up, then falling back to your own pace. When you wanted company, there was someone there. When you wanted to be alone, you slipped into the spaces between. Each of us was as alone as he or she wanted to be.

I never walked with Ursula again. As things worked out, I spent an extra day in Puente la Reina because of a tick and fell behind her for good, though I continued to see her name in the registers of the refuges, always gaining another day on me. I hope her Camino was a happy one.

One more thing I took from that day five years ago: the memory of a certain moment when the view of a long stretch of road opened up below me and I saw a straggling trail of pilgrims crossing the fields and pastures. They were far enough away as to seem barely human—tiny, upright figures picking their way across the face of the land—yet not so far that I couldn't recognize each of them, one by his hat, another by her walk, her stick, the colour of her shirt. And though it was not something I could see, I knew them well enough to understand that they all had their own hopes, stories, reasons, sadnesses, odd notions—the same as I did. We were alone in our selfhood, but united in our experience. Whatever we were looking for on the way to Santiago, we approached it over the same earth. Wherever life took us when this was over, we would be together in the road we had shared. I date from that moment a change, or the beginning of a change, in myself: the change from a walker to a pilgrim.

Life is a pilgrimage and a pilgrimage is a life. It is a metaphor, but for a few weeks we were living it. The Camino was our life, and the people we shared it with were our family, friends and colleagues. Some we liked more than others, but that made no difference. There was only one road, we all had to share it, and in the end it would take us all to the same place. This was life, compressed in time, heightened in effect, stretched across a Spanish landscape.

A Missing Bar

You cross the spine of the Sierra del Perdón, leaving the wind turbines behind, and descend to a sparser, drier, more "Spanish-looking" land. At the centre of the first village, Uterga, in the shelter of its three trees, stands the well. It is the hub of civic life, the bus stop, the playground. The proud inscription proclaims: *De Pamplona a Puente, en Uterga la mejor fuente*—"From Pamplona to Puente la Reina, Uterga's well is the best." It is for a watering hole of another kind, however, that I remember Uterga: a cool, cavernous bar on the street level of an old stone house, with arched doors that open on the Camino, and walls inside papered with postcards, letters and photos of pilgrims.

I may be giving the impression that the Camino is nothing but a bar crawl (which it is for some, and the world's longest), so let's be clear what a bar means in the Spanish context. The traditional Spanish bar, be it in the tiniest village or the heart of Madrid, is a home with an open door, the living room of the community, where it's as natural to see mothers chatting while their children race between the legs of the tables as it is to see men watching soccer. For pilgrims, bars are the source of life-giving morning coffee (the Spanish do not separate the functions of bar and café), of groceries in villages too small for a shop, of meals, of shelter from sun, wind, snow and rain, of toilet facilities. A bar is a place to meet new friends and old, a place where, if ever you want to set your backpack down for a few hours, it will be safe until the end of time, and where, every now and then, you will be given something for nothing, because you are not only the bartender's customer, you are his guest.

The first time I arrived at the bar in Uterga, on that hot July afternoon in 1999, the long tables were lined on both sides with heat-dodging pilgrims and laden with pitchers of water and wine, baskets of crusty bread, plates of sharp cheese and smoky ham, bowls of olives and pimientos. Most of all there was *alegría*—laughter, high spirits, good fellow-ship. I sat for a few minutes, drank as much wine as seemed prudent in that heat and, before I left, signed the big guest book that lay open on the table.

Two weeks ago, I wanted to show Michiko this bar, but I couldn't find it. I was sure I knew where it was, it just wasn't there. Was my memory playing tricks? There *was* a bar in town—a spanking new place with a pebbled terrace and pot lights in the shape of scallop shells—but it was not the bar I knew. Had I transplanted another town's bar to Uterga? Or had it shut down forever, like my *jai alai* bar?

Today I intend to solve the mystery. I walk from the top of the town to the bottom. No bar. I come back to check the side street where the church stands. No bar. Then I see an old man coming up the road.

"Excuse me, sir, wasn't there a bar here once?"

"The bar? Over there." He waves me towards the new place.

I raise my voice three notches. "Not that bar, another one. Four or five years ago."

He blinks his rheumy eyes. "You were here five years ago?"

"Yes, and I remember a bar, in an old house, with long tables inside."

Now he smiles. He takes my elbow and turns me to face a white stone house with balconies on the second floor, iron grates over the windows, and ivy and rose vines climbing the walls. There is a handsome arched entryway and a stone bench out front where, with a little effort, I can picture pilgrims with wineglasses in their hands. "This is the place you mean, young man. This was *my* bar." He admires the house for a moment. "So you remember the long tables."

"Yes, I do. And the guest books."

He nods. "Ah, the guest books. Young man, I still have those guest books. Every one of them. Full of messages from pilgrims from all over the world. *Todo el mundo* stopped at my bar. We had rooms upstairs, too. Did you stay with us?"

"No, I only stopped for a glass of wine."

"The wine was good, wasn't it?"

I don't need to tell him. Of course the wine was good. "Why did you close your bar?"

"My daughters went away to college. It got to be more than I could handle on my own. And then . . ." He nods at the swank new place smack across the street. "It was time."

When he takes my hand, his grip is firm, his eyes gleam with pride. He could ask for nothing better than to be remembered as one who provided strangers with good wine, clean rooms, an honest welcome. I decide that if nothing else comes of this Camino, it's worth it just to have put a smile on his weathered face.

A Tick

The morning after that glorious day of my first Camino, when I walked from Pamplona and felt myself a pilgrim, I woke up in the refuge of Puente la Reina with a tick on my knee. It was a tick the size of a peppercorn. I had no idea when it had attached itself to me, but it had made itself quite at home. I had no prior experience with ticks, but I thought I knew who would have.

Montse was a tall, willowy, fair Catalan pilgrim with dark hair that hung around her huge, clear eyes. She always wore an orange tie-dye wraparound and sandals, and walked with a stick even taller than she was. I picture her sitting in streams on hot days, or resting cross-legged on the grass, eyes closed. She made no distinction between persons, talking to the children along the way with the same earnest, solicitous respect she paid to pilgrims, hospitaleros and bartenders. She was a doctor, and I heard, though never had it confirmed, that she was doing the Camino as treatment for a broken heart. I found her presence calming and wanted to know her better, but when I was around her I always felt a little in awe and at a loss for words. So I looked on this tick with something like gratitude. It gave us something easy to talk about.

"Ah, a *garrapata*," she said. The Spanish word, with its echoes of "grip" and "grapple," seemed just right for the thing on my knee. "I've had dozens of these. All you need is olive oil."

Her long bare feet slapped against the tiles as she ran to find the key to the kitchen. A minute later she was back with a cotton swab doused in oil. She went to work, swishing the tick back and forth, telling it to let go in her most persuasive voice. I sat back and enjoyed being ministered to.

"They can't stand olive oil. You just need a little. Then you coax them out. Their stinger is like a corkscrew, you see, so you twist them. Come on now . . ."

Soon a circle of onlookers had gathered. As Montse laid on the oil, enough now to toss a salad, they started to pitch in their two cents' worth.

"You know what they really can't stand? Raw onion."

"I've heard garlic works too."

"I use a cigarette myself. The trick is not to burn them, just put a fire up their ass."

"I'd be afraid to try that. You might kill it."

"Oh, you wouldn't want to kill it."

On this point, at least, everyone agreed. A dead tick's stinger festered inside you, bringing fever, headaches, delirium. No, you wanted to negotiate with a tick. Make it recognize its best interests.

Montse stopped swishing. She looked troubled. "This isn't working."

The others leaned in. I felt like the subject of an autopsy. "It's not dead, is it?"

"It's hard to tell."

It was hard to tell indeed. Ticks are not expressive. The committee debated, then decreed that I should go to the town medical clinic. Living as we did in our little pilgrim world, it never crossed anyone's mind that the chances of finding a doctor on duty at 7:30 on a Sunday morning in a town with a population of 2,100 were slim. But the Camino provides. A tall, stooped fellow in a medical gown was standing at the door of the clinic smoking a cigarette when I arrived, looking as if he'd already heard that a tick emergency was coming in. It turned out he was waiting for a French girl with a twisted knee, but once he had seen to her, he sat me on a bed and slathered the little limp parasite in olive oil. He made a phone call, lit a cigarette and came back to give the critter a flick.

"It's dead," he muttered.

"I told you that," I said.

He found a pair of tweezers, took hold of the drowned tick and delicately began to turn its body. I relaxed. Clearly I was in the hands of a master.

"Shit."

"What is it?"

"It broke."

After what I had heard from the experts at the refuge, I expected the delirium tremens to set in at once. "Do I need an antibiotic?"

"Probably not," said the doctor. "Fifty percent of the time with ticks, nothing happens. The other fifty percent, you get a fever that lasts a day or two. If you do get sick, come back and I'll give you something."

It was mainly the prospect of coming down with a fever halfway to Estella in 35-degree heat that kept me from walking that day. But it was not the only reason. After five days of Camino, my feet and legs were a mess. My glorious walk of the day before had left me crippled. The backs of my ankles were chafed, blisters had bloomed on my toes, and my heels ached every time they touched the ground. I was happy for a pretext to take the day off.

Half of the problem was my shoes: too tight, and without the heel and arch support I needed. (My cotton socks didn't help either, absorbing my sweat, then rubbing against the skin.) The other half was that I had never been in the custom of walking twenty-five thousand steps a day with a thirty-pound weight on my back. That was a kind of exercise I had only done before in dreams, or over the level terrain of maps and books. Why had I assumed it would come naturally?

Of course, I didn't want to lose a day in Puente la Reina. I had momentum, I was making friends, I had a plane ticket with a fixed return date. But I also had very sore feet. I spent a dull, solitary day at the refuge, shooing off flies and waiting for the sweats to break out (there was never a sniffle). Then, late in the afternoon, German John appeared unexpectedly. He had not gone ahead that day, but back to the mysterious chapel of Eunate, some kilometres before Puente la Reina, where he had passed his hours in peace and prayer. When I told him about the tick, he shook his head.

"You put olive oil on it? Olive oil suffocates them. If only I had been here . . ." From his bag, he produced a first aid kit the size of a tool box. After rummaging a moment, he picked out a tiny plastic instrument that looked like the bastard progeny of nail clippers and a corkscrew. "It's to take ticks off dogs. You slip the head over the tick's body, tighten it and then . . ." He turned the attachment at the top. "Unscrew!"

I asked if he had anything in his wonder box for feet.

"What's the problem?"

A half-hour later, my feet had been rubbed, creamed, salved, buffed and bound. All they needed was a ribbon. What was better, John had equipped me with blister pads, gauze bandages and helpful tips to keep me hobbling on. I lost a day in Puente la Reina, but without it I would have lost more. I might not have made it to Santiago at all.

Our Lady of the Bundle Buggy

We all benefit from the charity of the towns and villages where we stay, and as pilgrims we are enjoined to give as well as to receive. So why are the pilgrims in the refuge of Puente la Reina showing so little charity to the homeless man who has snuck into the refuge to snatch a few hours of sleep?

"You're no pilgrim, you're a disgrace!"

"You have no right to be here!"

"Get out or we'll call the police!"

The little hobo holds his own, muttering back in a slurred voice the imprecation *"Me cago en Dios,"* "I shit upon God"— just to let us know that this business is strictly between him and the Deity.

The issue with the scruffy intruder is not his presence but his smell (and what a theme that is becoming on this Camino), a long-unwashed odour that invaded the dreams of the sleepers at his end of the room when he slipped in from the street an hour ago. Of course, it's easy for me to moralize from over here (I caught a whiff of him as he went by, so I know why they're howling). And I have to confess some chagrin, since the empty bed the little man is occupying was mine. I abandoned it an hour ago, after the Brazilian pilgrim in the next bunk started to snore like a cement mixer. Like Lazarus, I took up my pallet and walked—to the far end of the dorm, where I pitched it on the floor.

The storm rages through the night. Things settle down for a bit, everyone snatches some sleep, then the curses and threats start again. The sleepers at my end of the room wake up and yell at the complainers to be quiet. And at some point I do something that in retrospect I can only call cowardly. The hobo has stamped out of the room—to look for a bed elsewhere? But here he is, coming back, hacking, shuffling, swearing under his breath. As he steps into the room, shame prods me. It's my fault that the other pilgrims can't sleep. I set myself in the little man's path.

"Please, señor, you cannot sleep here."

This stops him dead. My words have punctured the membrane of his solitude. He looks up into my face. And then he barks with wounded pride, "What the hell do you mean I can't sleep here? *Éste es mi país!*"

This is my country. An argument I cannot answer. I step aside. The night goes on.

You will appreciate, then, why I leave Puente la Reina this morning without stopping to admire the splendid churches or the sigh-inspiring bridge that gives the town its name. I'm starting to wonder if walking the Camino is strictly consistent with writing about it. Couldn't I maybe use a little distance?

The Camino's response to this rhetorical question is María. She must be in her late sixties, this woman in battered white sneakers walking ahead of me at the edge of the highway, pulling a bundle buggy. Despite the heat that will soon hit bread-baking levels, she is draped in a long blue raincoat. She flashes a smile when I say good morning.

"Excuse me," I say, pointing at her buggy, "but are you walking to Santiago with that thing?"

"My *changuito*? Of course. Do I look like I could carry a backpack?"

"But the road is very rough today."

"Yes, it was rough on the way from Roncesvalles too. When it's like that, I walk on the highway."

Today's road, as I know from my recent walk with Michiko, has been torn up by construction. The busy highway is no treat to walk on either. There is a long flyover with almost no shoulder to it.

"I'll manage. Who would want to run over a poor old lady like me?"

"Can I help with your buggy?"

"No, thank you, I don't like people feeling they have to help me. It was my choice to come here and walk the Camino, and I'll do my best with God's help."

I make one last feint at being the Samaritan. "It's going to be a hot day."

"Yes, isn't it wonderful? It's raining back in Argentina. Well, you enjoy your walk. Maybe we'll see each other again."

We go our separate ways, she toddling up the highway, I tromping down the pilgrim footpath. I'm concerned about her, but I feel I've done my best. I'm also a little relieved. María has taken some of the weight of the world onto her bundle buggy. When I think of her trundling to Santiago with her buggy and her smile, it's pathetic to complain about a little heat or a bad night's sleep.

The morning passes, the beautiful, still towns succeed each other and María's image fades. Then, in Villatuerta, the last town before Estella, as I sit in front of the church, a pilgrim approaches. His bare legs are long and sinewy and he has a red bandana wound tight as a poultice around his skull. He speaks with a German accent.

"Hello. Did you see María?"

"María?"

"The lady from Argentina with the buggy. I haven't seen her since this morning. I'm going back to check if she's okay. Can I leave my bag with you?"

He unburdens himself of his enormous pack. There is a guitar case lashed to the outside. My conscience coughs. I tried to be the Good Samaritan when I met María this morning, but this pilgrim is the Better Samaritan.

"Sure, I'll keep an eye on it."

It's only after he's out of sight that I hear the echo and remember that it was in Villatuerta that another Samaritan turned back to help.

Harry's Story

Today's pilgrims mostly think of the Camino as a break, a few weeks of healthy exertion and renewal before they resume their lives. They carry return tickets, and it doesn't cross their minds that they might not live to use them. Pilgrims in the old days were more circumspect. They set out prepared never to come home.

In the pioneer days of the Camino, it was mostly nature that dealt the fatal blow. Pilgrims froze in mountain passes and drowned crossing rivers, were poisoned by bad meat or water, were killed by wolves, or simply gave in to the effects of long exertion and poor nutrition. As the Camino was "civilized," the Grim Reaper got a hand from humans: treacherous innkeepers and toll collectors, ferrymen who "lost" their pilgrim cargo, wandering bands of mercenaries, and sick pilgrims seeking cures who turned the road into a highway of contagion. If a pilgrim was wealthy, he could hope to be buried with some ceremony, but the poor pilgrim, if he was fortunate enough to be buried at all, was laid to rest under the stark epitaph *Aquí yace un peregrino*—"Here lies a pilgrim."

Though it is rare today, pilgrims still die on the Camino. Not by the hundreds, but a few every year. Their modest memorials can be seen from the Pyrenees to the place, less than twenty-five kilometres from Santiago, where "Guillaume Watt Embraced God at 69 Years, 25th August, 1993." Of course, a person can die anywhere, but a death on a pilgrimage is seen in a special light. In the old days it was believed that the good pilgrim was one step from heaven.

The day I heard the story of Harry and Catherine Kimpton was a Saturday. It was the 2003 spring meeting of the Little Company of Pilgrims and there were fifty or so of us scattered over ten rows of plastic chairs in the basement of St. James Humber Bay Anglican church. Toronto has had its own Camino gatherings since 1994, when Father Ben Lochridge came home from a life-altering pilgrimage with a pilgrim's longing to share his experience. Some of the early meetings drew three attendees. These days the church parking lot is always full.

As usual, Barbara and Anthony Cappuccitti had lined up an interesting slate of speakers. Marina from the Spanish tourist office was going to talk about the esoteric Camino. Sue Kenney was there to tell us about sorrow stones. Bob Crew of the *Toronto Star* was back from Spain with stories and slides. And then there was Harry Kimpton. Harry looked as if he'd just roused himself from his couch. The moustache and glasses, the unbuttoned cardigan, the softness around the middle—everything about him said "Dad." He was introduced by Marina, who seemed to know him well, and the two fiddled with the mike for a minute to get it down to his level. Then he pushed his glasses up his nose and thanked us all for coming. He didn't waste words explaining why he was speaking that day. He just told his story.

"Last year, my wife and I began to talk about doing something different. She had just retired, and my career was winding down. We had some time for ourselves. And both of us were feeling that we didn't like the direction things were going in this world. We had heard about the Camino, and the more we talked about it, the more it sounded like something we should do.

"Well, we started out in France, from St-Jean-Pedi . . . Pierre-de . . . I never can get the name of that place straight. And that first day, crossing the Pyrenees, was no picnic. Somehow we made it over the mountains to Roncesvalles. And that was where our adventure began. I'll never forget the wonder of the next days. The things we saw and heard. Sometimes we would just stop and listen to the wind blowing through the grass. I'm sure that all of you who have been on the Camino have done that. It was something we hadn't done for years, something we'd never found time to do. And now it was coming back to us, the joy and freedom of just being alive. We even watched the ants! Imagine. I don't think I've ever paid attention to ants before. So those first days on the Camino were something very special for us.

"Now, on the fifth day we were walking from Puente la Reina to Estella. We were coming down one path and there was a Spanish man coming along another path parallel to ours, and he was whistling and smiling and walking along at a great pace. And it happened that we came at the same moment to the point where the two paths met. Of course, we didn't know any Spanish and he didn't speak English either, but we said hello in our own languages and smiled. Then he kept on walking at his speed and we at ours.

"Well, it was very hot that day, and Catherine was having a hard time. She wasn't one to complain, but anyone could see that she was feeling poorly, and I guess the Spanish man picked up on that. He had gone up the road ahead of us a good fifty or hundred yards, when all of a sudden he stopped and turned around and came back all the way to where we were. And when he got to us, he had a bandana tied around his neck, and he took the bandana off and he tied it around Catherine's forehead.

"Well, we looked at him and he at us, and we didn't have the words to thank him, but I think he understood what we wanted to say. And then he started off again. Pretty soon he was out of sight, and we were wondering how we would ever catch up with him to return his bandana. Then all of a sudden there he was, coming back again. We didn't have any idea what he was up to, we just kept walking till we met him. Then he took hold of Catherine's backpack, just like that, and he slipped it off her shoulders and put it on himself. Of course, he already had his own pack on, so he had to carry hers in front. But he just shrugged like it was no big deal, and then he took off again and left us behind.

"I looked over at Catherine and said, 'How are you feeling?' And she smiled and said she was feeling pretty good. The going was much easier now, and we felt lighter just knowing that there was such kindness in the world. We walked on for ten minutes or so, and then we saw our Spanish friend at a rest area by the highway, waiting for us to catch up. We couldn't talk to each other, but words weren't necessary. It was like we were already old friends. And there we were, standing

by the roadside, smiling and wiping our foreheads, when out
of the corner of my eye I saw a car coming. It was coming
very fast, and as I watched, it seemed to come off the highway
towards us. Without thinking, I took one step back and felt it
brush my leg.

"The car hit Catherine and the Spanish man. Catherine
was killed instantly, and the man was terribly injured. The car
stopped in some bushes and the doors opened. Two young
men got out, and I attacked one of them. I didn't know what I
was doing. I was shouting and going on. Then the ambulance
came and the next thing I knew I was in hospital with things
all over my chest. I wasn't injured, just a graze on my knee
where the car went past me. But I was in shock.

"When I came to in the hospital, there was a man sitting
by my bed. He told me that he was from Ottawa, and he had
been at the refuge in Estella and heard what happened. He
said he spoke Spanish, and was there anything he could do to
help? Well, there I was in hospital in a foreign country where
I didn't speak the language. My wife was dead and I had
to somehow bring her body back to Canada. And here was
this man, a total stranger, who had come to help me. And I
thought to myself, 'This is Jesus Christ.' I don't know how
I would have got through the next few days without him. He
gave up his pilgrimage for me. When I got back to Canada,
he was the first person I called, and he continues to help me.

"In the end, I only spent a few days on the Camino. I lost a
great deal in those few days, yet I brought a great deal back
with me. I believe that, if I lived, it is because God saved me.
I stepped back and I didn't die. I was given a gift. Now I have
to give something back, whatever I can. I smile more than I
used to. I'm always smiling at people. People I know, people
I don't know, it doesn't make any difference. I give them a
hug if they let me. I want them to know how lucky they are to

be alive. I can only think that's why God saved me. To give something back. Thank you all for listening."

There was a warm round of applause. Harry acknowledged it with a smile, gave Marina a big hug and went back to sit down on one of the plastic chairs. He had given witness to the mystery of life and death. Now he was just an elderly gentleman in a cardigan, and the mystery was ours to grapple with.

I marvelled at Harry's capacity to turn his tragedy into an affirmation of life's goodness and God's love. Another man might come to the opposite conclusion, for the whole thing came down to timing—a minute earlier, a minute later, and that day in June would have been another happy, life-affirming day on the Camino de Santiago. And the act that had set the clock ticking was the act of a Samaritan, an act of pure kindness.

A few weeks after Harry spoke to us, he was back in Spain. In his working days, he had been a bricklayer; now he was going to build a monument for his wife. People from Estella helped out, and the memorial was completed in time for the anniversary of the accident. In attendance at the dedication service was the Spanish Samaritan, only recently recovered from his injuries. Afterwards, he and Harry walked the rest of the Camino together. Or rather, he and Harry and Catherine, the silent companion.

Catherine's memorial stands by the highway just after Villatuerta. It is a simple stone cairn, a metre high, topped with a figurine of the Madonna as a young girl. The plaque, in Spanish, bears the inscription "In memory of Mary Catherine Kimpton, Canadian pilgrim, who died tragically in this place at 4 p.m. on the 2nd of June, 2002. May she walk forever in fields of gold." When Michiko and I passed two weeks ago, someone had placed a rosary in the hands of the figurine.

Other pilgrims had left tokens—a cross made from twigs, a scrap of cloth, coins from their countries. There was an empty tin can at the base that Michiko filled with yellow wildflowers.

They are still here today, dry, fragile, bright in memory.

Research

Estella's Plaza de los Fueros is the epitome of a Spanish plaza. The lungs of the city, it inhales and exhales the Estellans at intervals through the day, drawing them together then puffing them back to their homes. In the morning, they come for the open-air market; after noon, everyone converges here for coffee and spirits; from five, it is the mothers who come to sit at the outdoor cafés while their children turn the plaza into a soccer pitch (the trees around the perimeter are set at the precise distance to serve as goalposts); between eight and nine comes the grand pre-supper *paseo*, when the whole city meets, promenades, flirts, caffeinates and gets caught up on what's happened in the several hours since everyone saw everyone last. After the evening meal, I'm sorry to say, I have no idea what happens. I have always had to run back to the refuge by ten.

The Camino Francés, the French Camino, is an apt name for the road we are walking, not only because it originates in France and has always teemed with French pilgrims, but because it was largely built and settled by the French. Estella, first populated by immigrants from the province of Auvergne, is only one of the Camino's "French towns." It was established in the eleventh century, a time when Spain's Christian rulers were asserting control over lands they had battled over for centuries with the Muslims, lands that formed a natural corridor clear across Spain to Galicia. Once this corridor was secured, the number of pilgrims leaped, and with them the need for roads, bridges, churches, hospitals, inns and all the services a pilgrim requires. The tiny Spanish kingdoms lacked the skills and the numbers to meet the demand, so they called on the French for help. They responded in waves, lured largely by economic initiatives (the term *franco*, a designation used for all foreigners, implied both *French* ethnicity and *freedom* from taxes). In a few cities, such as Pamplona, the newcomers retained their identity and privileges for generations. But the greater number assimilated rapidly—and soon were just as anti-French as the old Spaniards.

With all this history, plus the fact that the Estella pilgrims' association has played a leading role in the revival of the Camino, this would be a great place to do some of that *research*—since research is something I feel I should be doing. (It's a dull, nagging duty that comes with writing books.) The hospitalero could probably point me in some interesting directions, but when I arrive at the refuge he is caught up in a dispute with some pilgrims over their credentials. Suddenly someone rushes in from the street. "Has anyone seen my wallet? I left it outside on the bench and now it's gone!" A crowd of pilgrims rush out to join the wallet hunt. Among them I recognize my nemesis, the Brazilian cement mixer from last night.

Things are a little chaotic right now. Maybe I'll go for a walk and check in later. A few aimless steps take me from the refuge to the bridge. Then my legs carry me down the long, narrow street to the Plaza de los Fueros. I find a seat at a café with a view of the action, order a glass of wine and wonder what it's like to spend an hour or three every day here for your whole life, from being pushed in a carriage, to kicking a ball, to trailing your secret love at a discreet distance, to minding the kids, to sitting on a bench with a big cap on your head and a cane between your knees, shooting the breeze with the same people you've known since the beginning.

In fact, wouldn't it be nice to spend a peaceful night right here in the plaza and forget about research and snoring and night intruders? The thought startles me. The first time I did the Camino, I disapproved of pilgrims who didn't stay exclusively in refuges, nor was I alone in my rectitude. I remember hearing it whispered that a certain Brazilian pilgrim sometimes slept in a hotel. In the eyes of some, this was no better than sleeping in a brothel. And now here am I, a mere four days into my walk, contemplating a night in a private room. Can my pilgrim conscience live with this?

I find that it can. Without shame or hesitation, I call at the *pensión* just off the plaza. The rooms with a view are taken, but up some back stairs in a disused part of the building there is a box of a bedchamber with a bare light bulb dangling from the ceiling. The bedsprings click against the floor when I sit on the mattress. At least I can't be accused of spending the night in a harem. Thank you it's lovely I'll take it.

So far my ideas for research have not been panning out. It's hard to hit a target when you're in motion, but if you stop to take aim, you stop being a pilgrim. So maybe I'll just let the Camino decide what it wants me to say about it. In keeping with this resolution, I shall adopt a new line of research for this evening in Estella. Two weeks ago, when Michiko and I had supper at the Bar Casanova, the man at the opposite table told us he had eaten there twice a day, lunch and supper, for the past fourteen years. Tonight I will go back, equip myself with a bottle of wine and see if his run continues. After that, I'll stick around to see what happens in the Plaza de los Fueros after ten p.m. And that will be my research for September 29.

Del the Optimist

The man from Bar Casanova showed up all right. He had no recollection of me at all, though he did remember "the Japanese woman." And now I can tell you what happens in Estella after ten o'clock. Not much. Not on a chilly Wednesday in September, anyway.

I sleep until eight a.m. Magnificent. At night silence is golden. But by morning it turns to lead. Where is everybody? It's lonely here. By the time I've had my coffee and toured the morning market (buying a string of local sausage that will make me the friend of every dog from here to Burgos), I'm two hours behind pilgrim time. Tardiness has its benefits, however. For the first time in many Caminos, the famed monastery of Irache, just beyond Estella, is open when I arrive.

There is one other pilgrim in the pure white Baroque chapel, María's friend from yesterday, in his cut-off denim shorts and red and white bandana. He's pacing around the church, checking camera angles. Seems Charley is a photographer. He's been walking since May, all the way from Budapest, doing a photo essay for an Austrian magazine. After a chat, he gets back to his picture taking while I go looking for the door to the monastery's famous cloister. When our paths cross again a few minutes later, Charley's eyes are shining.

"I have been walking for five months," he says in a hushed voice, "and this is the most beautiful church I have seen. So pure. So spiritual. It is the first place where really I can hear the silence. I must play my guitar."

And under the bemused eyes of the custodian he opens his guitar case, takes out a balsa wood travelling model—"I made it myself," he tells me as he tunes—and starts to sing—what else?—"The Sound of Silence." His voice is good, and the guitar fills the church with brightness, so I try not to wonder if sound is really the best tribute to silence, or whether a song that compares silence to a cancer expresses exactly what Charley intends. When he's finished, Charley packs up his guitar and says, "I feel great now. Did you see the cloister?"

"No, I couldn't find the door."

"It's right over there." He points to a massive door near the back of the church that looks as if it could only be opened by an aged priest with a gigantic key. "Just give it a push."

I do. One touch and the door is open. Beyond lies the secret garden and the silent gallery where monks once paced and prayed. The fountain is overgrown with moss, the yard unkept. A single bird is singing. I wonder how many secret gardens I have missed in life because I didn't give a door a little push.

After Irache, the path runs through forest, a rare treat. A little climb and a pause to look back. On the shoulders of the hills across the way stand trees and a lonely hermitage. A purple mist rolls over the bare bluffs to the north. To the northeast, where I came from three days ago, ranks of mountains recede like memories.

It was around here, in October 2002, that I met Del. That was my second Camino, when I was gathering stories of miraculous Virgins. A cold coming I had of it, and a lonely one. Only seven of us set out from Roncesvalles, and there were many nights when I slept alone in refuges and days when I hardly met another pilgrim. So I was glad when I heard footsteps coming up the path behind me.

"Hello, are you a pilgrim? I suppose you would be, wouldn't you? And you speak English? God, it's been ages since I spoke English to anyone. I haven't seen anyone since this morning." He was a young man with a crisp, cheery Midlands accent. The words fairly exploded out of him.

"Where are you coming from?" I asked.

"Puente la Reina."

Puente la Reina was a day's walk before Estella, which I had recently left. If Del had seen no one for hours, it was because he had left them all behind.

"That's quite a walk."

"Well, I've only got twenty-eight days for the Camino, that's the absolute most I could get off work, so I wanted to cover as much ground as I could at the beginning just to have a cushion."

"So this is your fifth day?"

"Fourth."

Three days before, Del had leaped off the train in St-Jean-Pied-de-Port and hit the ground running. That first day, he attacked the Pyrenees after noon and only a lift from some friendly French motorists saved him from a chilly night on a mountainside.

"It doesn't seem quite the way to start a pilgrimage, does it, hitching a ride, but I'd have never made it to Roncesvalles before midnight otherwise. And in the end it was well worth it just for the chance to meet the local people. It was extraordinary, because these fellows in the car, I mean, we didn't have a single word in common, but we were still able to communicate. Just goes to show we're really all the same beneath the skin. And the people in Roncesvalles, well, everyone's been lovely. It's been just an incredible experience, and a very important one for me personally."

I wondered how Del had found time for so many life-enhancing encounters at the rate he was moving. His second day's walk from Roncesvalles to Pamplona had covered nearly fifty tough kilometres. Today he was tacking on another forty-five. If he kept up this pace, he could walk to Santiago and back again.

"I could almost, couldn't I? Not that that's what I had in mind, but it's a rather thrilling notion, isn't it? Maybe I'll do that next time. Say, are you ready to get walking?"

Del slowed down for me, but I still had to double my pace to keep up. As we went, I learned a great deal about his life, his job, his girlfriend, his thoughts on the Camino. Somehow I wasn't surprised to find out he was a radio call-in host. Talking was his job, and he was thrilled at the prospect of spending four weeks in silence. So thrilled that he couldn't stop talking about it.

"The Camino is an amazing chance really, a once-in-a-lifetime, to see who one is and what's important to one. Which is not to say that I'm in the least a *religious* person, at least not in any sort of institutional way. Though before I started on the Camino, I did receive some very definite signs that this was something I was *meant* to do . . . But that's not exactly what you'd call *religion*, is it? And yet at the same time, I think I can say that I'm quite a *spiritual* person. I have *questions*, you know—all of us have questions, I suppose—and this pilgrimage is a way of addressing them and having the time and the space to sort some things out once and for all."

"How's it going?"

"Well, you'd be amazed how many of my questions have already been answered. There's no limit to what you can learn in even three days if you open yourself up to it. Like those French chaps who picked me up on the highway. They didn't have to do that. It was pure kindness, and it taught me something. You know, I promised my listeners—and my listeners have been incredibly supportive—I promised that I'd keep a journal on my website so they could follow along and share in all I'm learning as I go. Because that's what the Camino is all about, isn't it? Learning and sharing. Do you reckon there's an Internet café in the next town?"

After an hour or so, I told Del I needed a break and if he wanted to go ahead, that was okay. He said he'd see me that night and shot off up the trail like an epiphany-seeking missile. I watched with relief. It wasn't that I didn't like Del, I just couldn't stand him. Or rather, I couldn't stand his certainties: that he was becoming a measurably better person with every step he took; that after four weeks on the Camino he'd have all the answers to life's big workbook of questions; that his experience would be just what he expected it to be and give him exactly what he thought he needed. There were no real discoveries here, only confirmations of what Del already knew. "Slow down and shut up," I wanted to tell him. "Stop walking the Camino and let the Camino walk you."

I felt cranky after I talked to him. When I started walking again, I found myself parroting things he had said. I even cast a bit of the *mal de ojo* on him, wishing him misfortune. Nothing grave, just a bit of tendinitis to throw him off schedule, a run-in with an obnoxious Spaniard, anything that would give a jolt to his certainties. But I knew he'd just put a happy spin on it. And maybe that was what galled me. That even if he was fatuous, he was optimistic and nothing seemed likely to change that. Was I perhaps jealous of Del's cheery faith in things?

I can hear his voice now, a little staticky, like he's on the air, refuting me in his very positive way.

Well, Bob, I don't deny it for a moment. I set out from a place of optimism and I find things that tend to confirm that optimism and maybe that's a self-fulfilling prophecy, but there you have it, that's how I'm built. Now you—and I don't mean this in a critical way— but you seem to start from a place of doubt and then find things that confirm your doubt, and there's nothing wrong with that, because at the end of the day we all want to be right, don't we? Even if it gives us no great joy . . .

I'm working on my reply, but it's already too late. Del's gone on to the next caller.

The Girls

The young women parked on the steps at the edge of the village of Villamayor de Monjardín would look at home on a *Vogue* cover: "Camino chic: Who says a pilgrim has to be a frump?" Everything matches, from the spiffy straw hats and silver scallop-shell earrings to the capri pants (one's in grey, the other blue). I don't see any matching backpacks. Have they already checked in somewhere?

"Yeah, we're at the refuge. Not exactly the nicest place we've been . . ."

"There's a hole in the ceiling and this *huge* spider web . . ."

"And the bathroom door doesn't really close . . ."

"And there's no windows . . ."

"But the ladies were nice . . ."

"Yeah, they were, weren't they . . ."

"And I've been laid up for three days with tendinitis, so this is it for today . . ."

Do they not know about the other refuge? The one a hundred metres up the road, with the clean, hot showers and the windows overlooking the valley?

They take one look at each other—"Can you wait here?"—and they're back in a wink with their matching backpacks. "Let's go before someone sees us," says Nuala. We tear up the street as if we're running out on a bill.

There is a turf war being waged in Villamayor de Monjar-dín, a battle for pilgrim hearts and euros. For eight years, the Dutch Evangelical refuge in the handsome stone house at the top of the square has served passable coffee with a side of John's Gospel. ("Maybe you'd like something to read while you're walking . . .") But the evangelism is soft-sell and the village is a wonderful place to cool off after the nine-kilometre walk from Estella.

Starting this summer, however, there is a new game in town, a refuge situated just where the Camino enters the ancient burg. As the girls have pointed out, the new place leaves much to be desired, but location is everything, and the welcome is so warm that many pilgrims who sit down "for a minute" end up staying the night.

"No, we're not happy about this," a lanky Dutch boy told me when I was here two weeks ago with Michiko. "No one spoke to us. One day the refuge was just there. And they are aggressive, the way they catch pilgrims on the way into town."

I saw him later that day hanging out at the well before the village, handing out pamphlets "just to inform pilgrims" that there were two refuges in Villamayor de Monjardín. I had just come from the new place, where the Spanish hospitalera was telling horror stories about how the Dutch made you sing psalms before they fed you and how "all the money" went to Holland. All what money? The pittance they made off the pilgrim trade wouldn't buy a sandwich at Schiphol airport. In the Dutch boy's opinion, it wasn't about money at all.

"No, from what I understand, our refuge belongs to one family and the new refuge belongs to the parish. It's some kind of local rivalry. Village politics."

Village politics. Now there's a concept. Imagine, these quaint little frozen-in-time postcard villages have lives, passions, *politics*. You could probably spend a year in one of them untangling the histories of love and hatred, alliances and power plays as old as Spain itself. Sadly, we have only a single night here, and if I have to take sides, I'm on the side of the Dutch, if only because the view from their refuge is better.

But then, the view means nothing to me today because I'm not staying here. It's too early in the day to stop walking, and besides, I missed Aaron, Inácio, Carmen and Maribel last night. I need to catch up on the developments of the past twenty-four hours. So I'll just drop these girls at the door of the Dutch hostel, then I'm off to Los Arcos.

"Will you stay and have a glass of *tinto* with us?" asks Kara. Well, that is an attractive offer. One little glass of red wine. I'm not really big on drinking and walking, but it's only noon, and Los Arcos is just twelve kilometres away. We settle down with our glasses on the shady porch. I learn that Nuala and Kara are Londoners, mid-twenties, former employees of Toni&Guy, the international salon. Last month they quit and set off in search of adventure. The Camino is Episode One, with future chapters possibly involving Barcelona, Japan, Australia, the United States and an ocean cruise to South America. They will work as they go and come back when they do.

With the first glass of wine under our belts, we consider the economics of the situation. Clearly, it makes sense to share a bottle. I'll have one more glass, it's too hot for walking yet. Can I top you up? Thank you. The Spanish hours pass in their inimitable fashion till I sense that we're nearing the point where a decision will have to be made. To stay or to go. Then again, if I keep putting off the decision, the hours will decide for me.

In the end, I stay in Villamayor.

That night, in the bar, I hear—or half-hear over the racket of a tableful of Spanish pilgrims—Kara and Nuala's Camino saga.

Her name may conjure up shamrocks and leprechauns, but Nuala McBride is Indian on her mother's side, and it's her mother's side that shows through in her mocha skin and dark, glinting eyes. When she speaks, her hands do little dances, the words rush out like flocks of swallows, then she catches you over her glasses with that arch gaze and you find yourself agreeing with—whatever it was she said. The fair and languid Kara provides a low-key counterpoint, mellow, wry, with a growl in her voice that suggests she has eternally just got up. As you watch the two of them light each other's smokes and finish each other's sentences, it's hard to believe they've only known each other for the two years they claim. Separated at birth is more like it.

Nuala tells the story in her elliptical fashion. Kara sits back, arms crossed, interjecting qualifications. I listen, enchanted, mystified and increasingly drunk. From what I can make out, everything started at a London book-signing by Paulo Coelho, author of a popular book on the Camino. Instead of presenting Coelho with his own book to sign, Nuala inadvertently handed him a SpiderMan comic that she had picked up for her nephew. Coelho grabbed her arm, and (subsequently? consequently?) the bones of that same arm were shattered in a fall. ("The specialist said, 'Normal people don't break their arms like that. Only babies fall down that hard. Adults are supposed to have protective mechanisms.'") At any rate, everything that has happened so far is somehow thanks to—or the fault of?—Paulo Coelho.

Nuala was several weeks recovering from her accident, time she spent visiting the Chapel of the Miraculous Medallion in Paris, where the Virgin Mary once appeared to a nun. There Nuala had an extraordinary experience, the details of which she promises to tell me someday (the Camino is long), but which I have yet to hear (the Camino leaves much untold).

She came home with a sackful of Miraculous Medallions (Kara shows me hers: an eerie green holograph that takes Catholicism to new places) and a determination to walk the Camino.

And here we are.

These women are mad and inspiring. They are optimists, but not of the Del variety. They have no agenda, no 28-day plan. Their Camino is a brightly illustrated book of adventures, a big one they have to hold in two hands, and they never know what will happen next till they turn the page. They are pilgrims on the Camino of uncharted tomorrows.

But there, I said they have no agenda. I've forgotten the party. The girls have made one misstep. On their second day, fresh out of Roncesvalles and full of pep, they decided that an all-nighter on the beach at Finisterre would be just the way to wind up their pilgrimage. Together with a wonderful black girl from California named Saffron, they picked a date, wrote up a bunch of notices and then asked bicycle pilgrims to post them in refuges along the way. The very next day, naturally, Kara came down with tendinitis. They were pinned for three days in Estella, lost touch with Saffron (who is somewhere up ahead, pumping the big event) and now find themselves having to rush. Even Kara and Nuala hear time's winged chariot at their backs.

We step out into the cold night. The sky is riddled with stars. We are the last ones into the refuge, whispering, tipsy, stifling giggles. The other pilgrims are asleep. No one, thankfully, is snoring.

Déjà Vu

To make amends for yesterday's half-day vacation, I'm up and walking before the girls open their eyes. Three hours of cut wheat, brilliant in the morning sun, the faded greens and browns of olive groves, low hills on either hand. There are new mountains to the northwest, higher than the Pyrenees at Roncesvalles. New wind turbines, too. Michiko and I had a game: How long will it take to walk there? How many hours? Days? My mind drifts from this moment back into the past, tacks forward into the misty dawns of the future. This is what we're made for, I think. Walking and daydreaming. Where are the yellow arrows that will point the way back to our lost innocence?

I catch up with John from Derry. He's walking with Sandee, a steady-headed senior from New York State who describes herself as a Christian educator. When I ask why she is doing the Camino, she knocks me down with an answer so detailed and precise that the only part I can repeat with confidence is that she first heard about it while hiking the Appalachian Trail. She and John were talking to "the other Canadian," Tony Bush, yesterday, so the big guy isn't far behind.

The sun climbs the sky and by noon the temperature is in the mid-thirties—just where I like it. Walking in the heat is a taste I acquired on my first Camino, when I found that on a hot afternoon I could have the road all to myself. The Spanish learn from childhood to pull down the shutters and stay out of the midday furnace, and pilgrims with sense emulate them, many starting at five a.m. to arrive at the next refuge before the heat sets in. Having no sense, I walk. My survival strategy is simple: I go slowly, keep my head down and hope the sun doesn't notice me.

After Los Arcos, the road to Sansol goes on forever. It starts out running straight as a beam of light towards the towers of the village, then peels off to the right as if to say, *Such a handsome place, let's admire it from another angle.* The detour would be less like torture if there were more than three trees in these eight kilometres, but three trees there are, or three at least that are close enough to the road for pilgrim use. The first is an almond tree so small you must crouch to fit in its umbra. The second and third stand side by side by a burbling brook, creating their own microclimate. Ten metres on either hand is inferno, but in their shade there are singing birds and a breeze. Once, in the paralyzing July heat of my first Camino, I stopped here for a nap. Later, at the refuge of Torres del Río, I mentioned my snooze to a Brazilian girl.

"Ah, that was you," she shot back. "I could have killed you. The only shade for eight kilometres and you were hogging it all."

Today the shade is being hogged by a middle-aged French couple. When I remark on the trees, the gentleman replies with Cartesian precision, "Poplars. They indicate the presence of water."

From Torres del Río, it's a dry, rough, rotten, up-and-down walk to Viana. Along the way, I pass the spot where Michiko took a tumble last month, tearing her pants and skinning her knee. An involuntary "ouch" escapes me, as if the pain were somehow in the place itself. By now there's hardly a step of the Camino that doesn't recall to me a feeling, the pain, satisfaction, weariness, laughter, doubt, exhilaration of some past moment. The mind has this power, to transform a landscape into a trail of memories, turning every tree and hill and stone into a window on the past, on *our* past.

In the kitchen of the refuge in Viana, Lualla from Vancouver is making a cup of tea. Her face is so familiar that I do a double take when I see her. Where do I know her from? Then I realize that Michiko and I met her last month in Villamayor de Monjardín, where she was taking a break from the Camino to help out at the new refuge. She just got back on the road today. She invites me to sit down for a cuppa with her and Lorraine, a yoga instructor from South Africa with a shaved head and a Modigliani face.

As I tell Lualla about my adventures since I saw her last, Lorraine leans closer and closer towards me, her gaze becoming intense, feral. Finally I have to say, *"What?"*

"I'm sorry. It's just your whole routine. It's like I've heard it before, and recently, every word, every detail. I just can't remember who it was, and I'm wondering whether it was anyone."

Lualla breaks into a laugh. "We were talking about déjà vu just now and saying how many times we've both felt it on the Camino. Looks like you've brought some in with you."

Lorraine tells me to please go on with my story, but within minutes that look is back.

"What is it now?"

"The way you took your notebook out of your pocket."

"Don't tell me you've seen my notebook before."

"I have. And the way you took it out of your pocket and opened it. Everything."

I ask if I should go on with my story. "I mean, you've heard it already, right?"

Lorraine grins. "Yes, but Lualla hasn't, and I promise not to ruin the ending."

I want to talk more with Lorraine, but people start coming in and then it's time to eat and soon it's time for bed. My bunk adjoins hers, however, and when I wake at four a.m., she's doing yoga exercises. She raises her legs slowly to ninety degrees and wiggles her toes. Inhale. Pause. Exhale. Amazing control, they wave like anemones. I lie still, falling into her breathing pattern. Inhale. Pause. Exhale. *So what's this* seen-it-before *all about?* I ask her in my thoughts. Since I started this Camino, I've been in a near-constant state of déjà vu—like today when I came to where Michiko fell, or when I saw Lualla in the kitchen. But for me it's different; I really have seen these things before. Lorraine hasn't seen me or Spain or anything here, not in this lifetime anyway. Inhale, pause, exhale.

I know the feeling she means. I got it as a kid, the sense of having lived this moment before in all its details. I've heard there's a rational explanation for it, just some crossed wires in the brain. This may be true, but it still doesn't explain why we like it so much, this certainty that we've been somewhere before. Is it that pilgrim longing again, to feel that no place on earth is foreign to us? That everywhere is our spirit's home, and wherever we go, we will find our memories, moments and stories waiting for us in the trees and hills and stones? I'll have to ask Lorraine what she thinks in the morning. Inhale. Pause . . .

When I wake again at six, Lorraine's bed is empty. Her bag is gone. I won't see her again, not on this Camino anyway.

PART II

This Is Camino

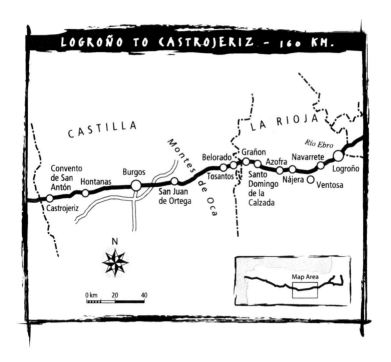

LOGROÑO TO CASTROJERIZ - 160 KM.

CASTILLA

LA RIOJA

Río Ebro

Belorado

Grañon

Azofra

Navarrete

Convento
de San
Antón

Hontanas

Burgos

Tosantos

Santo
Domingo
de la
Calzada

Nájera

Logroño

Ventosa

Castrojeriz

San Juan
de Ortega

Montes de Oca

N

0 km   20   40

Map Area

The Eternal Pilgrim

Logroño is the capital of La Rioja, the capital of wine. The pilgrim approaches the city from the Pico Sacro, passing along the way the home and madly barking dogs of the legendary Felisa, who for nearly twenty years dispensed "figs, water and love" (the motto of her *sello*) to every pilgrim who stopped at her impromptu welcome desk. Like so many who live by the Camino and devote their lives to it, Felisa never walked it herself. I remember her warm smile, her strong, generous laugh. Since her passing in 2002, at the age of ninety-one, her daughter, María Teodora, carries on the family tradition.

I cross the bridge over the slow-flowing, coffee brown Ebro and follow the yellow arrows to the old city core, a medieval *urbs* of straight, narrow streets shadowed by tall buildings that once were stately but are now dilapidated. At the gates of the refuge, I bump into Tony Bush. "Come on," he says, "I'll take you for a coffee." Poor Tony still hasn't figured out the Spanish phones and he's having a hell of a time all round. For a couple of days he was walking with two retired ladies from the States, but one of them quit on doctor's orders and now he's on his own again. "Everyone's faster than me," he laments. "I didn't come all the way to Spain to be lonely." Slow though he is, there was still enough iron in his legs to carry him thirty kilometres from Los Arcos today.

Back at the refuge, Kara and Nuala fly by me on the stairs. "I went for a motorcycle ride this morning," Nuala calls back. Never a dull moment. I stick my head hopefully into the kitchen. Not every refuge has a kitchen, but when there is one it's the place to be. Pilgrims often cook food in vast quantities, so any time you venture in you are liable to hear the magic words "Grab a plate and join us!" Sure enough, someone's cooking now. He's the same man I saw earlier at the reception desk, where he was welcoming everyone with a hug and a handshake. Thin as a stick, with skin of tanned leather and a wide gap-toothed grin, he looked like some harmless local character, someone the staff put up with. In the kitchen, however, he cuts a different figure, singing and talking to all and none as he chops parsley, shells shrimps, skins potatoes, cracks eggs. Ten minutes of steam and sizzle later, he's making the rounds with a platter of fritters. "Go on, have another. Good, aren't they?" And once he has our attention, a proposal: "I used to be the cook on a ship. I'm making fish soup tonight. Three euros each, to pay for the wine. Who's hungry?" Hands shoot up all over the room.

No one has seen José before. "I came from the other direction. I went to Santo Domingo de la Calzada yesterday to see my brother, but he wasn't home, so I came to Logroño today. I have friends here." Is he coming back from Santiago? "Santiago?" He dismisses the holy city with a wave of his hand. "I've been to Santiago enough. I'm walking to Rome. I'm going to be there when the Pope dies."

He steps out for a moment, then he's back with a fistful of laminated pages. He tosses them on the table in front of us and gets back to his cooking. The sheets go round from hand to hand. They are newspaper clippings from Germany, France,

Portugal, Spain, Gibraltar: the story of José the sailor in five languages.

Ten years ago, José's fishing boat, the *Revolución*, capsized in the North Atlantic. Of the seventeen men on board, only he lived to tell the tale. For nine hours he clung to the bodies of two drowned companions as the waters surged and crashed around him. At last he felt his flame dying. He raised his eyes to the stormy heavens and swore to the Virgin Mary that if he lived, he would spend his life on a pilgrimage of thanks. Moments later the helicopter arrived. Since then he has travelled 45,000 or 50,000 or 58,000 kilometres (the newspapers vary), on foot and sometimes bicycle. To Santiago, Rome and the shrine of Saint Olaf in Norway. To Jerusalem, India, Tibet. He has met the Pope, the Dalai Lama, Mother Teresa. In Syria, on his way to Jerusalem, soldiers broke his legs for taking a picture. After three months in hospital, he got up and went on walking. He is walking still. He is the eternal pilgrim.

José's story races through the refuge like wildfire. Pilgrims lead their friends by the hand into the kitchen. "Him, that's the guy." But José doesn't let it distract him from his soup. Pilgrims approach to tell him that his life is an inspiration. He grins and adds some salt. They ask for a picture. He glances over his shoulder, one hand still stirring the pot. It's only when he lifts the cauldron from the stove and brings it bubbling and fragrant to the table that he succumbs a little to pride. "This food," he announces, "you cannot buy with money. No restaurant in Spain serves it. The king can't eat this food. This . . . is fisherman's food."

As we devour our soup, we know that we are living a moment. We'll be telling this story for the rest of the Camino, and beyond: "I had supper one night with a kind of super-pilgrim, a man who's walked everywhere . . ." It's like eating

with one of those heroic statues of medieval pilgrims you see
in the plazas of Camino towns. The only thing is, there's
nothing heroic about José. To all appearances, he's just a
regular guy who happens to cook a mean fish soup. It's hard
to know whether to be impressed or disappointed that his
remarkable life has left him so unremarkable.

After supper, a group of Spanish pilgrims claim José. I
pop out with Nuala and Kara to the celebrated Calle Laurel,
where every door opens on a bar and every bar has its trade-
mark *tapa*—desiccated hams, surly cheeses, shrimp, octopus,
garlic-drenched mushrooms. The patrons stroll from bar to
bar like pilgrims to the shrines of saints, tippling from minia-
ture glasses of Rioja wine.

Kara shares her take on José. "What gets me is that he can
survive all these years being a pilgrim. And I don't just mean
in the sense that people give him things. It's the taking, too. I
can't just *take* things from people. I mean, if it's Nuala, okay,
I can pay her back. Or my dad, I'm going to pay him back
too . . . one of these days. But when people I don't know
give me things—like Saffron, that American girl, she gave me
this really cool cigarette box, and the first thing I thought was,
now I have to give her something back . . ."

"Of roughly equal value," I offer helpfully.

"See? You know what I mean."

I do. Like Kara, I was brought up to the tune of "The
Lord helps those who help themselves," a popular number in
the Protestant world. José walks to a different beat: "Provide
neither gold nor silver nor copper in your money belts . . .
for a worker is worthy of his food." A pilgrim like José is,
to this older way of thinking, a worker, bringing proof of
heaven's mercy to the world. He is a postman of prayers too,
carrying the intentions of the people he meets to their holy
destinations. In payment for this holy labour, it's only reason-

able that he accept some donations for maintenance: a little food, lodging, a euro or two. And the occasional drop of wine. For as we make our way back to the refuge, we see José at the end of a long table of Spanish pilgrims, a glass in his hand and a grin on his face.

The Footprint of the Goose

It was in Logroño last year that I met Luisa Rubines. Luisa was a tornado with ringlets, an angular, intense young Galician woman, always halfway to somewhere, who had gone to London some years before to study English and ended up staying there and opening her own photo studio. Now she was back in Spain, taking photos for a solo exhibition at the Museum of Pilgrimages in Santiago on the subject of the esoteric Camino. I had been trying for days to find out more about her project, and at last our paths crossed where they were always most likely to, in the plaza of the Church of Santiago. The object of our mutual curiosity was laid out on the pavement before us: the seven horizontal rows of nine squares, numbering one to sixty-three, that make up a life-sized game board of the Camino de Santiago, the Goose Game of Logroño.

It's a novel monument with interactive appeal. You'll often see pilgrims—not to mention local children—pacing its squares, fourteen of which feature stylized marble images of famous stops along the Camino: Roncesvalles, Puente la Reina, Estella, Logroño, León . . . Other squares depict sights welcome to pilgrims: a tavern, a well, a bridge; while others still contain more enigmatic images: a labyrinth, a prison, a pair of dice. Saint James awaits the pilgrim in the sixty-third square, but to reach him you must first get past the Grim Reaper in square fifty-eight. Portrayed here and there along the way are the pilgrim's walking companions: pairs of waddling geese.

The Goose Game has been played by European children for centuries. You'll sometimes see it in refuges along the Camino. Its first recorded appearance was in Renaissance Florence, but the arcane symbolism of the game suggests a pre-history; one theory has it arriving in Italy with Greek scholars fleeing the fall of Constantinople. The Goose Game resembles Snakes and Ladders—roll the dice and move your piece—but with more elaborate rules. Land on a bridge and take an extra turn. Venture into the labyrinth and go back twelve squares. A night in the tavern costs two turns. Land on Death and it's back to square one. The goose squares are "safe" squares, inspiring the Spanish expression *de oca a oca*, meaning "from one place of refuge to the next." *De oca a oca* was also the name Luisa had chosen for her photo exhibition.

Geese have their footprints all over the Camino de Santiago. The sign of the *pata de oca*, the goose's foot, which looks like an inverted peace symbol, has become the unofficial symbol of the hidden Camino, the *yin* to the yellow arrow's *yang*. You see it graffitied on walls or formed from pebbles on rocky paths. In the mythology of the Celts, who inhabited much of Spain before the Romans came, the goose is a messenger between this world and the next, and a guardian of wisdom (a far cry from our "silly goose"). It is even claimed that a pagan pilgrimage to the Atlantic Ocean "on the trail of the wild geese" predates the Camino. It's a theory that can't be substantiated, but it possesses a sheen of mystery and a ring of spiritual truth.

I had always puzzled over the Logroño Goose Game. Who was behind it, and what were we to make of it? For while this work of art fills a public square, there is no plaque or inscription to account for it. If I had been on my own that morning last October, I would be puzzling still. But by good fortune Luisa's piece and mine had landed in Logroño on the same turn, and we went sleuthing together. At city hall, Luisa turned on the charm and in no time we were seated in an office of the planning department. The amiable gentlemen there served us coffee, answered our questions as best they could, then referred us to someone who could answer them better: Carlos Muntión Hernáez, editor of the La Rioja cultural review *Piedra de Rayo*. He gave us the key to the riddle in the form of a remarkable manuscript, handwritten and illustrated by a local priest named Rafael Ojeda, entitled *El juego de la oca: memoria y proyecto*—the blueprint for the Logroño Goose Game. Father Ojeda had arranged its publication because he felt that the public work (unveiled in 1991) did not live up to his conception and he wanted to set the record straight.

After such brilliant detective work, I felt like Indiana Jones as I broke open the document that night. But within minutes I was feeling something more like vertigo. For Ojeda, the Goose Game and the Camino are both metaphors for a journey of transformation that concludes in square sixty-three, Santiago, with the rebirth of the pilgrim goose as a swan. He has aligned the Game and the Camino with the cosmos and ancient wisdom through a system of significant numbers, the twenty-two figured squares of his board corresponding to the twenty-two letters of the Hebrew alphabet, twenty-two cards of the Tarot, twenty-two miracles of the Apostle James as recorded in the *Liber Sancti Iacobi* . . . What is a humble pilgrim to do with so much wisdom? I stuffed the manuscript away in my bag and went to bed.

But as I returned to it from to time, I began to see a use for its formulas, not as prescriptions but as trial balloons, invitations to find or to forge relations between the flotsam of the day-to-day and the enduring symbols of the universe. "Let's think of the Camino as a game," Ojeda seems to say, "a subtle game, laid out on a world-sized board by an all-knowing games master. Now let's look beyond the Logroño we see with our eyes, with its refuge and churches and the bar where we ate tonight, and see it as something more: as the fourth *oca* in the journey, the tavern; as the Hebrew letter *zain*; as the Cart in the Tarot deck. Let's see it under the sign of Gemini, whose meaning is law and realization, corresponding to Saint James's miracle of giving life through water. Let's *play* the Camino and see what happens."

It sounds like madness, but then, what *is* the Camino? A little world with its own rules; a self-imposed suspension of normal life. Is this rational? Or is it not a kind of game? There are attractions to seeing the Camino as a game board, a labyrinth, a mystery: a mystery has a solution, a labyrinth has a centre, a game has winners. In a game, even death is just a setback.

On the title page of Ojeda's manuscript, in blue and red crayon, is written the motto *Sólo se aprende jugando*. "You only learn by playing."

Una Piedra en el Camino

My Camino last fall was not meant to be a continuous journey but a series of two- or three-day walks linked by bus and train, a greatest hits package. First I would walk from Puente la Reina to pay my respects at Catherine Kimpton's funeral cairn. Then I would take the bus ahead to Burgos, from where I'd walk to Castrojeriz, and so on . . . It was a plan that would not have pleased me on my first Camino, when I was more of a purist, but I had walked the Camino twice by then, so I thought I had earned the right to take some liberties. My plans could not begin to unfold, however, until I got around a certain obstacle—the girl sitting in the doorway of the refuge in Puente la Reina playing a didgeridoo.

The instrument was rigged up from a length of blue plastic plumbing equipment and duct tape. Its weird thrum and buzz came at me from every direction at once. The girl playing it was no more than twenty, with olive skin and the almond eyes of a Gothic Madonna. A white kerchief pulled her hair back chastely from her forehead. I've already confessed that I hold the first pilgrim I meet in almost superstitious regard. If this girl was a portent, it was going to be a strange Camino. As I debated whether to say "Excuse me, can I get past?" in English or Spanish, she looked up and said, "Wanna give it a try?" in fluent American. Giving it a try was the last thing I wanted to do, but the instrument was already in my hands. "It's easy. Just do this." She pursed her lips and blew. *Thp-p-p-p-p-p-p-p.*

The ring of beeswax around the mouth of the tube was sweet and humid with spit. Resisting an urge to gag, I forced out a few alarming squeals, attracting the attention of the middle-aged French pilgrims down the porch. I offered the instrument back to its owner. "That was fun," I lied. She didn't take it. Apparently she assumed I would want to succeed as badly as she did.

"Your lips are too tight. Relax your mouth. Watch. *Thp-p-p-p-p-p.*"

I tried again, this time producing a more baritone flatulence.

"That's better," she said. "Keep doing that."

She ran inside, abandoning me to the smirking French pilgrims. Was I now "it" in some bizarre game of tag? To my relief, she was back in a jiffy with a small package. Sitting cross-legged on the porch, she unwrapped it and produced one by one an ark load of twisted-wire animals—dogs, giraffes, rabbits, foxes, an elephant . . . "Did you make these? They're cute." I picked up the rabbit. It *was* cute, but it was also a trial run, like the didgeridoo.

"I thought I could sell them to pilgrims, but now I see that nobody really wants more stuff to carry, so I'm thinking of mailing them to Santiago and selling them there. You don't want to buy that rabbit, do you? That's okay. How much do you think I could get for them?"

"Five euros?"

She gnawed on a fingernail as she did the math. "I guess I'm going to have to sell a lot of them."

"Maybe you can try busking."

"What's that?"

"Playing the didgeridoo for money."

"Do you think I'm that good?"

"Do you think the Spanish know?"

The thought encouraged her and she went back to her droning. I stepped around her into the refuge. My Camino was under way.

I didn't see the didgeridoo girl the next morning. Instead, I walked out of the refuge and into an ambush. Three women named María were waiting to frogmarch me through a day of food, wine and song. I told them the story of Catherine Kimpton when we reached her memorial and the Marías said a prayer for her. When we got to Estella, we went for a glass of wine with two pilgrims from Bilbao. One was a friendly, gangly fellow with a big Adam's apple, an easy smile and a sleeve that hung empty at his side. When I asked what he did for a living, his friend answered for him.

"He's retired. He lost his arm in the saw two years ago and now he lives on his pension. It's bad luck he's walking with me. If he was by himself he could take his time, but I'm back at work in three weeks, so we need to get to Santiago fast."

As the talk ricocheted around the table in rapid-fire Spanish, my attention faltered. Then I realized that one of the Marías was calling me.

"Ro*bert*! Ro*bert*! Yoo-hoo. We're telling Ramón about the guy in the wheelchair. You saw him, didn't you? He was in Puente la Reina last night."

No, somehow I had missed him and his wheelchair. But when we got back to the refuge after supper, there it was, tucked behind the front door. It was a rudimentary contraption, flimsy-looking. It made me think of one of the didgeridoo girl's wire sculptures. Yet it was not hard to read nobility into its frailty. It was a plucky little horse ready to carry its rider into battle. The one-armed pilgrim from Bilbao shook his head. "I can't believe he's doing the Camino in that thing. He must have balls like this," and he cupped his hand to show how big. "Is he travelling by himself?"

"He has a friend with him," said one of the Marías. "There's a girl, too."

I lay awake that night thinking about the man with the wheelchair. What drives someone to roll eight hundred kilometres over hills, mountains and baking plains? Was he raising money for charity? Trying to prove something to himself and the world? Maybe he was taking his injured body to Santiago in hope of a miracle, like pilgrims of old. When I tried to picture him, I kept casting up images shot through gauze of a man patient, wise with a wisdom born of suffering, possessed of an inner strength that belied the weakness of his body. A hero. Then I peeled back the gauze, thinking, "Or maybe he's just someone who wants to do the Camino." A regular guy, like the one-armed pilgrim I had eaten dinner with, whose empty sleeve was not a sign of martyrdom or a badge of honour but just an empty sleeve. To know which he was, I would have to meet him. Which meant I wouldn't be taking the bus to Burgos tomorrow after all.

I was up late next morning, and the wheelchair and its rider were already gone, but I had a good day walking with Hiro, a young Japanese man studying in Spain, Belén and Mari, lively friends from Alicante, and Raúl and Mathilde, a beautiful young couple who had met and fallen in love somewhere between Roncesvalles and Pamplona. I arrived in Los Arcos that evening to find a crowd gathered on the porch of the refuge. Someone was singing in a voice that swung cleanly from oaky baritone to quivering falsetto. Edging in, I saw the singer, a roly-poly boy-man with cherub's lips and a round, smooth face. Beside him, leaning back with his eyes closed and his fingers joined, was the man in the wheelchair.

The singer was a remarkable mimic. He did Whitney Houston, Madonna, Michael Jackson, Elvis, all with perfect pitch and inflection, yet without knowing a single word of their songs. He just made their sounds. When he started on Tom Jones, I thought I would help by teaching him the words to "Delilah." But he was a better Tom without them; the English only hobbled him. While the singer sang, the man in the wheelchair held court, like a king with his jester, teasing the girls in a low, whispery voice. He was a handsome man, his face both smooth and jagged, cut from flint, then polished. His blue eyes had a still, avian intensity. He was dressed in a grey woodsman's toque and a sleeveless jacket whose pockets looked as if they ought to be jammed full of cartridges. I could see him with a rifle in his hand, scrambling over rocks, crouching in the underbrush, taking aim. Somehow this hunter had become a tethered falcon.

After a while, the man in the wheelchair had had enough of pop tunes. "Come on, Paco," he said. "Sing a Spanish song."

"What do you want to hear, Julio?"

The song Julio requested was an old Andalusian lament. The singer stands at the foot of the Cross, weeping, waiting for Christ to speak, but Christ says nothing, the implication being that either God doesn't listen or he doesn't give a damn. It was Julio's favourite. He listened with his eyes closed, then clapped gently at the end. "Bravo, Paco, bravo."

I stuck around after the party broke up. Julio was happy to talk about his journey so far, the places, the food, the women. It soon became clear that his Camino was not a crusade or a quest but a road trip, an escape from the tedium and limitations of life in his little sea town. This was the best adventure available to someone in his condition; it offered cheap places to stay, highways and paved roads to roll on, and always a crowd to cheer him on. So he was not the sort of hero I had imagined, but one of a more Spanish variety: a *pícaro*, an adventurous rogue.

All the time Julio talked, Paco held himself aloof. There was a prickliness about him that seemed like the pre-emptive scorn of one who fears being scorned. He only smiled when the door of the refuge opened and the girl with the didgeridoo stepped out.

"Are we having supper sometime, you guys?"

"Don't tell me you're hungry again," said Julio. "We just ate."

"I'll fix you something," said Paco.

I hadn't seen the girl since Puente la Reina and she showed no sign of recognizing me now. She just kissed Paco on the cheek and skipped down off the porch.

"Where are you going, Lupita?" asked Julio.

"Down to the river to play my didgeri."

"Don't go yet. Paco, sing 'El Rey.'"

Paco started in on the old mariachi song about a guy who has been jilted by his girl and tries to put a brave face on it. Then Julio joined in and the song suddenly took on new meaning.

"*Una piedra en el camino*"—a stone in the road—"taught me that my destiny was to roll and to roll." *Rodar y rodar*, to roll and to roll. It was Julio's theme song. The girl sat down and sang along to the end. Then she jumped to her feet.

"You guys are beautiful. See you later."

So the didgeridoo girl was part of the entourage. Somewhere on the way she had fallen in with them, forming one of those spontaneous families you so often meet on the Camino. I wanted to hear her story—what was she doing alone on the Camino?—and to follow the adventures of Julio. So it looked like tomorrow, once again, I would not be taking the bus.

My sleep was interrupted three or four times that night by a long, hollow hum that rose gradually to a high keening. Was it the didgeridoo girl still out on the bridge, serenading the river? I bumped into her next morning as she was taking down her laundry.

"Was that you I heard last night?"

"People keep asking me that. I swear to God, it was the plumbing."

I grabbed the opportunity to find out more about her. "So you're from Mexico, Lupe?"

"Yeah, but my name's not Lupe, it's Maite. Those guys don't think that sounds Mexican enough, so they call me Lupita. They think it's funny." Clearly, she thought it was funny too, though it was part of the game not to admit it.

"Where did you meet Julio and Paco?"

"In Zubiri, four or five days ago. God, it feels like a year." And before I could ask another question, she had scooped up her clothes and was gone.

I didn't see her or her friends that day. They must have been sticking to the highway for Julio's sake. But that night in Logroño, I saw the familiar wheelchair tucked behind the door of the refuge. They had arrived late and the only beds left were on the third floor. Poor Paco, carrying Julio up and down all those stairs. When I found them, Julio clasped my hand in his strong fingers.

"Good to see you, man. Sit down."

Paco thrust a beefy hand into his satchel and came out with a scrap of paper. It was the lyrics to "Delilah" that I had scratched down for him. "Listen, Bob, I've been practising," and he began to wail, watching out of one eye to see if I approved of his pronunciation.

"Almost there," I said, not having the heart to tell him to ditch the words and stick with the sounds. His look spoke eternal gratitude.

Maite was lying with her eyes closed on the bunk opposite Paco. After he sang, he reached over and touched her hair.

"Julio," he said, "we should give Lupita a break. We're wearing her out."

"Lupita!" barked Julio. "*Lupita!*"

"What?" Maite grumbled, without opening her eyes.

"Paco says we're wearing you out. Is that true?"

"Let me sleep, Julio."

"I'm worried, Paco. I don't think Lupita's getting enough sleep. Lupita, what do you think?"

"Shut up, Julio," Maite laughed, pitching her pillow at him.

Julio held it up like a piece of evidence. "You see, now she's getting cranky."

"Leave her alone," said Paco with a scowl. It seemed excessive. Maite could hold her own against Julio.

We talked for a few minutes till lights-out. I was about to go downstairs when I noticed something missing. "Maite, where's your didgeridoo?"

She shrugged. "I gave it to somebody."

The next morning was when Luisa Rubines and I went on our Goose chase around Logroño, so Navarrete, a dozen kilometres on, was as far as I got that day. The refuge of Navarrete is housed in a magnificent fifteenth-century building. There is a long arcade out front, and after a communal supper in the kitchen a bunch of us went there to enjoy the evening cool. It was after nine and there was no sign of Julio and company. I assumed they had gone beyond, to Nájera. Then I heard voices and the trudge of feet. They had arrived. Paco climbed the ramp of the arcade and slumped against a column. He looked about ready to cry. Maite headed into the refuge without a word. But Julio rolled right up and started to work the crowd.

"Robert, have a taste of this. It's a Mexican beverage I purchased for Lupita, but she doesn't want to share it with me." The big bottle of tequila was more than half empty. "Man, did we have a day. Tell Robert about our day, Paco."

"You tell him, Julio."

"Barbecued chicken. Wine. Tell him about the wine, Paco."

"I don't want to tell him about the wine, Julio."

"*Una maravilla*. Here, try this. Right from the bodega." He produced a big plastic bottle of mouth-puckering red. "Robert, please be so good as to offer a drink to the young English lady with the blue eyes. She looks thirsty."

"I'm Scottish," said the girl, taking the bottle.

"My sincere apologies," replied Julio with a smile.

As more pilgrims filtered down from the kitchen, the bottle went round. Julio kept teasing the Scottish girl and bantering with the Spanish ones. The only person he couldn't charm was Paco.

"Let's have some music. Sing us a song, Paco."

"I don't feel like singing, Julio."

It was hard to tell that Julio was drunk. Propped up in his wheelchair, he looked the same as ever. His voice had its familiar low timbre, and he cajoled Paco to sing in the tones of a parent reasoning with a difficult child. But there was an edge, too. Paco *would* sing. Julio was *el rey*.

When I ran up to the kitchen to grab some glasses, I found Maite sitting alone. I didn't need to ask about her day, the words came pouring out.

"You wouldn't believe what we went through today. Julio was impossible. This morning he decided that he wanted chicken for lunch, real chicken. So we found a farm and had them kill one for us. Then we had to figure out how to cook it. Julio sent Paco for firewood and we ended up using a garbage can lid as a barbecue. They're army guys, they know how to do this stuff. And then Julio had to have wine with his chicken. But not store-bought wine, it had to be from a bodega. We spent half the day just getting the stuff for lunch.

"The thing is, I can't tell you how much I laughed. It was crazy doing all that just for lunch, but those guys are *alive*. They decide to do something and then they do it. They don't worry about whether it makes sense. It's just that Julio never wants the party to be over. It took us two hours to go the last kilometre today. He said he didn't feel like rolling the wheelchair himself, so Paco had to push him, and then Julio kept jamming on the brakes. One time he fell onto the ground. He thought it was hilarious." She chewed on a nail.

"You know, everybody treats Julio like a hero, but if there's a hero, it's Paco. He never complains. He always tries to make Julio happy. And Julio abuses him. I watch him: when he gets to the top of a hill, he lets go of the brakes and coasts to the bottom, then he waits for Paco to come and push him up the other side."

I went back to the porch feeling a little sobered. Julio was still needling Paco to sing, to smile, to talk. But it was nearly ten and the partiers were starting to drift to bed. A minute behind me came the gaunt, elderly French hospitalero (the very one who welcomed me this year in St-Jean-Pied-de-Port).

"All right, everyone," he called. "Upstairs, time for bed!"

Julio looked the hospitalero coolly up and down. "And who are you?"

"I am the hospitalero."

"Tell me, hospitalero, where are we?"

"Where are we? We are in Navarrete, and it is time for bed."

It was just as Maite had said. Julio didn't want the party to end.

"Listen, Mr. Hospitalero, we are in *puta* España, and no *puto* Frenchman tells me when it's time to go to bed in my country."

There were a few uneasy laughs. Then Paco stood up. "Don't pay any attention to him, sir, he's drunk. Come on, Julio, we're going in."

"No, Paco," said Julio in that low, even voice, "I'm not going in until someone tells me whose country this is."

"Then you can sleep out here," snapped Paco, and he turned and rumbled up the stairs like a bowling ball.

The hospitalero pointed at Julio. "Look, maybe I am a *puto francés*, but I am the *puto francés* who must get up tomorrow morning to unlock the door, and I am the *puto francés* who must clean up your mess after you leave, and now this *puto francés* is telling you it is time for bed."

"You French son of a whore," growled Julio, putting up his fists as though he meant to fight the skinny old man. The hospitalero only shook his head and went back up to the reception. This infuriated Julio. He yelled after him, challenging him to come back and fight, ranting about the "French mafia" on the Camino. The few of us left on the porch tried to cool him down, but it was no use, all we could do was wait for him to shout himself hoarse. Before he did, with a last, pathetic effort, he pulled himself upright, put his hand on his heart and rasped out, "*Viva España! Amén!*" Then he was finished.

At the reception desk, the hospitalero was hanging up the telephone. "I have called the next refuge. If he refuses to sleep here, they will drive over and pick him up." I admired his composure. When I told him that Julio looked ready to come in, he went to his room so the coast would be clear when we brought him through.

I went back down to the porch, where Julio was now smiling mildly. "Where did everybody go?" he asked. "It's only ten o'clock."

"Can we take you upstairs?"

He didn't say no. By this time there was only me and the Scottish girl's boyfriend. We went to either side of the chair and Julio placed his arms on our shoulders, like a child reaching to be picked up. I took a wheel in one hand and the chair back in the other and braced for the lift. I was scared. Julio, in my mind, was such a solid piece of work that I doubted I had the strength to pick him up, much less carry him up the stairs. I breathed out, straightened my legs . . . He weighed nothing at all. Like a cabinet you thought was solid oak that turns out to be balsa. Years of disuse had wasted his legs down to twigs. They swayed from side to side as we carried him up the stairs.

Julio was a long time preparing for bed. He went about his business quietly, methodically. I could almost hear his slow, determined pulse. I couldn't be angry at him, not with the memory of his lightness in my arms. I didn't know what to feel about him, whether to laugh or cry. His outburst had been crude and insulting, but in the end it had hurt no one but Julio himself. He would be forgiven, his arrogance excused because of his disability. It must have infuriated him that people felt pity for him. Yet at the same time, he was willing to use his weakness to manipulate them. Julio was not a hero, or not the sort of easy-to-admire one that I had wanted him to be. He was more complicated than that: foolish, wise, proud, insecure, pathetic and admirable. Just like the rest of us. It made me weary thinking about it, weary and sad. Maybe it was time to catch that bus to Burgos.

Before I got out next day, Maite caught me. "I've decided I'm not walking with them anymore. I've let myself become part of Julio's story, but his story isn't mine. I'm going to miss them and the fun we have, but it's time I found my own Camino."

I sensed she was asking me something. "You can walk with me today if you like."

"Would you mind?"

We stopped for a coffee first. The woman behind the bar was laughing when we came in; Julio was back in form. If he felt any remorse for the night before, he didn't show it. Instead, he went on about the indignities *he* had suffered. As for Paco, he just sat, eyes averted, muttering, "Shut up, Julio." When Maite said she would see them later, Paco hugged her as if she were leaving on a ship for America. To me he gave a nod and a look.

As we left Navarrete behind and headed out across the yellow-brown fields of grain, Maite began to tell her story. "I was a flamenco dancer in Mexico, one of the best in the country. It got to where there was nothing more I could learn from anyone at home, I needed to come to Spain. I entered a school in Seville, but the flamenco artists here don't really want to share their secrets. There's a wall against people from outside. All they teach us is technique, and I already know the technique.

"At first, I felt like I had thrown away a year of my life, because I put off university to do this. But then I started to think that maybe there was some other reason why I was meant to come here. I met this guy from Barcelona, the one who gave me the didgeridoo. He was living in Seville, playing in the streets. All day we would just walk and walk around the city, talking. Then one day he told me about the Camino. He said, 'You like to walk, why don't you go on a pilgrimage? You can walk every day, like the Aborigines.' He gave me a book about how the Aborigines in Australia walk and sing until they find their dream."

"When did all this start?" I asked.

"Well, I came from Mexico in July . . ."

And this was October. The lifetimes we can live in three months. The book about the Aborigines was called *Voices of the Desert*. I smiled to think that she had come to the Camino looking for a solitary walk in the desert, then wound up with Paco and Julio. Julio was a rolling stone, *una piedra en el camino*, wanting nothing more than to push on from adventure to adventure, scrape to scrape. He answered each hunger as it arose, and took each day as it came. Maite, meanwhile, was out to "find her dream." She believed that there was a design to it all and hidden meanings to be mined; that these days were adding up to something beautiful and important.

There could hardly be a less likely pairing, but for a few days at least they had been family.

This was Maite's spiritual journey and, much as I wanted to help her, there was nothing I could do to guide her on it. But I thought there was something I could do for her on another plane.

"That's quite a limp you've got."

"It's my blisters."

"Let's see."

She sat in the tall grass and took off her runners. Her feet weren't too bad. There were blisters on her little toes and her heels were chafed. In my bag I had what she needed: breathable gauze bandage, stick-on blister pads, antiseptic, lotion. The good things that German John had once given me. She talked while I daubed on the lotion and wrapped her up.

"You must think I'm stupid for not taking care of myself, but it's because of that book about the Aborigines. The author goes walking with them expecting some kind of instant religious experience. But she isn't used to walking in her bare feet, so for the first month all she can think about is how much her feet hurt. She has to get through that pain before she can even begin to reach a spiritual level. I was expecting the same thing, that it would take me a few weeks to get tough."

I was taking some of the edge off that toughening experience, but she didn't seem to mind. When I had finished the first aid, she took a pouch out of her pack and spilled some shells and beads into her hand. "Which one do you like?"

I pointed to the shiny white seashell. She took a ball of string from her pack, cut three strands, then set to work braiding them. She strung the seashell on, then took my arm and tied the bracelet round my wrist.

"That's for you," she said. We were even.

We went slowly that day. I walked ahead, Maite dawdled

behind, her eyes cast down as if her dream might be lying beside the path. Now and then I'd stop to let her catch up and we would chat for a minute, but we had said all we needed to say, and soon we would be walking again, alone with our thoughts. It was night when we arrived in Nájera, too late to go to a restaurant, but Luisa Rubines was at the refuge and she threw us together some vegetables and instant noodles. Then she and I started talking about the Goose Game and Father Ojeda's manuscript. Maite listened carefully at first, then began to ask question after question. When I brought the manuscript out of my bag, her eyes lit up.

"Is it okay if I take a look?" she asked. I said yes, and she tucked it under her arm and disappeared up to the dorm.

Paco and Julio had been sitting all the while at the far end of the common room. You could see it hadn't been a happy day. After Maite left, Paco came and sat down with me. We had never spoken much, so I asked him about his music. He told me he was the singer in a band. They had been together for five years. He held up the fingers to show that it wasn't three years or four, it was five. I wanted to ask more, but Paco had other things to talk about. He took a card out of his wallet. It was the membership of a tae kwon do association.

"You know tae kwon do? I have a black belt. Fifth level." Those fingers again. Not third, not fourth. Fifth. Another card appeared from his wallet. "I used to be in the army. Now I do security part-time. This is my licence. It allows me to carry a gun."

I thought he might make a gun with his fingers, but he didn't. I let him know that I was impressed, and since we were playing show and tell, I brought out the copy of my book that I was carrying and told him I was a writer, a harmless sort of fellow really. We shook hands and he went back across the room.

If Paco was warning me off Maite, he didn't need to. Tomorrow, without fail, I was going to take the bus to Burgos. I had followed Julio's story far enough, and finally I had heard Maite's. It was high time for all of us to get on with our own Caminos—or maybe to begin new ones. For I had been wrong in thinking that there was nothing I could do to point Maite on her spiritual path, even if my intervention had been unwitting. When I woke in the wee hours of the morning, I could see her four bunks away, in the glow of her night light, rapt in study of the Goose Game.

The next morning, I said goodbye to them all. Paco sang "El Rey" one more time, while Maite joined in and Julio smiled his sing-me-a-lullaby smile. Who knew how long it would last, but for the moment they looked like a family again. Later I would see them once more, this time in a local newspaper, an interview from the day of the barbecued chicken. The photo showed the three pilgrims by the highway, Julio smiling, chubby Paco looking tough with his crossed arms and wraparound shades, Maite—whom the caption identified as Lupe Sánchez—squinting into the sun. I was struck for the last time by how frail Julio's chair looked, and by his shoes, which sat primly side by side on the footrest like empty shoes left at a doorway.

It was months later when I sent Maite an email. I didn't really expect an answer, but this is the one I got.

Hi Bob!! Good to hear from you. I have a great story to tell you about my camino. After you left us in Nájera Paco and I took off in a car and went all the way to León. I walked to Manjarín and here is where my camino really started. I met two guys soon to be temple knights who are rebuilding an old church dedicated to Maria Magdalena,

this town is somewhere between Ponferrada and Manjarín. It has been abandoned for 50 years now and they
are trying to bring it back to life by turning it into a place
where people can develop spiritually. In the Goose Game,
Ponferrada is the labyrinth. The only way to get out is
going back, so without knowing I went back there. Then
I took off to Santiago, Fisterra and Muxía. I died in Fisterra where I burned my past and felt the roundness of the
world. I have found nothing but love all over from nature,
from people. It is everywhere, every time I felt hunger I
was blessed either with an apple or with castañas, or corn,
and the best part is that there are blessings for all of us.
My biggest lessons love, faith, trust. I don't want to walk
towards fame cause there's no heart there, so now I'm
going to try to help others with my given talent which is
to feel the dance, so I want to be a dance therapist. Life
is as round as the earth. I have so many things I would
like to share with you about my camino cause it has been
a beautiful experience, I'm in Barcelona now not really
knowing why but my heart seems to know a whole lot
more than my brain so I guess soon I will find out. Right
now the only house I have is the world and my body so
please keep in cyber touch.

    Maite

Out there on life's game board, the dice were being cast,
the players were making their moves. Sometimes they landed
on the wrong squares, but that comes with the game. *Sólo se
aprende jugando*, "You only learn by playing." I felt sorry for
Paco. He had been in love with Maite, but he was never destined to be with her for more than a few squares of her journey. And I wondered what had happened to Julio. Did Paco
come back for him? Or had he kept rolling along by himself,

una piedra en el Camino? I sent an email to Maite to ask. This time there was no reply.

Pepe

My Camino so far has been much about memories and see-ing old places once more. It's time to let it find its own shape. A look at the map has revealed an intriguing prospect for the next few days: a series of villages, neatly spaced at twenty-kilometre intervals, that fall between the traditional pilgrim stops. They are likely to be less crowded than the big towns, and I've stayed in none of them before. Ventosa, which lies on an alternate route a kilometre off the main road, is the first.

On the way, I catch up to two girls who are singing walking songs in what sounds like German. The harmony is lovely, and I linger behind them to enjoy it. But when one turns back and sees me, the singing stops.

"Go on," I beg them. "It's lovely. Are those German songs?"

"No, they're Swedish."

"So you're Swedish?"

"No, we're German. But we like Swedish songs."

"Well, don't stop. I'll just walk back here."

They make a couple of false starts, but I've broken the mood.

"We don't want to make noise," says blonde Regina. "It's a pilgrimage, after all."

"Don't worry," I tell her. "I only heard you when I was right behind, and then I thought it was nice."

"But it's those English girls, you know? They have a CD player and they listen to music while they walk. It kind of bothers me, and I don't want to bother people."

So Nuala and Kara have a boom box. Clearly, they have been sent to test me. This is another thing I disapproved of once upon a time. As a pilgrim, you came to listen to the Camino, you didn't bring the noise of the world with you. But the Camino has tempered my judgments. Or maybe I'm just willing to let those two get away with anything.

The other German girl, a carrot-top named Jacquie, walks a little closer to me, lowering her voice as if someone could hear us out here. "If I tell you something about the English girls, can you keep it a secret?"

"Sure."

"I call zem ze Spice Pilgrims."

I have heard that the hospitalero of the refuge of Ventosa is a great guy, but today he stalks the beautifully restored stone house like dynamite looking for a spark. He growls at me for eating in the dining room. He shouts when pilgrims come in without ringing the bell. He throws his hands in the air when pilgrims ring and then *don't* come in. Thinking it best to keep out of his way, I retreat to the bright upstairs dormitory, where a young black woman is sitting on a bunk, massaging her legs and looking annoyed. She comes straight to the point. Linda is nothing if not direct.

"So you've done this before? Then tell me something. How long is it before you start to like walking? Is it seven days? I've heard it takes about a week to get used to it and after that it's not so bad."

"Depends what you don't like about it. Is it your feet? Is your bag too heavy?"

"My feet are fine. My bag is as light as I can get it. I just don't like walking. All my life, I've never really walked anywhere. I've always taken a car or the Tube."

"Then why . . . ?"

Well, it was a number of things. An itch to see Spain, a BBC documentary about a man who did the Camino with a donkey, the fact she's a practising Catholic. Right now she has a gap between work and study, so it seemed like an ideal time to go.

"But when do I start *liking* it?"

Linda has two problems with walking. The first is impatience: "I just want to *be* there. I don't want to have to *get* there." Tough, I say. The second is a shortness of breath when she starts in the morning, accompanied by a gripping chest pain and the feeling she's about to pass out. I concede that's a *good* reason to not like walking.

"Do you think it would be okay to have a car take my bags to the next place and I just walked?"

"Why not? If that's what you need to do."

"But wouldn't that be cheating?"

Here's one more clue that the Camino is a game, this idea that we can "cheat" on it. What constitutes cheating on the Camino? Most pilgrims would say driving, though most could then come up with cases (injury, mountain storms) or conditions (not staying in the public refuge) that would make driving acceptable. Ideally, of course, cheating should be a matter between a pilgrim and her God, but unfortunately there is a finite number of beds on the Camino. If you arrive at a refuge to find them full of pilgrims who snuck a ride, or whizzed by you because they had no packs to weigh them down, "cheating" becomes more than a matter of conscience.

Linda, however, is clearly not one to abuse the system, so

I put on a serious face and say, "The only person you can cheat on the Camino is yourself."

I've been dying to use that one.

Olga's on the main street is the place to eat in Ventosa. When the tractors come home from the fields, the patrons shove their tables close to the wall to let them pass. Everyone from the refuge is here. I'm sitting with Kara, Nuala and Pepe, a jowly, sixtyish Spanish man in a red and black mackinaw with grey eyebrows that bristle over the rim of his sunglasses. There's Alfred from Austria in his Tyrolean hat, and Marta, his Catalan girlfriend. There are two Israeli pilgrims, a lanky Italian boy, the German girls, and Linda-who-doesn't-like-walking. There are also the quiet, blonde, fair-skinned English art college students whom I think of as the Weird Sisters— though there are only two of them and they're not sisters. As a pilgrimage, a project and a performance, they are walking the Camino in the demure white pilgrim shifts fashionable in Chaucer's day. In every village, the Spaniards stop in amazement to watch them pass. They make an especially ghostly impression in the misty dawn and at twilight. One of them explains (with academic footnotes) that their process is meant to result in two "artifacts": dresses soiled with the dust of the Camino.

Spanish restaurants are required by law to serve a *menú del día*: three courses and wine for an economical fixed price. Apparently this is a legacy of General Franco, and it may be his greatest. The slate of first dishes usually includes salad, soup, pasta or legumes; second comes meat, usually pork, beef or fish, with tripe or rabbit occasionally making an appearance; *postre* may be a piece of fresh fruit, or else yogourt or ice cream presented without apology in its original plastic packaging. Washed down by an unlabelled bottle of the local red (or light, white *viño joven* in Galicia), it's a cheap, filling, savoury way to stoke a pilgrim's furnace.

Olga's, however, is more diner than restaurant, with a menu that doesn't venture beyond the bare staples: pig, potatoes and eggs. This leaves the vegan Kara and Nuala in a bit of a bind. Vegetarianism is considered somewhat subversive in Spain—the sort of pleasureless vice practised by northern Europeans. So far the girls have staved off starvation by doubling up on vegetable dishes and salads, but Olga's has no vegetables or salads except as trimming at the edge of a carnivore platter.

"*Somos vegetarianas,*" Kara informs the waiter. He waits for more information. "We don't eat meat products." He shrugs. Is that my problem? After protracted negotiations she orders a combination plate without meat—or at least she thinks that's what she's ordered. What comes is two plates of fried eggs.

Grinning unhelpfully through this performance is our Spanish companion, Pepe. Pepe speaks no English, and the girls' Spanish hasn't progressed much beyond "*Dos tintos por favor,*" so the communication passes through me. At first it passes in a desultory way, the girls not being sure how to take this grandfatherly Spaniard. Luckily, I've taught enough beginner English classes to know how bridges are built.

"Do you have pictures of your family, Pepe?"

Out they come. We gather around. There are the wife, the two handsome sons, the daughter—the chest tattoo peeping out from under her blouse pleases Kara and Nuala enormously—the first grandson, only nine months old ("Oh, he's a*dor*able").

"Bob, ask him why he's doing the Camino."

Pepe makes me work, mumbling, eliding his syllables. It takes three or four listens before I'm sure I've got it right.

"He wants to strengthen the bonds with his family. A while ago he was thinking of becoming a monk. He's doing the Camino to redirect his love towards his family."

This tugs a gasp out of the girls. For those of us who can't say in twenty words or less why we're doing the Camino, a statement of purpose such as Pepe's or Tony Bush's evokes real admiration.

"How's it working out?" asks Kara.

"So far, so good."

Pepe doesn't seem the monkish type. In fact, he's an ex–truck driver, pensioned off a couple of years ago due to hearing loss and currently occupied as—in his own words—an *ama de casa*, a housewife. He's not thrilled about cleaning and shopping and making meals while the other members of the family are out earning. He misses the travel, too. "But that's life," he says.

Night brings a chill and we move into the bar. It's Sunday and half of Ventosa is here, putting back the bacon and eggs. Wine flows from giant casks. Pepe cements his standing as a cool old dude by showing the girls the cigarette-rolling techniques he picked up in the armed forces. I relax and get to know the new pilgrim crowd. A couple of days ago I was still racing to catch up with Aaron, Maribel and Inácio; now they're like people I knew in another life. At ten o'clock, a dozen of us are still laughing and drinking. It's the kind of night that could last well into morning, if it weren't for the long arm of our hospitalero. When we ask for one last bottle of wine, the bartender tell us, "Sorry, but if you're not all out of here by ten, we're in trouble."

The Con

Next morning, the weather of the hospitalero's mood gusts to intermittently cheerful. Maybe he's trying to make up for being such a grouch yesterday. Maybe he's happy to see our backs. This Holy Year of 2004 has been wearing. It's not just the old story of too many pilgrims, not enough beds. It's a story of too many partiers, too many "tourists," too many people trying to beat the system. When Alfred, Marta and I ask for details, the hospitalero is happy to oblige.

"Fall usually isn't bad. Summer is the worst. You have the university students who give up their apartments to save rent and live by bumming along the Camino. Always some story about why I should let them stay for free. But just last week there was a couple from Austria—middle-aged, nice backpacks, good shoes. They show up late at night and say they have no money. So how did they get here? Oh, well, they're 'real pilgrims,' they live on charity. It was too late to send them to Nájera or I would have said 'Camino!' and shown them the door.

"I mean, there are limits. I'm not here to subsidize thieves. A couple of years back there were two Germans who camped all summer outside Roncesvalles, telling pilgrims their money had been stolen. Plenty of pilgrims helped them out. I say, better just to rob them than to prey on their goodwill. And then there's that sailor rogue, José, with his stories about going to Tibet and Jerusalem and kissing the Pope. A total fraud."

"José the sailor?" Our jaws bounce off the floor. "We met him the other night in Logroño."

"And who knows where you'll meet him tomorrow. He takes the bus up and down the Camino, sleeping for free and getting pilgrims to pay for his drinks. He picks the refuges where the hospitaleros rotate so that he isn't recognized. He doesn't come here because he knows I'd never let him past the door."

"But what about the shipwreck?"

"Those tales were discredited ages ago. Now you're going to say, 'But it was in the newspapers.' Well, take another look. The papers just printed what José told them. If it's a good story, do you think they check it out?" He pats his cheek to indicate the *cara dura*, the "hard face," of an inveterate liar. "He's shameless, that one. Shameless."

Well, here's something to think about on the way to Nájera. José is a fraud—or alleged to be one, I should say. Though I see no reason to doubt the hospitalero. He lives on the Camino, he knows its characters. And he's right about the newspaper stories; everything was José's word. What I'm finding interesting now is my own reaction. Shouldn't I feel indignation, anger, disappointment? Instead, what I feel is admiration. What a con! Not for José the paltry, predictable hard-luck story. He made a legend of himself, then got the press to print it up for him. And the wealth of detail—the frozen shipmates, the broken leg, tea with the Dalai Lama. I have to confess professional jealousy.

I'm burning to tell somebody, and I get my chance an hour from Ventosa when I catch up with Linda. She is affronted by the news, but not mortally.

"The cheek! I think it's a shame he lies to pilgrims. It wouldn't be so bad if he had corporate sponsors and he lied to them."

But with the German girls it's a different story, and it isn't José they're angry at. "That hospitalero doesn't know what he's talking about," snaps Regina.

"He seems to know José pretty well."

"How do you know? Who knows why he says such things? Besides, José's story was in the newspapers."

"They just quoted what José told them."

Jacquie purses her lips and nods, but Regina isn't buying. "It's not right. I think this hospitalero has a problem with José. Or maybe he's just a cynic. He doesn't want to believe that what José says could be true."

Obviously others are more heavily invested in José than I am. The way I see it, I gave him three euros for fish soup and a story. I'd call that a fair deal. But others have given him something more—a bit of their trust—and in exchange they've received a ray of hope, a confirmation of faith, maybe even a hero.

I decide not to press the point with Regina. The fact is, I don't know that José is a fraud, I only have the hospitalero's word, so it's a matter of faith on my side as much as it is on hers (I notice how ready I am to accept a story that confirms my skepticism). And in a sense, it doesn't make any difference to a believer whether José is telling the truth, any more than it makes a difference whether Saint James's body lies in Saint James's tomb. What matters is the potential José represents. Proving that he is not the eternal pilgrim doesn't prove that there isn't such a person out there somewhere; proving it isn't James who lies in James's tomb wouldn't prove that there are no miracles.

The Matchmaker

Pepe is waiting for me at the desk of the refuge in Azofra. "That's him," he tells the hospitalera. "That's the young man. Mark him off the list."

"Your friend was worried about you," says the hospitalera with mock reproach. "He made me hold a bed for you."

It was an unnecessary precaution—there are still thirty beds empty. Pepe drapes an arm around my shoulder. "What kept you? Those English girls? Come on, I'll show you your room." He plonks my hat on his head and takes off down the hall with my bag and stick. "This place is like a luxury hotel. Two to a room. I saved you a bed at the other end of the hall from me so you won't hear me snoring." He swings back the saloon doors of one of the cubicles. "You're the first here. Spread your things on both beds so people will think someone's with you. Come on, I'll show you the toilet and showers."

He ushers me into the washroom and gestures like a real estate agent showing off a property. "Nice, clean. Good facilities. Happy? Now take your time, clean up, and when you're ready, we'll go to the bar."

"I'm ready now."

"Then come on."

Before the bar, we stop at the general store. I lay my purchases—an apple and an ice cream bar—on the counter behind Pepe's. He slides them up with his and says something to the cashier. He's already treated me to wine in Ventosa; I can't let him start buying my groceries.

"It's okay, Pepe, I have money." He pretends not to hear me as he chats up the cashier in his booming voice. Or maybe he doesn't hear me; he *is* deaf in one ear.

When we're back in the street, he turns to face me with those eyebrows flaring and plants a fat finger on my chest. "Listen, Roberto. I know you have money. But I'm never going to do the Camino again. This is a once-in-a-lifetime, you understand? So if I want to buy you an apple, don't give me a hard time."

At the bar, he ascertains that I would like a glass of red, orders a name-brand Rioja instead of the cheap, local stuff, then pays up front to be sure I don't get up to any tricks. As for Pepe, he indulges in *sin—sin alcohol*, that is, non-alcoholic beer.

"Doctor's orders. My ulcer." He pulls a vial full of pills in all colours and sizes out of the pocket of his mackinaw. "Grown-up candy."

"That's all for your ulcer?"

"And my heart condition." He slugs back a handful. "My brother died of a heart attack when he was fifty-eight. I'm fifty-eight this year."

Pepe's details fall into place. His Camino is more than what he told us last night. It's a prayer for life, for health, for more time to see his family grow. As he sips his beer substitute, he asks about my parents, my siblings, my wife. He wants to know when we're going to have kids. He tells me to behave myself with the English girls.

We've just ordered supper when Tony Bush comes in. I've never been much of a matchmaker, but it occurs to me that this might work out. They're both retired men of similar vintage with health concerns and families. Maybe they'll hit it off. But tonight, Tony looks as if he's been drawn and quartered. After ten minutes he's still panting and wiping his brow. He'd like to have a chat with me in English, but he's not up to the game of nod-and-gesture communication with Pepe, and I don't want Pepe to feel left out. The conversation flags. Pepe's attention wanders to the soccer game on the TV. Tony, sensing he's put a damper on things, falls silent.

I thank the heavens when Kara and Nuala breeze in. They relate their day's scrapes in colourful detail. Pepe perks up. But all the time, Tony concentrates on his meal. When he's finished, he stands and says good night. I should coax him to stay, but I don't.

There's a quiet moment after he leaves, then Nuala turns her lasers on me. "Bob, you were quite rude just now. Is that the right word? Yes, I think I can say that you were *rude* to your friend. You looked positively relieved when he got up and left."

I pause to realign my jaw, then bleat, "But I don't know how to cheer him up."

"Well, you might have introduced us to start with—"

"I thought you knew each other."

"—and you should have told us he was feeling down. We would have cheered him up. We'll cheer him up the next time we see him, won't we, Kara?"

"Oh, definitely."

I make two resolutions: to give Tony a lift the next time I see him, and never to underestimate my Spice Pilgrims.

Tourists and Purists

At seven-thirty next morning, the moon is still beaming, the stars burning like ice. In the tiny square by Azofra's fountain, Linda sits shivering. Last night she stayed in a private refuge with supper included, so we missed her at the bar.

"You're out early," I say.

"My hospitalero kicked me out."

"He what?"

"I was having breakfast and I asked how soon he wanted me to leave. He said, 'Right now, please. I have things to do.'"

We walk down from the town with daylight's first glimmer at our backs.

"He's quite the character. German. He's had this place for seven years now. I think he's just fed up with the Camino. The pilgrims don't live up to his standards. He has these little tests, you know. Like when I got there yesterday, he carried my bag up the stairs. I thought he was being nice, then he told me he always picks up pilgrims' bags to make sure they're heavy enough. He said that one time there was a lady who had nothing in her bag but a pillow, so he sent her away. Then, after supper, he saw me looking at a book about the Camino. He got really indignant. 'Don't read about the Camino,' he said. 'Live it!'"

"Sounds like a purist."

"Yeah, I think he had the idea when he started that he was going to be meeting like-minded people. Seeker types, you know? But it's a private refuge and he charges seven euros, so of course it's the pilgrims with money who stay with him—*tourists*, he calls them. Now he says he wants to sell out and buy a house in the mountains."

I get a laugh out of Linda's description of her disillusioned hospitalero, but I empathize too. He came to the Camino chasing an ideal and found himself knee-deep in grubby reality. I know what it's like to be—or to consider yourself—a purist, a guardian of ideals. For strangely, on my first Camino, once I had decided that I was a pilgrim, I became the most pilgrimly of them all. Or maybe that's not so strange; I was a typical convert, burning with the fire of my new calling. Suddenly I was full of strict notions about how a pilgrim should—and shouldn't—behave. Some of my ideas you might call Franciscan, but others were definitely "Teutonic": Romantic notions filtered through Hermann Hesse of pilgrimage as a journey of the spirit, a pure, solitary, monkish seeking. It took a while before I truly accepted that people came to the Camino seeking different things in different ways, and that a pilgrim couldn't be measured by the weight of her bag, or the hour she got up in the morning, or how many kilometres she walked in a day—or whether she walked at all.

One of my orthodoxies the first time I did the Camino was, "Thou shalt not ride in a motor vehicle." Yet in Nájera last October, after I said goodbye to Julio, Paco and Maite, I went to catch the bus to Burgos. It wasn't anything I needed to justify; it had been my plan all along to walk only parts of the Camino, and the only way to do this in the two weeks available to me was to use buses and trains to bridge the gaps. Still, I couldn't say I was enthusiastic about taking the bus. Not for dogmatic reasons, just that it seemed like a waste of a day I could spend walking.

Of course, I also regretted leaving behind the pilgrims I had met and grown attached to in the previous week—not only Julio, Paco and Maite, but Luisa Rubines, my Japanese friend Hiro (whose feet were so badly mauled by his walking boots they looked as if they had been sanded), Mari and Belén, Ferrán from Barcelona, and Raúl and Mathilde. Raúl was a curly-haired young Basque, an actor and filmmaker, and the only person who has ever told me his mother was a witch and meant it in a good way (she is the local dispenser of spells and traditional herbal remedies). His partner, Mathilde, was a striking farm girl from the south of France. Whenever I met them on the road, they would share with me the nuts, figs and other goodies Mathilde had spotted with her country-bred eye. She told me her mother had named her after a character in a book, which Mathilde had chosen never to read; no one else was going to write the story of her life. She had dropped out of her university science courses and now her goal was simply to keep walking—to Santiago, then on through Portugal to the south of Spain, where she would look for winter work.

On my way to the bus stand, I wondered if I would ever hear the end of Mathilde and Raúl's story, or see Luisa's photo exhibition, or walk this way again. I had an hour to kill till nine, an hour when everyone else was walking. At last the bus arrived. I threw my stick and bag in the luggage compartment and climbed into the beast. It roared and snorted through the narrow city streets like a bull in a maze, then broke out onto the highway. After a week on foot, the speed was dizzying. The land raced by my window in fast-forward. Sometimes I saw pilgrims trudging along beside the highway. How strange. I was moving twenty times faster than them, yet my body felt paralyzed. In the low-humming, climate-controlled speed capsule of the bus, I drifted in and out of waking. We passed from cloudy zones to sunlight and back to cloud again. By eleven-thirty, when we arrived in Burgos, we had covered five days' walking in two hours.

I stepped down into the heat of the day and felt my body again. It was wound tight as a spring. My legs wanted to stretch, but I wasn't done with vehicles yet. I went to the train station: there was a departure for Astorga at one. Perfect. I'd be there by late afternoon, spoil myself with a big meal, then wake early the next day to walk under skies of deepest azure to the Montes de León. In the meantime, I had an hour for a stroll and a bite. Except I didn't feel like eating. I didn't know what I felt like. Inside me, something was objecting to this whole project, not on the grounds of orthodoxy, but on the grounds of what felt right. I went to the river and stood for a while on the bridge listening to an inner voice. *Take what the Camino gives you*, it said. *Finish what you've started.*

The walk from Nájera to Santo Domingo is not dramatic

like the walk from Astorga to the Montes de León. There are no mountains ahead, no breeze in your face, no high blue skies. It is hot and sere. But I wasn't on the Camino only to fill my eyes. I was here for the walking, the step-at-a-time, the slow unfolding, the sharing of the road. I had those things with the pilgrims I knew. What did I hope to find ahead that wasn't mine already?

At the bus station, the driver was revving up for the trip back to Nájera. I called for him to wait while I bought my ticket. He didn't ask me any questions. I was a pilgrim, there was no accounting for us. I slept all the way back, my mind and body uncoiled. At two-thirty, I hit the ground and covered the twenty-three kilometres to Santo Domingo de la Calzada in four hours. When I arrived at the refuge, Mathilde was in the kitchen, peeling a sack of potatoes she had foraged.

"I thought you went to Burgos," she said.

"I came back for something," I told her.

We shared a beggars' banquet that night. Mathilde's potatoes and Belén and Mari's cabbage, shredded and fried in olive oil with lashings of salt. Raúl made a big salad, Hiro and I took care of the wine, others brought bread and grapes to the table. That night I slept like a good pilgrim, and the next morning I went with the rest to see off Belén and Mari. Their Camino was over for that year. Mine was back on track.

As I walked that day, I thought about my aborted bus plan. What had made me turn back? All I could say was that I had broken one of my rules of the Camino. It was not a rule based on any external standard of orthodoxy, nor was it a rule that I would impose on anyone else; it was part of my personal, unspoken pact with the road. You learn the game by playing it; you learn the rules by breaking them.

Saint Domingo and the Chickens

Santo Domingo de la Calzada is a town named after a saint named after a road. *Calzada* means "roadway," and Domingo was the saint who built it. Born several kilometres from here, he was a self-taught engineer who spent his life in a frenzy of marsh-draining, bridge-building and tree-cutting as he cleared a pilgrim path through La Rioja. His symbol is the scythe, with which it was said he could level a forest in a morning. In the village that bears his name he built a pilgrims' hospital, a church and the bridge over the river Oja. When he was in his seventies, King Alfonso of Castilla set him the chore of repairing all the bridges between Logroño and Santiago. He was approaching the century mark when he came home to build his own tomb. Not even death could slow him down. He established a posthumous reputation as a healer, and even took on a new office as Spain's patron saint of public works.

You see him all around town. He looks like a man to reckon with, even with those ridiculous chickens pecking at his feet. Ah yes, the chickens. In Santo Domingo you can buy chicken bookmarks, fridge magnets, letter openers, silverware. The emblem of the local sports club is a chicken perched on a soccer ball. There are even real ones on display in a giant case over the inside doors of the cathedral. If they crow while you're there, it's good luck.

The story of the chickens goes like this. Once, a pilgrim family stopped at an inn in Santo Domingo de la Calzada. The innkeeper's daughter took a shine to the handsome young son, but the boy, faithful to his pilgrim vow of chastity, resisted her. The spurned girl slipped a silver plate into his bag and reported a theft. These being days of swift justice, the hapless boy was hanged at once. His distraught parents went on to Santiago to pray for his soul. But unbeknownst to all, Saint James had held up the innocent boy's body so that the hangman's rope would not choke him. He was holding him still, and probably getting a little tired of it, when he spoke to the parents in a dream. The parents raced back to Santo Domingo de la Calzada and burst into the home of the judge just as he was sitting down to a chicken dinner.

"Our son is alive!" they cried. "Cut him down at once!"

The judge scoffed. "Your boy has been hanging in the square for a fortnight. He's no more alive than the chickens on my plate!"

And with that, the fricasseed poultry carcasses started capering and clucking about the dining room. The reunited family made a joyous pilgrimage to Santiago, and everyone lived happily ever after—except the innkeeper's daughter, the local judges (who were required to wear a symbolic cord around their neck for many years after) and the chickens.

Since my scolding from Nuala, I've been watching for Tony Bush. I'm going to be encouraging when I see him today. But Tony saves me the trouble. When we run into each other in Santo Domingo, he slaps me on the back. As we walk across the square, he's waving at other pilgrims, calling out their names, taking charge the way a big guy is supposed to. Looks like he's got his groove back. I walk with him to the Benedictine sisters' refuge where he's staying tonight, then hit the road for Grañón, my next "place between." This is the first Camino when I won't spend the night in Santo Domingo, but I'll grab a souvenir from the bakeshop before I leave town: a box of *ahorcaditos*, tasty almond-filled confections in the shape of a hanged man with a scallop shell on his chest.

The Secret Door

At the refuge of Grañón, Linda is waiting to pray. "That's one thing that bugs me about Spain: they keep the churches locked except for Mass. You'd think in a little place like this, people would want to go in and pray sometimes. What else is there to do?"

When the doors finally open, a crowd pours in. Pepe, Linda, the German girls, Alfred and Marta, even Nuala in a demure, flowery cashmere sweater that she brought along just for occasions like this. Looks like the Camino is still a Catholic pilgrimage after all.

Grañón has a reputation as a Catholic place, where pilgrims are encouraged to pray and reflect on their spiritual journey. Bibles and theological tracts are close to hand in the common room, and the donation box carries the charitable message "Leave what you can, take what you need." Kara and I agree that the word *need* offers a lot of room for interpretation. I have heard that this refuge is funded by the wealthy and secretive Catholic organization Opus Dei. I can't confirm that, but what I *can* say with certainty is that if a tired pilgrim pulls one of the big leather chairs up to a window on a sunny autumn day when a liquid breeze is stirring, and looks out over the benches in the park below, the dry fountain, the willow trees, the sculpted bushes, he will wake up before he even knows he is sleeping, his pen still perched between forefinger and thumb.

I hear a *clink clink* of cutlery being laid out, and footsteps treading between kitchen and dining table. The good pilgrims are home from Mass. When I open my eyes, the table is set.

There are twenty of us at dinner tonight, including two hospitaleros and the parish priest. The hospitaleros serve up heaping platters of salad, tortilla and pasta. It is Austrian Alfred's birthday and Marta has procured a cake for the occasion. It's a night for her to celebrate as well. Her first time on the Camino, she gave up at Santo Domingo de la Calzada because of her knees. Now she's made it to Grañón, seven kilometres closer to Santiago.

After supper, the priest, a tall fellow with an easy, secular manner, stands to extend an invitation. "I'm going to open the church now for a special pilgrims' prayer. Everyone is welcome to join us, but if you don't feel like it, that's fine. There's no need to change clothes for the outdoors—we will enter the church directly from the refuge through *a secret door*."

There are oohs and aahs. It almost makes me want to go and join the fun. This is often a moment of indecision for me. Sometimes I feel comfortable praying or going to Mass with the others. I experience in a different way what it is to be part of the pilgrim body, and even when I'm not involved, a church is a good place to open your mind and let the thoughts blow through. But tonight I'm not in the mood. There's more than one way to give thanks, anyway. That mountain of dishes piled up in the sink, for example.

Many hours later, long after the dishes are dry and the prayers prayed, the door to my bedroom opens and I hear someone enter. The main sleeping area of the refuge, in the loft above the dining room, was full when Kara, Nuala and I arrived today, so instead the three of us are sleeping on the floor in the all-purpose room downstairs. I sense the intruder inching through the dark towards the girls' side of the room. The tread is heavy, masculine. Is he a thief? A pervert? Should I cough? Speak? Do something manly? I lie tensed, ready for anything. Then I hear the click of a latch, the sound of a door opening and the creak of footsteps on a wooden floor. A cool gust of air touches my face. Then the door closes and all is still.

Next morning, Pepe catches me on my way out of the washroom. "Come on," he says, "let me show you where I slept last night." He leads me back to my own room, then to the door the night visitor passed through. He opens it and I feel at once the coolness of a great hollow space. A few steps, and we're standing on a platform high above the altar of the church. Of course. The secret door.

I peer over the railing, down to the empty pews below. The view is impressive. Pepe's sleeping bag is still on the floor beneath the statue of the Virgin.

"First time I ever slept in a church," he says, with the chuckle of a naughty schoolboy.

No Country for Young Men

In the valley below Grañón, a rusty plough claws potatoes from the earth. Men follow in its wake, stooped from the waist, scooping the spuds up by the sackful.

"This is poor country," says Pepe. "In other places, they would have machines to pick them up." The potatoes remind me of Mathilde and last fall's wonderful feast, and I tell Pepe. He enjoys the story, but objects to my choice of words. "You said your friend *stole* the potatoes for the meal. That's not right. If she took them to sell them, or if she kept them all for herself, *that's* stealing. If she only took enough to eat, there's nothing wrong with that."

I love Pepe's moral clarity. His sense of justice is firm but not rigid, his judgments fall on the side of mercy. This is the first time we've walked together and we won't be together for the whole morning. His pace is too slow and I'll start to stiffen up. But it's fun to talk to him for a while. The heat of the day is coming on and I've stripped off my jacket. He'll keep wearing that old red and black mackinaw with the collar turned up no matter how hot it gets. He's talking about his family, the one he was born into. Nine siblings from a village near Seville who are now scattered all over the country. It's handy for visiting. "I never have to pay for a hotel. Listen, the next time you come to Spain, bring your wife and we'll go see my sister in Asturias. That's my favourite place. Incredible. The mountains, the ocean, the seafood." I wish I could make a reciprocal invitation, even as a gesture, but Pepe swears nothing will ever get him on an airplane. Clearly, this is destined forever to be a one-sided relationship—and that's fine with Pepe. Like most Spaniards, he can't conceive of how anywhere could be better than Spain.

I like to imagine Pepe and myself making it all the way to Santiago together. I get something from his company. He is a distant echo of my father, another sociable man of moral clarity who talked too loud because of his bad hearing and wore a mackinaw. His life ended before sixty, like Pepe's brother's. It's novel to have a friend the age of my father, or the age at which I last remember him.

In Redecilla del Camino, the first village of the province of Castilla, the tourist office is already open at the indecent hour of nine. My heart goes out to the girl who stamps our credentials. The otherwise still-sleeping village is ramshackle. After the white house-fortresses of the Basque country, the proud hill towns of Navarra and the wine-rich pueblos of La Rioja, everything here looks old and tired. Franco-era tractors rust in the tall grass. I leave Pepe rolling a smoke on the doorstep of an abandoned and crumbling house and walk on.

In the Plaza Mayor of Viloria de Rioja, birthplace of Santo Domingo de la Calzada, a slide and a teeter-totter wait glumly for a child to happen by. The town's three dogs don't even bother to lift their chins off their paws as I pass. The only signs of life are the floral extravaganzas on the doorsteps. The building that dominates the square must have served as the town hall (the *ayuntamiento*) when such an institution was needed. I am sitting on the bench out front when the German girls arrive.

"What town is this?" asks Regina.

"Viloria de Rioja." Such a quixotic roll of syllables.

"You're sure this isn't Castildelgado?"

"No, it's Viloria de Rioja."

"But this is the second town after Grañón."

"No. It's the third."

"It can't be. We've only walked through one town."

"Sorry, you've walked through two."

"How do you know?" I'm not sure how to respond to that one. "Look, my guidebook says it takes two and a quarter hours to get here, and it's only been one and a half."

"Maybe we should go back and walk slower this time," says Jacquie slyly.

There are many villages like this one on the Camino through Castilla-León and Galicia, places that vanish swiftly from memory and soon will be vanishing from the maps. The young move to the cities, leaving their parents as the last cus-todians of the old homes, the old ways of life. Some villages survive as bedroom communities. Others are kept breathing only by the Camino.

Suddenly, Viloria de Rioja creaks to life. A shutter rises. A door opens. One and two at a time, the ancient residents converge on the square. Some ascend to the porch of the *ayuntamiento* and lean out over the railing as if there were a view to take in. A few minutes after ten, a white car pulls up. A young woman jumps out, calling apologies for being late, and trots up the stairs to unlock the big doors. For the first time I notice the plaque outside: *Consultorio de atención primaria*. This is the local health clinic and today is the weekly round.

Five hours later, a dozen of us are shivering outside the sanctuary of the Virgen de la Peña, high on the hill overlooking Tosantos. Like the old folks this morning, we are waiting for the lady with the key. We have been told that the señora will come to unlock the church at four. In the meantime, we are ideally situated to appreciate the turn in the weather. The Spanish summer that seemed set to last forever ended abruptly at noon, with lashing rain and a bitter wind. The rain has subsided now, but the wind is still up to its mischief. Pepe hikes the collar of his mackinaw to his ears and warms himself up in his usual way, by gabbing.

"Do you know what this is, Roberto?" He pulls a medal on a chain from inside his shirt. I do. It is Our Lady of Fatima. "Did you know that Fatima is in Portugal? That's the only place I've ever been outside of Spain. To the shrine of Our Lady. Three times, my wife and I."

I've been to Fatima too and—though I don't phrase it quite like this to Pepe—I found it dour, gloomy, full of fire and brimstone, with not a trace of Pepe's merciful Catholic spirit, and definitely not the sort of place you'd take your wife for a foreign getaway. Pepe has no idea what I'm talking about.

"It's a very spiritual place," he corrects me. "You can feel it."

And here comes the señora with the keys, right on time. She wears a thin cotton dress and an unbuttoned cardigan.

"Fresquito, no?"—"A little chilly, eh?"—she says with almost Canadian nonchalance. She unlocks the doors and we crowd into the chapel. The sanctuary is a clean, cozy cave scraped out of the tufa hillside. The walls gleam white under the electric lights. There are just enough seats and standing room for a village. Our Lady of the Peña gazes out from behind a solid ceiling-high grid. The security seems excessive, but a Spanish village can never be too careful. *Nuestra Señora* is the holy protector and mother of the land, and in the old days a common strategy of intercommunity warfare was to steal a rival town's Virgin. It sounds like a shameful ploy, but it was easily rationalized: if Our Lady permitted herself to be stolen, it showed she wasn't happy where she was.

Our Lady of the Peña explodes in this bare, simple setting, with all manner of crowns and beams of light projecting from her head. Before her grate, covered in plastic sheeting, is the festive platform upon which she has, since time immemorial, been borne down to the village each May amidst great rejoicing, then back again to her lonely hermitage in September.

While the rest of us stroll around the narrow shrine or sit on the benches facing the Virgin, Pepe talks with the señora. His voice reverberates around the walls of the cave. Anyone who came here for silent prayer is out of luck. But I think he wouldn't care even if he knew how raucous he was. The Virgin is family; there's no need to be hushed in her presence.

The señora beams at a memory. "When we were children, we used to ask why the Virgin had to live here through the cold winter. Why did she only come to the village in summer? Then our grandparents would tell us, 'The Virgin comes down to watch you while we are out working in the fields.'"

Spiritual Topography

Evening at the refuge of Tosantos is similar to evening in Grañón, but with extra helpings of prayer. There is an air of piety, slightly forced, that is different from what I have felt elsewhere on the Camino. They really do make you sing for your supper. The table talk lacks spark without Nuala and Kara, who must have stopped back in Belorado. A pity, for last night's register bears the signature of Saffron, the American girl who was their partner in planning the end-of-the-road party. At least the trail is still warm.

After supper, as at Grañón, we are invited to prayer, though here *enjoined* might be the better word. That's fine. Someone else can do the dishes tonight. I troop up with the rest to the prayer room in the attic. No secret door tonight, just a slope-ceilinged room with wall-to-wall broadloom, a splash of stained glass and the calming air of a yoga studio. The chairs are arranged around the centre, where Francisco, the resident priest, presides.

We start off with readings from the Bible in our various languages—German, Spanish, French, Italian. Linda handles the English. Then Francisco hands each of us a scrap of paper, as if we were going to play a party game. "Who speaks German? English? I have a French one here, who wants it?" But when we unfold the papers, it's not movie titles or secret identities we find, but prayers that past pilgrims have written out and slipped into the wooden prayer box. In our hands are their hopes, reflections, words of encouragement, cries from the heart. One by one, each of us reads out the prayer that has fallen to us in the language in which it was written. There is no translation. That would take too long, and it's really not necessary; whatever the prayer, our response is the same. *Amen.* My prayer was written by an Irish woman who stopped here two weeks ago.

"Please pray for my mother who is slipping into the darkness of dementia. Give us the strength to be patient and understanding and keep our love for her in front of us."

Amen.

When the prayers have been read, Francisco speaks. He has much to say and often the Spanish eludes me, but the kernel is this:

"On the first part of the Camino, the landscape is always changing. There are forests, mountains, rivers. There are beautiful towns and bridges. There is always something to catch your eye and take you out of yourself. The novelty of the experience distracts you, as do all the new people you are meeting, the human relations you are forging. Pain distracts you too. The pain of your feet, your legs, your shoulders. At the end of every day your body is tired from this unaccustomed effort. Your mind is tired too, from trying to process so many new things. With all these distractions and weariness, it is hard to focus on the things of the spirit.

"But now, most of you have been walking for a couple of weeks. Your body has made adjustments. It no longer requires all your attention. Your mind too has passed through the initial stages of wonder and commotion and settled into the rhythm of the pilgrimage. This means it is free to think other thoughts.

"In a few days you will come to the *meseta*, a broad, flat land that stretches to the distance in every direction. A place where there are no longer visual distractions, where there is nothing to look at but the sky above and the far horizon.

There, you will begin to look into yourself. That is where the first part of the Camino—the physical part—ends, and where the spiritual Camino begins."

It is a breathtaking idea. The hundreds of millions of years, the geological ages, that lifted the mountains and levelled the prairies were all ordained by God for the sake of pilgrims. This is the Camino as spiritual topography—beginning in the mountains with the wonders of Creation, the joy of fellowship, the consciousness of the body; then progressing by degrees to simplicity, solitude, the silence of wide spaces. And this in turn is meant to prepare us for a third stage, to which Francisco only alludes, over the mountains to Galicia and the tomb of Saint James.

Francisco grants us a silent moment to survey the vista he has opened for us. Then he switches off the lights, sets a candle before a Byzantine image of the Virgin and begins to sing "Salve Regina" in his sweet, wavering voice. The rest of us join in, or hum the haunting melody to the Queen of Heaven as best we can. Pepe's voice rises above all the others, loud, off-key and full of love.

Sticks

I'm away from Tosantos before first light, walking through a string of silent villages, then into a bowl of mist so soupy it pearls my pilgrim beard. Little by little the darkness beyond the mist resolves into a wall of trees. I have reached the Montes de Oca. This range of hills on the frontier of the ancient kingdoms of Navarra and Castilla was once among the most feared stretches of the Camino. *Se quieres robar, véte a los Montes de Oca*, said the proverb: "If you want to be a thief, go to the Montes de Oca."

Today, the region is a tree farm, parallel ranks of oak oak oak oak as far as the eye can see, then oak oak oak on the north side, pine pine pine on the south . . . The trees are cut back too far from the road to offer shade, or even the sensation of walking in a forest. Soon I'm wishing I'd waited for Pepe or Linda to keep me company. Then I spot a message penned on a waymark that could have been put there just for me: *Party at Finisterre—October 30th, dusk to dawn!* Saffron was here. Late in the morning, the trees give way to a barren upland of ferns and gorse. Then an enormous white building appears ahead. Who would build something so grand out here in the middle of nowhere?

San Juan de Ortega spent his early years helping Santo Domingo de la Calzada rebuild the Camino's bridges, but his story really began when the ship that was bearing him back from a pilgrimage to the Holy Land nearly sank in a storm. Juan promised to build Saint Nicholas a church if he survived (the story has a familiar ring . . .), and he kept his promise, erecting a haven for pilgrims where one was needed most, in Ortega, "the place of nettles," in the midst of the Montes de Oca. At first the thieves of the forest, reluctant to lose their pilgrim prey, removed by night the stones that Juan laid by day. But in the end, good prevailed and the monastery and pilgrim hospital were finished.

With what relief the medieval pilgrim must have approached this refuge of bright stone, and how pleasant it still is today to arrive on a sunny day and see pilgrims parked under parasols at the *taberna* with glasses of beer in their hands. Thanks to Father José María Alonso's decades of devoted service, San Juan de Ortega remains a functioning refuge. True, the dorms are unheated and the pilgrim must somehow survive a day without a shower, but it's worth it for a bowl of the *cura*'s homemade garlic soup and to spend a night under the starry skies.

I'm not staying tonight, but I will sit down for a quick one with Alberto and Roberto. The former is an Italian teacher from Logroño. The latter, with his handsome leather safari hat, hails from, and is now returning to, the end of the world: Finisterre, on the Atlantic shore. When I say I've been there, he asks if I know his bar.

"Which one is that?"

He thrusts out his chest to display a T-shirt emblazoned with the name *La Galería*. He is a born marketer. Inexplicably, I can't recall any bars in Finisterre.

"Then you haven't been to La Galería, because you'd remember if you had. It's a cosmopolitan bar, a place for travellers, pilgrims. We show local art, there's a lending library . . . Come by when you finish the Camino."

I'm tempted to have a second glass with the two Bertos, but seconds lead to thirds, and I have some walking to do today. In fact, I hope to make it to Burgos. That's forty kilometres, about twice what I've been averaging on this Camino, and a fair distance for my feet. I know that tomorrow I'll feel it, but I don't know what else to do. I've been worrying about my little black notebook—my beautiful, burnable, stealable, loseable, far-from-waterproof little black notebook, first gift of this Camino. If anything happens to that book, I will lose all my notes, so for the sake of my peace of mind I need from time to time to sit for a few hours in front of a computer and commit my words to the ether. By walking to Burgos today, I'll get a jump on the pack. Then I can work through tomorrow without falling off the pace. So I bid the Bertos a reluctant *buen camino* and walk on.

After San Juan de Ortega, the forest is real forest for a while, close and shady, till it opens out into pastures. Cows watch placidly as I roam off the trail to the edge of the highland, from where you can see the whole world, or most of it. I can recommend no better place to sit in the sun with the wind kicking up your collar. One year ago, on another afternoon of ambitious intentions, I lay down for a moment in this very place. When I opened my eyes, the day had flown by and there was nothing to do but go back to San Juan de Ortega for a bed and a bowl of garlic soup.

It was the following morning, as I stepped from the frigid refuge into the frigid outdoors, that I noticed a walking stick standing just by the door. I was, not atypically, the last one out that morning, so there was no one behind me who might have been the stick's owner. It was a hazelwood beauty, some inches taller than me, slim and limber. I tossed her in the air, caught her as she fell. She was light and fit my hand nicely. Around the top, the bark had been peeled away and the words "Nino 2003" written in black marker pen. I thought maybe the stick was the walking partner of an Italian called Nino, so I said, "Come with me. If Nino left you here by mistake and he comes looking for you, I'll save him some walking."

But no one came back for the stick, and I had been walking without one, so I adopted it. It proved an agreeable walking companion, so you'll understand why, two days later, in Burgos, when I saw a girl striding away from the refuge with a stick in her hand labelled Nino 2003, I set off in pursuit. "Hey you! Hello! That's my stick!" I was about to tackle the startled pilgrim when she directed my attention back to the refuge. There, by the door, stood a row of walking sticks, lined up like billiard cues, all signed Nino 2003. So Nino was a brand! Then who was the designer?

I found out last month, when Michiko and I met him

in Logroño. We knew his face already; you see his photo in every refuge and bar along the way, that stern-looking pilgrim in medieval robes releasing a dove from his hand. But we didn't know his name till that morning: Marcelino Antonio Collantes—a.k.a. Nino. He wasn't wearing his robes when we met him, just a T-shirt and jeans, and with his thick beard and his paunch he looked more like Fidel Castro than a super-*peregrino*. He had set up a table in the park, from where he was dispensing figs, biscuits, water, dried gourds and scallop shells, along with this year's line of walking sticks: Nino 2004. In exchange for what we took, he asked only that we sign his book and submit to a bear hug and a rough kiss on the cheek. "No money, *peregrinos*. The Camino takes care of me."

Nino was happy to tell us about his endless peregrinations on all of Spain's Caminos, and of the conferences and gatherings he was invited to. "I am a simple pilgrim with no education, yet I speak at universities." He posed for a picture with us, stamped our credentials with his personal *sello*, dedicated a gourd to the two *peregrinos canadienses* and generally carried on like a rock star. When Michiko and I walked away, it was with new sticks in our hands.

I've never brought a stick with me on the Camino; I've always found one along the way, or had one given to me. It's part of the journey. My first stick was the one John Kennedy from Long Island tossed me one day as we scrambled down a slope. "Here, take this before you fall on your ass," he said. It was an ungainly stick that some other pilgrim had cast aside, and I would have done the same if I hadn't felt sorry for it. I was never satisfied with it—one day in Castrojeriz I nearly sliced a thumb off trying to whittle it down to size—but somehow we made it to Santiago together. There, with a twinge of regret and a sigh of relief, I left my silent partner at the doors of the cathedral. I couldn't help going by later to see if it was still there. It was, and I had to slip away because I felt it was looking at me reproachfully. Next morning, it was gone.

In 2000, when I went to write about the Virgins of the Camino, Little Miguel found a stick by the path on the way down from Roncesvalles and offered it to me. It had a V at the top that was handy as a thumb rest and for hanging hats, cameras and laundry. I called it my goose-footed stick, and it was my partner every step of the way from Roncesvalles to Santiago, then on to Portugal, Barcelona, Italy. In Vigo, it received second-degree burns in the line of duty when I left it leaning against a radiator with damp socks hanging from it. In Lisbon, I retrieved it from the hand of an elderly gentleman who had seen it outside the place where I was eating lunch and assumed it was free for the taking. "A very good stick," he said, sounding like someone who knew. In the end it flew back to Canada in the baggage compartment of an Air France jet, though I wonder, when I see it standing in the corner of my apartment, if I shouldn't have left it on the Camino for someone to find. It's a wild thing, after all, from the slopes of the Pyrenees, and should be out walking.

Last year was Nino 2003, and now Nino 2004. Though the fact is, I'm walking with Michiko's Nino and not my own. When we were selecting our sticks, Marcelino told me that a sturdy fellow like me should carry *un gordo*—a "fat one"—and I trusted his judgment. But after a couple of days I knew that it was Michiko's stick, long, light and springy, that I wanted in my hand. So before she flew home, we made a deal: I could use her stick as long as I brought it back safe and sound. It was a good arrangement, not only because I got the stick I wanted, but because it was a way for Michiko to be with me on the Camino.

The deal was struck, however, in Madrid, on the eve of Michiko's flight home, which left me with the question of what to do with my own Nino. It was not, after all, a stick that I could just dump somewhere. I thought the right thing would be to bring it to the Camino and give it to someone who would appreciate it. And that was how I found myself, after seeing Michiko off at the airport, sitting on the Madrid metro with not one but two fine walking sticks between my knees. At a certain stop a middle-aged woman got on board. Grabbing instinctively for a pole as the train lurched forward, she got hold of my sticks instead. The expression on her face as the "pole" gave way and she pitched into my lap was worth the trip to Madrid.

"Oh, but what wonderful sticks," she said when she had stopped laughing. "I'd love to have a stick like this for walking in the country."

"You do a lot of walking?"

"*Hombre, sí.* Every weekend I take my daughters to the Sierra, where I grew up."

"What do you think of this one here?" I asked, handing her my *gordo.*

She hefted it doubtfully. "For me it's a little heavy," she said. "But my older daughter is a big girl. She could handle a stick like this."

"Then it's hers."

There was just enough time before her stop to tell her the story of the stick so that she would know what a treasure she had. Then she strode off the metro at Avenida de las Américas, stick in hand, an urban pilgrim.

The Capital of Aching Feet

The pilgrim of old knew Burgos for its life-sized cow-skin image of the crucified Saviour, renowned for the verisimilitude of its tortured flesh. An artifact of a cruel age, it implied intimate and detailed knowledge of all the sufferings a human body might endure. The faithful swore that the image's blood circulated, its hair and nails grew, its tears fell. It is said that when Queen Isabella, with customary temerity, asked for a nail as a souvenir, the Christ's arm fell limply to his side. The nail was promptly replaced. The image was renowned for its miracles. "On the day we saw the Christ," reports Schaseck, who travelled to Santiago in the 1460s as secretary to the Bohemian nobleman Leo of Rozmital, "a child who had been dead three days, a child with two broken legs, and a man with St. Anthony's fire were all cured. We were told this was nothing out of the ordinary." When Schaseck asked where the Christ had come from, this is the story he was told:

Once, long ago, some pirates captured a ship off the coast of Spain. There was no one on board and no cargo but a great chest that the pirates could not open. On shore, they found a hermit who advised them to seek counsel from the Bishop of Burgos, a learned Jew. When the pirates came upon the bishop, he was just waking from a nap. "What a strange dream I have had," he said. "I saw a crucifix in a chest on board a ship with no crew." The pirates bowed down in amazement and told the bishop their story. Then they went together to the ship. The moment the bishop stepped on board, the chest flew open. Inside was the Christ of Burgos.

It's a lovely story that contains a puzzling detail. How on earth could the Bishop of Burgos be "a learned Jew"? The answer is Salomon Halevi, the chief rabbi of Castilla, who converted to Christianity in the 1390s. The Pope at the time, scenting a propaganda coup, swiftly appointed him Bishop of Burgos. As Halevi's family claimed descent from the same tribe as the Virgin Mary, he took as his Christian name Pedro de Santa María. It was said that during his tenure as bishop, favour was shown to all who responded to the Ave Maria with the words "Holy Mary, Mother of God—and cousin of His Excellency the Bishop—pray for us."

Tales such as this open a window for us on the *convivencia*, the long "cohabitation" of the Peoples of the Book in Spain. It was not always a period of peace, but its tensions were creative, rendering artistic, architectural, literary, philosophical and cultural riches. In a time when the Christian king of Spain was proud to style himself "king of the three religions," the pilgrim on his way through Estella, Logroño, Burgos and the other cities of the Camino might have done business with Jewish and Muslim traders, peeked into mosques and synagogues, heard Hebrew and Arabic spoken in the streets. Tragically, Catholic Spain would expel the non-Christians who had for so long been part of its fibre, so that today there is only the occasional street sign or plaque to tell us that these stones were once the foundation of the Muslim bathhouse, this street the *judería*, or Jewish quarter.

Even stolid Burgos, known as one of the most conservative cities in Spain, had its dash of Levantine spice. During their time here, Baron Leo and his entourage dined at the home of a mighty count, where they were attended by beautiful maidens with coffee skin, dark eyes and an immoderate fondness (or so Schaseck tells us) for northern European men. Where can

I find an evening like that in Burgos today? I will end up instead, at the end of my long day's walk, at the jam-packed public refuge, where surely I will be serenaded tonight, though not by the sweet voices of dark-eyed maidens.

At least there's a friendly face waiting for me.

"Bob!"

"Inácio!"

We stagger into each other's arms like long-lost brothers. It feels like years since I last saw my Brazilian friend. In fact, it's been nine days. He has been pinned down here since two days ago by tendinitis and blisters. To help the hours pass, he's assumed the hospitalero's duties. He stamps my credentials and hauls my bag to the dorm, telling me all the while a tangled tale of how he got separated from Carmen on the way from somewhere, and how now somebody has somebody else's camera. I try to unknot the details, but my head is spinning from too much sun. I apologize and collapse on a bed. When I return from oblivion, another face from the past is smiling at me. What's Tony Bush doing here?

"My knee was acting up, so I took the bus around the Montes de Oca. I didn't want to do it, but I didn't want to get stuck in the middle of nowhere with a bum leg, either. And you know, Bob, when I look around, I don't feel so bad. Jacques over there has been laid up with tendinitis for almost a week. Inácio is crippled. There's some Brazilian ladies who'll probably have to give up, and those Italians, the ones who look like such tough guys, they can hardly walk. I've got lots of company, and all of them are younger than me!"

Tony's plan now is just to keep walking for as long as he can. When he starts to run low on time, he'll take the bus ahead to Sarria and walk the last hundred kilometres to Santiago from there, because it doesn't matter if you start your Camino in Vladivostok, they won't give you the Compostela unless you walk that last hundred kilometres. I tell Tony it sounds like a good plan and I hope he's going to take a rest before he starts walking again.

"Don't you worry," he assures me. "I'm not going *any-where* tomorrow."

Whatever Burgos was to the medieval pilgrim, to me it will always be the capital of aching feet. Francisco told us the other night in Tosantos that by this point of the Camino we were past our initial aches and pains. Looking around here, I see little to support that view. Nowhere have I observed so many pilgrims looking quite so medieval, hobbling about on chafed and bleeding feet, their blisters pierced and threaded, their knees and ankles trussed.

Walking is a mystery. There's no predicting who will have problems. We have all met, on the one hand, that perky seventy-year-old who covers thirty kilometres a day with ease and, on the other, that strapping young athlete whose feet were a disaster from day one. Some pilgrims, when they run into troubles, rest or adjust. Others drive themselves, deter-mined to overcome the pain, or convinced that pain is an integral part of pilgrimage, or trying to keep up with their walking companions or their itinerary.

On my first Camino, even after German John's treatment, walking hurt. It hurt most at the beginning and the end of the day, when I picked my way around the refuges with the winces and grimaces of a mime walking on thumbtacks. Clambering up and down ladders to top bunks, when the whole weight of my body fell on one narrow band of foot, was torture. Each morning's first few hundred steps were an act of faith, till gradually my tendons loosened up. These are symptoms of plantars fasciitis, and they can be treated. But I didn't know plantars fasciitis from planter's punch. I was just damned if

I was going to let anything keep me from walking. I had a variety of other pains, my favourite being the sensation of a large pebble lodged *inside* my foot, just behind the toes. A well-meaning woman assured me that a friend of hers had had the same thing and it would need to be operated on. I would probably be laid up for months. I thanked her for the information.

I had always seen myself as a walker, so I was not prepared for pain. If I had expected the Camino to be a test in any way, it was emotionally: would I be able to stick with it? As things turned out, that was the least of my problems. From my first step, my commitment to finishing was never in doubt. Instead, it was my body that threatened to "betray" me. I was reluctant to moderate my demands on my legs, feeling, like Maite with her Aborigines, that all they needed was toughening up. I felt ennobled, too, by my daily suffering. I was being the good pilgrim: stoic, single-minded, impervious to discomfort. In the end, I overdid it. For months after the Camino was over, my first steps of the day made me wince. They also made me smile. "Ah, Camino!" I would say.

A few technical adjustments have taken most of the hurt out of walking: bigger shoes (more room for the feet to swell in), gel-pad inserts to cushion my heels and raise my arches, wool socks instead of cotton, sturdy sandals for backup, blister pads and gauze bandages at the first sign of trouble (thanks, John). And I am easier on myself these days. I must have passed a test that first time.

Five years ago in Burgos, I spent the night listening to Karen, the Californian woman in the next bunk (who had warned me that *I* had better be a quiet sleeper), give a master class in snoring. I had finally succumbed to sheer exhaustion when I felt two icy wet hands gripping my forearm. Opening my eyes, I saw Karen's face hovering inches in front of mine in the half-light of dawn.

"Bob," she whispered. "There's a Canadian film crew outside. They want to talk to you."

"Your hands are freezing."

"Sorry, there's no hot water. Listen, I told them you'd come right away . . ."

I pulled the sheets over my head and she had the good judgment to leave me alone. But soon it was John Kennedy from Long Island who was shaking the daylight into me.

"Bob, there's a film crew from Canada outside."

Great. Karen had everyone in on the game.

"John," I said, "could you do me a favour and . . ."

I went back into a doze, but from the babel of voices outside, one word kept poking up its head. "*Canadá* . . . *Canadá* . . . *Canadá* . . ." Reminding myself that this was the Camino, where anything was probable, I ventured down from my cozy bunk, wincing with each step, and peered outside. A film crew was camped on the lawn.

"Are you the Canadian? Sorry to get you up so early, but we're doing this documentary on pilgrimages and we heard there was a Canadian here."

The show was being produced under the auspices of the Anglican Church of Canada. Affable, bearded Ben Lochridge, renegade priest and founder of Toronto's Little Company of Pilgrims, was along in a consulting role. I asked the interviewer if they could wait while I splashed some water on my face.

"That's okay," she said. "You look more like a pilgrim this way." Apparently pilgrims look decrepit.

They were seeing the Camino in reverse, working backwards from Santiago. "It was amazing talking to people there," the interviewer told me. "Their emotions were so raw. It was like they had just been scalded." I liked that word. I wondered if I would look scalded when I got to Santiago.

The camera ran for ten minutes or so as they tried to coax something usable out of me. I didn't have much to offer at that hour, though a couple of my banalities made the final cut. (I am identified in the video as "Canadian Pilgrim"—nice epitaph.) The only interesting thing I had to say, in my opinion, didn't make it. I mean the part when the interviewer leaned towards me, lowered her voice so the viewer would know that this was *a moment* and said:

"This must be a very spiritual experience for you."

My response came so fast, it surprised even me. "No," I said, "it's a very *physical* experience."

She looked disappointed, but what could I say? It wasn't my spirit that was doing the walking, it was my feet. And my feet hurt. Not to say that the Camino was all pain, but it was all, or mostly, *sensation*. Heat, weariness, pain, thirst—not to extremes, but well beyond what my body was used to. And then relief. The rest in the shade, the cold drink, the breeze that sprang up from nowhere, the sting in the mouth of sheep cheese, the gasp as I plunged my face into a cold fountain.

If there had been anything spiritual about my Camino to that point, it had come through the senses: the cessation of discomfort, and with it the unfocused reflex of gratefulness, that impulse to give thanks even when it was not clear to whom. Maybe that's where spirituality begins.

I sleep like a drugged man. In the morning, my heels are tender when they meet the ground, but it's endurable. I wonder if that trek yesterday was only about catching up with my notes or if I'm not still setting little tests for myself. I'll spend the next few hours immobile in front of a computer, then stop by the refuge in the late afternoon to say hi to Pepe and whoever else has shown up. After that it's an easy five-kilometre walk to the next refuge after Burgos. The closest thing to a day of rest.

Nothing in town opens till ten o'clock, so I hang out at the refuge, keeping Inácio company. He's getting frustrated watching the pilgrims hoist their packs and tromp away. "The doctor says I must rest for a week, but I will leave tomorrow even if I have to take the bus. I don't like to watch everybody go. It's not natural."

I see Tony Bush lacing up his boots. "Going to take a look around town, Tony?"

"No, I'm walking today. The knee feels okay. Don't worry, I'll know when I've gone far enough."

Saint Anthony's Bread

After my sedentary day in Burgos, I'm ready for another long walk today, thirty-five kilometres to Castrojeriz. I already have a date there for tomorrow night, when we will celebrate the twenty-sixth birthday of Miss Nuala Ann Tigerlily Saturnina McBride. But Castrojeriz has other attractions for me, enough to merit an extra day there.

Early rain gives way to pale blue skies of stunning clarity. The hills are sleeping lions, their flanks streaked with tawny stumps of burnt wheat. On the plateau, the roundness of the world touches the sky. I tie a kerchief over my ears to keep the wind out. A shepherd passing with his flock stops and points to my pack. "Good idea. Keeps your back warm." Looking back, I see his sheep spread over the hillside like the shadows of clouds.

The route from Rabé de las Calzadas to Hontanas is hours of dirt roads and bare uplands. No highway, no electric wires. No church spires on hilltops to mark the villages; they crouch in the valleys so the wind will blow over their heads. It's a strong wind today, stronger than it knows, like a big young dog that wants to gallop. Fighting it breeds energy. I break into a run, feed off the wind's power, then let it blow me over onto a pallet of wheat stubble.

I stop in Hontanas to warm myself by the fire at Casa Victorino. Victorino is a round, tightly stuffed man in his sixties. When I come in, he nods towards the *porrón*, the plump wine decanter with the long spout that sits on the bar. I hesitate, so he drinks first, holding the *porrón* a foot from his face and tipping it till the thin red stream leaps into his mouth. Then, with a twinkle in his eye, he shifts the arc to the bridge of his veiny snub nose, from where it washes down his cheeks to his mouth.

"And what will you eat today, *peregrino*?"

"What do you have, señor?"

"I have pork cutlets and fish soup."

He clears a space at the table nearest the wood stove, plops down a bottle of wine and retreats to the kitchen, locking the street door on the way. He returns with a tureen of crab soup and two sets of cutlery, ladling out one bowl for me and one for himself. He takes the first slurp.

"It's good," he tells me, in case I don't know what good is.

"It's very good," I reply.

He tops up my bowl. "If you want more, help yourself." Then he pivots to watch the TV. Before I leave, Victorino stamps my credentials with a *sello* that shows him pouring wine from the *porrón* onto his nose, with a slogan that reads, "Serving the pilgrim for more than twenty years."

After Hontanas, the road winds through a valley by a river lined with poplars. The light starts to fade, but the wind still wants to play. At last I see what I have been waiting to see: spanning the road ahead, the massive ruined arches of the Convento de San Antón.

The afflictions pilgrims bring with them to the Camino today are mostly of the spirit: doubt, alienation, boredom, stress, estrangement from family, disenchantment with work, lack of faith, and that all-pervading sense of something missing. In contrast to their ailing spirits, their bodies are usually well nourished and fit. This is a far cry from the old days, when the Camino was a walking infirmary, an endless procession of pilgrims seeking cures at the shrines of healing saints. There were many such on the Camino, some specializing in blindness, others in leprosy or infertility, but the most famous was Anthony, whose specialty was the disease that bore his name: Saint Anthony's fire. It's called ergotism now, an almost unknown condition, yet for centuries it was the scourge of northern Europe, tormenting its victims with gangrenous skin ulcers, convulsions and hallucinations.

The Convento de San Antón, the saint's "clinic," stood here, just before Castrojeriz. Nothing remains of it today but a few ruined walls and the angel-thronged arches that span the road. But long ago, those arches towered over the porch where pilgrims received the miraculous bread of Saint Anthony, stamped with the Greek cross or tau (τ), which was the sign of the Antonian Order. When pilgrims left the hospital, they took a tau with them for lasting protection.

The amazing thing about Saint Anthony's cure was that it worked. A pilgrimage to his shrine wasn't a faint hope or a last gasp, it was a safe bet. After a few days' rest and a diet of Saint Anthony's wonder bread, the sick were ready to walk the rest of the way to Santiago. Indeed, the saint's therapeutic powers were so strong that they started to work almost from the moment pilgrims entered Spain. Of course, science has an explanation for Saint Anthony's miracles. It seems the fungus that causes ergotism thrives on damp rye, and damp northern Europe was full of rye bread eaters. An ideal treatment for their condition would include exercise (a three-thousand-kilometre walk would be good for starters) and a lot of wheat bread, of the sort one eats in Spain.

It's not the first time science has rained on a miracle, but does science really have the last word here? Whether the pilgrims to Saint Anthony's hospital were deluded or not, the fact is, they came away cured. They got what they were looking for even if it didn't come in the way they expected. I suspect there are still many pilgrims who come to the Camino looking for a miracle cure—not for leprosy or Saint Anthony's fire, but for loneliness, depression, lack of purpose—and go home disappointed when they don't arrive in Santiago whole and healed. But maybe they don't realize that the Camino is still inside them, like Anthony's bread, quietly doing its work.

The tau is still worn today. You can get one from any shop in Castrojeriz, but if you like a touch of the authentic, go to the convent of the nuns of Santa Clara in the fields near town. The nuns are cloistered, so you will not see the hand that places your tau necklace on the lazy Susan and spins it out to you in exchange for your few euros. Hang it from your neck as a reminder that some miracles take time to unfold.

This Is Camino

There are places where arches or gates span the Camino within or at the entrance to cities, but only the arches of San

Antón stand alone among fields and hills. To pass through a gate normally signifies arrival or departure, a coming in or going out. Here there is no in or out. What lies beyond the gate is what lay before it. Trees, sky, the earth, and a road.

The first time I passed beneath these arches and walked the long, tree-lined road to Castrojeriz, I had company: Consuelo, a cheery, half-blind Catalan housewife; Joana, a brittle Portuguese *peregrina* who had issues with Jesus and his Father; and Loli, a good-looking, thirtyish Madrileña who observed the rest of us with amusement from an ironic cloud. As we walked, we made fun of Consuelo for always being in a hurry, and Consuelo teased Joana about a moody German pilgrim named Paul having *ojitos*, "little eyes," for her, which is a funny way of saying a crush, and Loli just smiled and shook her head. Then we saw Castrojeriz up ahead, so Joana said, "Let's sit down under a tree for a minute," and it seemed like a good idea because trees were something we hadn't seen much of that morning. She opened her bag and fruit emerged. Consuelo splashed some water from her bottle on each nectarine and apple as a symbolic cleansing before handing them around.

I had been walking with these women on and off for a couple of days, but of course, a couple of days is a lifetime on the Camino. Anyone would have thought, to see us loping along, talking and laughing, that we had known each other forever. Each of the women was alive to the pilgrimage in her own way. Consuelo was clear, happy and proud to be venturing out without husband or family. She knew what she was doing and why, though she never went into details, saying only that she walked the Camino to answer "a necessity of the spirit." Joana and Loli were anxious and alert. They were young and still looking for their road through life. But while Joana posed her questions in the language of religion—*What's God's problem?*

Why doesn't he tell me what he wants?—Loli's were framed in blanker existential terms: *What do I do after I finish doing this?* As for me, I was still working out what it meant to be a pilgrim, though I was stuck on the notion that it was something I had to do for myself. Which was why, though I couldn't imagine better walking partners than Joana, Consuelo and Loli, I meant to lose them the first chance I got.

That chance came in Castrojeriz, where I accompanied my three companions to the pilgrim refuge, got them settled in and then uttered as shameless a lie as any in the annals of falsehood: "My legs feel great today. I'm going to keep walking." My legs felt that day, as they always did, as if they'd been worked over with a stick. But it was not far to the next refuge, so I told my friends we would meet again in a day or two—which was likely enough—and I was free to walk on.

Except that now I didn't much feel like walking. I trudged to the end of Castrojeriz, learning on the way why the German pilgrims of old called it "the long town." The sun was beating down like a great hammer and there was a hill ahead, not very tall, but steep and shadeless and in the way. So I found a sheltered place to make my lunch, took out my pocket knife—and conceived a project for the hot hours ahead: I would whittle down my stick. It was a time when I was desperate to lighten my load in the hope of taking some pressure off my feet. Two days before, in Burgos, I had sloughed off four kilos of *stuff*, mostly paper. My bag still felt like it was full of hammers. Whittling my stick wouldn't make my bag any lighter, but even the illusion of lightness appealed to me.

My stick that time was not Nino, but the great hunk of lumber John Kennedy gave me. It posed challenges. The stone-hard knots that ran up and down its length could only be shaved away an onion skin at a time. The heat weighed, the cicadas whirred, the sweat pooled on my upper lip. I slipped into deep concentration, one of those moments when the physical seems about to burst through the membrane of the spiritual. Then the knife slipped, and my thumb proved a lot easier to pare than the wood. The blood flowed lustily despite all my efforts to staunch it, and soon it was clear that I would be joining the Camino's lengthy martyr roll if I didn't hurry back to the refuge.

The hospitalera chastised me: "Why don't you just find another stick? You can pick them up off the ground." When she had done with bandaging me up and chewing me out, I had no more desire to walk that day. I would be staying in Castrojeriz after all. As there was no sign of Joana, Loli and Consuelo, I took my notebook and went by myself to El Lagar, the little bar that stood opposite the refuge.

I stepped down into an oasis of stone, wood and shadow. A massive beam cut from a single tree and anchored by a stone counterweight arced across the room. A clutch of tables huddled in a well at the back. Bold paintings of rural life hung on the walls. Perhaps this was the higher end that today's events had served; I had been meant to find this place. The placid woman with thick glasses who stood behind the bar welcomed me with a smile, and I looked around for a table where I could write the afternoon away. All of them were free except the one where a stocky man in his late forties with apple cheeks and a red beard sat with a brandy snifter in his left hand and a cigar in his right. I hadn't seen him before, but I could tell he was a pilgrim by his skin-tight hiking shorts. I hadn't come looking for company, but he kept grinning at me like a demented Buddha till I decided the writing could wait.

"What did you do to your hand?" he asked with a heavy German accent.

"Cut it. I was whittling my walking stick . . ." I mimed the gestures. "Whittling, whittling, and then, *fwsssssh*, the knife slipped and—*woh*!" I showed the blood spritzing from my thumb with spasmodic clenches and releases of my right hand.

"*Katastroph!*" the man with the beard exclaimed. "Let me see." He shook his head. "You cannot make like this." With his sausage fingers, he undid the work of the hospitalera, sighing in dismay, as though she had used filthy rags for the job. Then he bound me all up again. I couldn't see any difference, but he was satisfied. "Is better now, *ja*? So what do you drink?"

"*Agua mineral,*" I said.

"*Cerveza!*" the man with the beard called to the bartender. He turned to me sternly. "In such weather like this, you must beer!"

So I beered.

"You smoke?" he asked, tendering me a cigar. "No? Never the pilgrims smoke. This is why I like the Spain people." He gave the bartender a cigar thumbs-up. She waved back, a cigarette wedged between V-for-victory fingers. "Is not good, I know . . . But I smoke each day only one. One Havana, and one glass Napoleon. Very good, Napoleon." He sniggered as if he was confessing to his first drink.

I finished my beer too quickly and Karl called for another. I was glad that I hadn't kept walking. Now and then, pilgrims peered in out of the heat, then tromped on. I pitied them. Two rheumy-eyed Spanish seniors came in and began to joke with the bartender, clearly men who knew how to kill an afternoon. Karl sat nursing his daily rations of herbal and liquid joy as he took me step by step through his journey so far—all fifteen hundred kilometres of it.

We walked out his front door in Bavaria one overcast day in April. Stopped at the shrine of Einsiedeln in Switzerland to pray to the Virgin for a safe journey. Pushed on through June, clear across France via the ancient pilgrim town of Le Puy, then southwest to the wall of the Pyrenees. Hiked up the north face and skiddled down the south and we were in Spain. I knew the way from here, following the yellow arrows from the green uplands to the parched wine lands and the fields of stunted wheat, till this afternoon, in the dead heat of late July, in a bar in Castrojeriz, where our two stories finally met, as they had evidently always been meant to.

This was Karl's second Camino. "Ah, yes, you must do it two times. The second time only to enjoy." And when he was finished walking all the way, not just to Santiago but to Finisterre on the Atlantic shore, he would do as he did the first time, "walk by the ocean and see again all the Camino, like a movie in my head. And then I walk home."

"You're walking back to Bavaria?"

"*Ja*, so I come home not until November. I hope my wife didn't change the lock."

When the two of us had talked enough, we slipped into silence. We had done our day's work of walking and now we were escaping the sun in the shelter of a place that felt as old as the road. We breathed in the coolness of the stone, admired the paintings, nodded at the bartender and the old men. We were two strangers far from home who had met and found a bond in the road we shared. A thousand years had prepared this moment for us, and all of the moments of a thousand years were alive in it. It was ancient and familiar to us, yet we had not lived it before and we would not live it again. It had a taste, a scent, a sheen all its own.

Then Karl began to laugh. His burly shoulders heaved with silent laughter and he swished the last drops of brandy around in his glass. When he had finished laughing, he said three words:

"*This is Camino.*"

There was nothing more to say.

The Well

As I walked the Camino last October, I kept thinking of Karl and the distant heat-struck afternoon when he said to me, *This is Camino*. The morning I got to Castrojeriz, I decided to stop for a coffee at *that* bar. It took a while to locate the place, but then I saw the bartender outside cleaning the windows. She smiled without surprise as I approached.

"It's you," she said.

"You remember me?"

"Some faces one remembers."

I had left a footprint on the Camino.

At that point, I had only three days remaining. It occurred to me that I could spend them right here. Only the night before, looking at Father Ojeda's plan for the Goose Game, I had noted that on his game board Castrojeriz is the Well. The rules say that if you land in the Well, you must stay till another pilgrim comes to pull you out. I decided to half-observe the rules. I would stay in the Well. But I wouldn't let anyone pull me out.

Those three days marked the first time I ever paused for breath on the Camino, the first time I felt myself a pebble in the river instead of a straw. I took a room in La Casa de los Holandeses, a *pensión* run by a Dutch couple who had come to this remote town looking for a quiet place to read. My window on the second floor looked out on the Camino, so that I saw the pilgrims' backs as they passed through town. The first morning, I sat at the window, calling out when I saw a back I knew: *Raúl! Mathilde! Ferrán! Hiro!* I had seen nothing of Julio and his entourage since my bus trip to Burgos, and I wondered if they would roll into town. But the circus didn't come, and though I kept my ears open, I heard no reports of a pilgrim in a wheelchair.

When the pilgrims I knew had passed by, I found other ways to entertain myself. I climbed up to the castle, roamed the farmlands near the town, walked back to the ruins of San Antón. Luisa Rubines was in town too; I would meet her on the street as she toted around her photographic heavy artillery. And once or twice a day, I would drop in at El Lagar for a drink and a chat with the owner, whom I now knew as Mila.

Mila was from Castrojeriz, but a career in art restoration had taken her off to the big cities for much of her adult life. Then, in 1998, she walked the Camino and found a new vocation: to apply her restorer's hand to the family *lagar*—the winepress—and make it a place of welcome. The winepress had been in the family since no one knew when, and up until the eighties, when the last of her siblings left Castrojeriz and the local farmers switched from grapes to grains, it had been in service. For centuries, this was where Mila's ancestors had rendered mountains of grapes into juice. The hulking machinery still stands: the twenty-foot beam, a single piece of lumber, that crosses the room from the front door to the well in the rear, where the fruit was crushed; the counterweight that anchors it, a stone about the height and girth of your average sixty-year-old Spanish man; and fixed to the stone, the huge wooden screw on which the beam was raised and lowered. Mila directed my eyes to a painting that showed how a wooden bed was attached to the end of the beam like a big square foot to do the squashing.

"So you didn't use to pull up your skirt and dance on the grapes?" I asked.

"Oh, we did that too," she laughed.

But the story of El Lagar ran deeper than the ages of Mila's family. This corner of Castrojeriz had once been the *judería*, the Jewish quarter, and tradition locates the synagogue of Castrojeriz on the site where El Lagar stands today. Evidence to support the tradition was discovered during the construction of the bar: "When they dug up the floor, they found a well. Synagogues were always built over wells so they would have fresh water for rituals."

The well, the sacred spring. Once, there had been a house of worship here. Then a place for making wine, that most sacramental of secular acts. Now the well flowed for parched pilgrims. We were drawn to it like dowsing rods even though we could not see or hear it bubbling, splashing, singing its ancient song beneath the stone.

The sight of Castrojeriz from the distance is unforgettable. The long, straight, tree-lined road, the hill rising from a peaceful landscape, the stump of the ruined castle keeping watch over the long brown town. As one approaches, however, certain unfortunate details come into view. The houses by the church are long abandoned, For Sale signs wave from their bricked-over windows like hankies from a sinking ship. Closer to the centre, there are fallen-in roofs and walls that tilt at gravity-defying angles. The gates of the grand churches that once stood open to pilgrims have been locked for years and show no sign of opening again.

Castrojeriz, once home to thousands, today shelters fewer than nine hundred souls. Even houses that have not been abandoned for good stand empty eleven months of the year, the young coming back with their Madrid-born children in August to spend the holiday in the old family home. For that month, the population swells by three thousand, and every night the streets are full of noisy city folk. Of those who stay on in September, many now reside in the massive seniors' home. Outside of work in the tourist and pilgrim trade, there is not much to keep young people here.

The paintings on the walls of El Lagar depict a different time, when people lived on the land and drew their sustenance from it, a time not yet gone, but going fast. I have mentioned the painting of the winepress. There are others: a shepherd driving his flock, a horse-drawn plough. The most impressive canvas depicts that most emblematic of rural events, the pig slaughter. Three young men hold the fated beast down while a fourth sharpens the knife. The women sit washing the entrails that will be stuffed to make sausages while the old men wait in the background, caps in hand, canes between their knees, hungry for their cutlets. The paintings all bear the same signature: *Alberdi*. "The painter from Burgos," Mila told me, as if it was a name one should know.

Last fall, after Mila told me the story of El Lagar, I made it my own, dragging in every stray pilgrim I found to explain the function of the beam, point out the grape-crushing well, tell the history of the building and generally show off my knowledge. One day I was giving two English pilgrims "the tour" when a Spanish man with a salt-and-pepper beard and a glint in his eye swept in the door and made straight for us.

"*Peregrinos!* Where are you from? *Alemania? Inglaterra?*"

When Jamie and Simon admitted to being English, a Grinchy grin crept over the man's face. He put his fingers behind his ears and pushed them forward. "*Carlos!* Eh? Charles! What a buffoon. And he is going to be your *king*! What a disgrace. Oh, England. Your country and mine, they have a history!

"And you," he said, wheeling on me, "you too are of the Grand Britannia?"

"No, Canada."

"*Canadá? Canadá!*" He closed his eyes and breathed in deep, as though he might catch a whiff of prairie wildflowers off my clothes. "Tell me you are from Saskatchewan! *Saskatchewan!* I love that name. So wide, so young. Not like Spain, where everything is old and narrow and stupid. Saskatchewan! It is in the west, no? The Great Plains? Tell me you are from Saskatchewan!"

"I'm not, but my mother is."

"*Qué suerte.* What fortune! The frontier! America!"

"Canada, actually."

"*Pffff!* The same. America, the New World, Saskatchewan!"

He punctuated this aria with jabbing fingers, tugged forelocks, extravagant shrugs. His every sentence seemed to end in something unspoken or unspeakable, something that could only be expressed by a huff, a snort, a wince. I was foolish enough to tell him that the New World was not as open and free as he thought. He fanned my quibbles back at me like a bad smell.

"You were born with a New World mind. You cannot comprehend the pettiness of the Spanish spirit. It is bad enough in Madrid and Barcelona, the great cities—but here!"

He was about to launch into this new theme, one that couldn't be very popular locally, when Mila sidled over to our table. "Juan, why don't you leave the pilgrims to talk?"

"We *are* talking. This young man is from Canada."

"Come over and say hello to me."

He executed one of his shrugs. "I wasn't staying anyway." Before he left, he clasped my hand. "You will come back tonight. I need to talk to people from outside. It's all that keeps me from going mad. Come back and tell me more about *Saskatchewan.*" And with that, he roared out the door.

"Who was that?" I asked.

In answer, Mila pointed to the painting of the pig slaughter. There was no mistaking it: the man standing behind the smoking fire was our friend with the salt-and-pepper beard.

"So he's a friend of the painter, Alberdi?" I asked.

"He *is* Alberdi," said Mila.

One year later and here I am, back in Castrojeriz and itching to get down to El Lagar to see what's been happening. I drop my gear at the refuge, head across the way—and am reminded again that things do not stand still. Several of Alberdi's bucolic paintings have been replaced by giant compositions of squares, blotches and jags in clashing metallic tones, a sort of visual experimental jazz. I don't recognize the woman tending the bar. Don't tell me Mila's sold the place?

"Mila? She's in the back. Shall I get her?"

I breathe a sigh of relief.

"You again!" says Mila. This time, I rate an *abrazo* (a big hug). She has a becoming new hairstyle, as I make a point of mentioning before I inquire about the paintings. "Do you like them?" she asks. "It's Alberdi's new style."

"Incredible," is all I can muster. "Incredible."

Mila has the same sweet, melancholy smile and quiet bearing. She's not happy with the business. The refuge across from El Lagar used to be the only one in Castrojeriz, but since the new municipal refuge opened on the main drag, fewer pilgrims have found their way down to her part of town. She sounds a little harried, like most members of the Camino service industry at the tail end of this Holy Year. The bar is packed with the early evening crowd and Alberdi is taking a nap right now, so I tell her I'll be back tomorrow to bring her some business.

Tonight I have an appointment with Alberto and Roberto, the two I met in San Juan de Ortega. We dine on grilled meat in a restaurant that is hot and smoky, like the innards of a great beast, with rude chunks of stone for flesh and warping lengths of raw timber for ribs. After a blustery day, it's a fine place for wine and talk. In the course of the evening, I discover in Roberto a kindred spirit: another writer afflicted by nostalgia. For several years he has written a column for one of the Galician papers, a chronicle of the passing scene with nuggets of local history and folklore mixed in. When I get to Finisterre, he says, he'll show me his journalistic scrapbook.

Trascendencia

By the time the Bertos and I toddled back to the refuge last night, the lights were out and everyone was sleeping. So it's not till now that I get a look at the pilgrim in the next bed. She is a black woman so slim and long that when she stretches, her feet poke into the aisle between the beds. She rolls over and blinks in my direction.

"Good morning, Saffron," I say.

Kara and Nuala's partner in crime is thrilled to hear that the girls are coming. "Cool. I was thinking of staying another day anyway. I like the vibe." Everybody likes that Castrojeriz vibe. We go for breakfast at the Brazilian bar. With her wool cap pulled down tight and her hair tied back in ponytails, Saffron looks like a Bill Cosby character. She admires my head kerchief. "You remind me of one of my homies from back in the 'hood." That's one I've never heard.

"The Brazilian bar" is really La Taberna, but the Brazilo-phile owner has hung a big Brazilian flag above the street door. Every year, when the pilgrim season ends, he closes up shop and heads for the South American beaches. I'm sorry to deprive El Lagar of the custom, but La Taberna is strategically located on the Camino. If Kara and Nuala stop anywhere, it will be here. So we hunker down, I with my *café con leche*, Saffron with her morning brandy.

"I'm a waiter back home, so I'm used to working till five or six a.m. and then kicking back and having a drink. It freaks the Spanish bartenders out. They always ask twice to be sure they heard right. I like my beer, too. I don't know about you guys in Canada, but that's the way we are in the States. I always carry a can of Carlsberg in my pack. It's kind of a ritual. Every day, when I get to where I can see the town where I'm staying that night, I sit down and break out my beer to celebrate. Course, it's usually hot by then.

"Why am I doing the Camino? Good question. Nobody else I know has ever heard of it. They all think I'm crazy. But I saw this pbs special, and after that, God just kept bugging me. Giving me signs. Like I'd meet some dude called Santiago. Or I'd call a wrong number and the voice on the other end would be talking Spanish. And I was like, first of all, I've never flown anywhere, I don't *do* flights. And then there was no way I could get the time off work. But God wouldn't leave me alone." She shrugs. Who is she to argue with God? But then, *what exactly is his point?*

"Shit happens to me that doesn't happen to anybody else. When I get home, I'm going to write a book about all the shit that's happened to me. I had a fight with a monk. I got attacked by a mob of pilgrims. I almost got eaten by dogs."

"What happened with the mob of pilgrims?"

"I threw a bottle into a field. I know that's bad, I was being a brat. But I was just mad at Los Arcos that day 'cause of something that happened there. So this Spanish pilgrim comes over and says, 'Do you speak English?' and I say, 'Yeah,' so he says, 'Who do you think is going to pick up that bottle?' Now, I wasn't in a mood for discussing, so I say, 'Well, you can pick it up. You look pretty fit.' So then he starts saying that I hate Spain and calling me a dirty American. So I tell him, 'Let him who is without fault cast the first stone,' and he can kiss my ass. And he says I don't know what other racist shit, 'cause it was all in Spanish, but before I know it, there's this mob of pilgrims yelling in my face like they're going to string me up. I had to get out of there or *somebody* would have got hurt. I mean, I know I'm not perfect, but I thought the Camino was about forgiving."

I commiserate, thinking at the same time that I wouldn't mind giving her a little bop for pitching that bottle away. But what was that thing about the first stone . . . ?

We keep warm at the Brazilian bar till ten-thirty. Then Saffron takes her bags to the municipal refuge while I check in at La Casa de los Holandeses. The Holandeses remember me. Yes, my old room overlooking the Camino is free. I pull a chair to the window, and it isn't five minutes before I see Kara and Nuala's matching backpacks passing by.

"Happy birthday, *peregrina*!"

"It's not till tomorrow. And what are you doing up there?"

"Watching over you. Hang on, I'm coming down."

I walk them to the refuge, saving Saffron as a surprise. The reunion is joyous, drinks are in order. It's a slow morning at El Lagar, and Mila gives me an extra-happy wave. Right now, the only customer is one of her old codgers. I catch a glimpse of him as I come up to the bar, a dismal, beaten-down fellow. Then he hears my voice and turns to me, his face breaking into a wide and utterly toothless smile.

"Aha! Mila told me you were back."

"*Alberdi?*"

"Pyorrhea," he says, reading my shock. "Gum disease. They pulled them out, every last one." He yanks his lips back in case I doubt him. "The denture won't be ready till next month. How can a man live without teeth?"

Something else is different. The facial hair is gone. He looks older without the bristle, and he's lost some of his vehemence. He even finishes his sentences. I assume the setback is temporary. I ask if there's some connection between the missing teeth and the violent new paintings. "Those? There's nothing new about them. It's the sort of thing that was big in the seventies. Colours. Blobs. What can I say? I get bored doing the same thing.

"It's for my own amusement, anyway. The fashionable thing in Spain today is lines. I don't want to paint lines. I came here to clear my mind, but the Spanish mentality pursues me. The Spanish mind does not aspire, it only looks back. 'Better to be the tail of a lion than the head of a rat.' This is how the Spaniard thinks." I sense a bit of the old madness creeping back. "But in America—!"

"Señor Alberdi," I break in before he sets sail, "come and meet my friends."

Saffron, Kara and Nuala have accommodated themselves at a table in the old grape-pressing well. I tell them that a few years ago they would have been up to their eyeballs in juice. They like that idea. Alberdi and Nuala hit it off immediately. She loves his canvases, the new and the old, and wants to know more about his "process."

"Come," says Alberdi, "I'll show you something." He takes us to a dark little room in the back with a half-dozen tables—for private parties perhaps, or a busier day than I have ever seen at El Lagar. He switches on the lights. On the walls around the room are genre paintings, each about a metre square. Hunting dogs, vistas of Castrojeriz, forest scenes, avenues in some city, probably Burgos. Away from the noise of the bar, our voices drop almost to whispers.

"Are these yours?" asks Nuala.

"Yes, they're all mine. These are the paintings people buy for their houses. If I show them a big canvas, they aren't interested. They say their walls are too small. And the 'serious' collectors only want lines. So these I paint to put food on the table, the others for my satisfaction."

"How long does it take you to paint one?" asks Nuala.

"A morning. But the big one in the bar, the pig slaughter, I worked on that for five years. Several times I changed the base, rearranged characters, added characters. I kept on till I was happy with it. But is it finished? Who can say?"

"Do these little ones give you any pleasure?"

"Pleasure, no. But I do believe in the concept of the artist as a skilled labourer. It's an idea that is almost lost today, that an artist should be capable of executing different kinds of commission. How medieval! But I take satisfaction in practising my trade. Still, when you are sixty-two years old and you have lost all your teeth, you begin to feel something is lacking . . . Don't get me wrong, it's not that I fear death, I was born dead. The caul was over my head when I came out of the womb and the doctor had to blow life into me. That is why I have no religion. Religions survive by making you fear death. Even Buddhism. Why was the first thing the Buddha saw when he went out into the world a leper? Why not a flower, a child, the sun rising? To make us afraid.

"No, no, the thing that lacks is transcendence. *Trascendencia*. I used to feel it in my work. It's something that flickers with age."

The three of us stand in uncharacteristic silence. That word, *trascendencia*, has left a wistful note hanging in the air. Then Alberdi turns out the light and the moment is over.

Back in the sunny bar, Kara and Saffron are making plans for the Finisterre party. Alberdi sits down with us and soon returns to his favourite theme. "The Spanish mind, rigid, hopeless!" He yanks his vanished beard in despair, then flashes a toothless grin, spreads his arms and declares, "But things are different elsewhere. Open spaces, open minds. *Saskatchewan!*"

This time I don't argue with him. He has a right to his Saskatchewan. We all do. The Saskatchewan of the mind.

In the Goose Game, Castrojeriz is the Well, and a well on the Camino is always a place of encounters. On my way through town, I hear a familiar voice calling my name.

"Hey, Tony Bush, you're supposed to be taking it easy. How did you get here?"

"Got here on my own two legs, what do you think?" He's standing straight, head back, cheeks flushed after the long walk into the wind. I've never seen him look better.

Later, at El Lagar, Linda blows in. She looks as beaten down by her day in the wind as Tony looked revitalized. "This is the last straw. I'm done, finished, fed up, knackered." Two glasses of wine and a dose of cajoling later it's, "Well, *maybe* I'll walk tomorrow, but only to the next town, just to see how it goes." By the time the pitcher is drained, she's promising to walk to León, *but not one step farther*. We'll see her in Santiago yet.

Marta and Alfred are next to arrive, then the Weird Sisters, John from Derry, Sandee. The German girls are making a final appearance; they have to be back in school next week. All of the gang from before Burgos are back together, all except Pepe. I ask around, but no one has seen him.

The girls, meanwhile, have made a useful friend in Kim, the Australian hospitalera, who has agreed to let them sneak out tonight to celebrate Nuala's birthday. In fact, she's coming along.

At a quarter to midnight, while the good pilgrims snore, five of us rendezvous in the plaza.

"Where are we going? Everything's closed."

"To the castle."

Kim leads us up a goat track through the moonless, mole-blind dark. Munchie, the refuge's puppy, bounds ahead. Coming down will be an adventure. The old castle, which looks so impressive from the plain, is only broken walls around some grass. Inside, a stone stairway leads to a lookout.

Nuala sizes up the surroundings. "All right, girls, this looks like the party room. Let's get to work."

The grounds are strewn with the refuse of past picnics. While Kara and Saffron forage for wood, Nuala gathers cardboard and scraps of newspaper. Then Kim puts it all together and in minutes we are squatting around a roaring bonfire. Kara breaks out the wine, but the birthday girl won't let her open it yet.

"I won't be twenty-six till 12:20 a.m."

It's smoky by the fire, so I climb out to the parapet. Nice drop from here. Behind me, the girls huddle in a chiaroscuro of black and gold. Ahead, silvery blue stars pulse in the still seas of the night. Burgos, forty kilometres distant, is a smudge on the horizon. My eyes follow the procession of yellow lamps that mark the trail of the Camino through Castrojeriz. For whom?

There's a crackle from the bonfire. Sparks spin past me to be extinguished by the night. I'm thinking about Alberdi and his "transcendence." I think I know what he means, that feeling of being in, and yet above, the moment. Of being outside oneself, yet still oneself, conscious, feeling, knowing what cannot be known. I know that the moment I'm living now, this conjunction of fire and stars and night, would have been a transcendent moment when I was younger. Or was that only something I strained towards because I wanted to believe in it? Now I find myself comfortably, if sometimes dully, settled in the physical: light, perception, bodies moving in space, and time like a dark river running through it all. Is there anything else? Does there need to be?

I remember the day five years ago when I met Karl in the town below. I see his childlike smile, the lazy line of smoke rising from his cigar. *This is Camino*, he tells me. Here is here and now is now and there's nowhere and no-when else to be. You want transcendence? Look around you.

My toes are starting to freeze. The night is not listening to my questions.

Nuala calls over from the fire. "How's the weather out there?"

"Cold."

"Then come here and warm yourself up, *peregrino*."

PART III

Alguien Que Busca Algo

CASTROJERIZ TO ASTORGA - 190 KM.

LEÓN

León

Mansilla de
las Mulas

CASTILLA

Hospital
de Órbigo

Reliegos

Carrión
de los
Condes

Astorga

Villar de
Mazarife

El Burgo
Ranero

Sahagún

Ledigos

Castrojeriz

Frómista

Boadilla
del Camino

THE MESETA

N

0 km   20   40

Map Area

The Meseta

Tink. Tink tink. It takes three or four little *tink*s before I'm fully awake. Is it the pipes? Termites in the beams? *Tink. Tink.* No, it's something hitting the window. I open the shutters to see Kara and Saffron in the street below with big grins and hands full of pebbles. "Nuala's at Mass," they yell. "See you at the bar."

The girls have declared today International Day Without Walking. They are holding court at El Lagar. When I arrive, the first round of *tintos* has already gone down. I am rash enough to join in, and before I know it, it's noon and the idea of staying one more night in Castrojeriz is looking attractive. Well, why not? I'm bound by no vows. I like this place. I like the company. What the hell . . .

At the stroke of noon, I pull on my jacket.

"Oh, Bob, you're not leaving."

But I am. I bid Mila goodbye till next time, tell the girls I'll see them up ahead, and I'm out the door. The first steps are a slog until I hit the sunlight, and then I know why I'm walking. The wind has died down, it's a warm fall day. This is Camino. I tear up the hill beyond Castrojeriz without breaking a sweat. I remember, the day after I met Karl, seeing him up here, sitting on his backpack admiring the wildflowers. He spread his arms as I passed.

"Van Gogh!" he cried. For Karl, every moment was Camino.

A long look back at Castrojeriz, then it's only a few hundred paces across the top of the ridge and I'm gazing out over a land that stretches flat as a tablecloth in every direction. The *meseta*, Spain's Saskatchewan, just a half-hour walk from Alberdi's doorstep. All right, it's not as vast as the North American prairies, but for walking purposes you wouldn't want it one step wider. Nor is it quite as flat as a tablecloth; there are ripples and furrows at the ends, where the cloth gets bunched up. But most of it is level, broad and bare.

Many pilgrims feel free to skip the *meseta*. *Nothing to see* is the usual explanation. *But that's exactly the point*, Francisco from Tosantos would say. *That's why God put it there. So that you will stop expecting the world to entertain you and begin to look into yourself.* That's one good reason for walking the *meseta*. Here is another: you never know where you will meet the most interesting person or hear the most important story or experience the most profound emotion. It might happen in some glamour spot such as Santiago or the Pyrenees. Or it might happen in Mansilla de las Mulas, Carrión de los Condes, Terradillo de los Templarios or any of the other drab, parched, improbably named towns of the *meseta*. You'll never know unless you're there.

Last year, I didn't walk the *meseta*. I came just this far with a British aid worker named Suzie, who was filling time before her assignment in Bolivia started. She had set out from Pamplona, expecting to walk for a week. Then the Bolivian army mounted a coup. Her agency thought it best to hold off till things settled down. Suzie kept walking. A week went by and Bolivia was still looking dicey. Suzie kept walking. She'd just been told that if all went well, in another week or two . . .

"It's like this whole coup happened just so I could finish walking the Camino."

"Do you really believe that?" I asked.

"Of course not, but isn't it nice sometimes to think that the universe revolves around you?"

I waved goodbye to Suzie from the edge of the ridge, watched her progress down the slope and across the plain till she was no more than a speck moving in the direction of Santiago, and swore that this year I'd be back. And here I am, picking up where I left off.

Once, the *meseta* was the Camino's Wild West, where warrior bands blew back and forth, Muslims from the south, Christians descending from their northern fastnesses on kidnapping raids. It is fitting, then, that the pride of Boadilla del Camino, the *meseta* town where I will stay tonight, is her *rollo*. Standing outside the church, this ornately carved stone column, ten metres or so in height, is reckoned to be one of the finest in Spain, pretty enough to have been featured on a postage stamp. And what is a *rollo*? It is the post to which accused felons were bound before the public reading of their judgments. To the accused, the *rollo* was a place of shame, but to those who sat in judgment, it was a source of pride, symbolizing the town's right to punish its own. One guesses it was a right exercised with gusto.

Behind unwelcoming walls, the refuge of Boadilla is the Camino's Club Med, complete with outdoor pool. The prospect of an evening dip is irresistible. My polar bear swim done, I find a table for myself in the bar and vanish into my notebook. Thanks to my long morning in Castrojeriz, I am back in pilgrim limbo. Everyone who caught up with me last night is now a half day ahead, the Spice Pilgrims are a half day behind and Pepe has fallen off the map. The faces around me are new, and though I had the will to break the ice on the

swimming pool, I don't have enough to break the ice of conversation. I guess I'll need some time to slip into this new
stage of my Camino.

A Thinking Stone

I wake with a start and stretch my arm blindly to the head of
my bed. Michiko's stick is there, right where I left it last night.
Thank God. But what a bizarre dream. I have to tell the first
pilgrim I see, a little bearded Frenchman with a twinkle in his
eye. In my dream, I have carelessly traded Michiko's stick to
some American pilgrims for an ugly blue stump of fence post.
It's not until the Americans are stick figures on the horizon
that I realize what I've done. Off I go across the wide *meseta*
in pursuit, desperate to convince them to undo the trade.
Before I can catch them, I wake up.

"What do you make of that?" I ask the little Frenchman.

"So let me see. The stick is your wife's? And you have
given it to some other pilgrims? And now you are afraid she
will be angry with you?"

"That's right."

He walks away with a shake of the head and a sly Gallic
chuckle.

Today is a day when a pilgrim can feel diligent. It's October 12,
feast day of Nuestra Señora del Pilar, the matron of Spain,
and a national holiday for everyone but pilgrims and bartenders. The towns are locked up and sleeping. The only
traffic on the highway is a herd of sheep. After Población de
Campos, the Camino cuts across the fields to follow a shallow

river, a peaceful walk beneath the poplars. But something has put me out of sorts. Maybe it was the break in Castrojeriz, but I've lost my rhythm. I am irascible, and my irascibility finds its objective correlative in the chafing of my bunched-up sock under my left sole. If I don't do something soon, I'll end up with a blister. But part of me seems to want just that.

—Sit down and take off your shoes.

—*I'll do it in the next town.*

—The next town is too late. Do it now.

With a huff, I sit down by the roadside, take off my shoes, slap a bandage onto the tender part of my foot and put on my sandals. I'm still getting a twinge with every step, but it should be okay. The problem now is that I have tied my shoes too loosely and they are swinging from my backpack. With every step I take, the left shoe gives me a hoof in the kidneys, the right a kick in the rear end.

—Can you tie those a little tighter?

—*I'll do it later.*

There it is again, that sulky little voice that's happy to be kicked in the rear end because that gives it an excuse to be angry. I sit down again to refasten my shoes, picking a spot on the riverbank with the idea that the running water will calm my spirit. It's a sweet little river, ten centimetres deep in the middle and a couple of metres wide, a Mississippi of the *meseta*. Clouds of butterflies rise and dip on the breeze. I take a few deep breaths. But there's still something grumbling inside, something that won't be placated. And that's when I think of Sue Kenney's sorrow stones. Sue is a pilgrim, author, filmmaker and all-round dynamo. She spoke at a Little Pilgrims meeting one Saturday about a discovery she had made on the Camino. Each day, as a kind of walking prayer, she would pick up a stone and fill it with her sorrow. At the end of the day, she would leave the stone by the wayside and walk away a little lighter. The idea of filling a stone not with my sorrow but my crankiness suggests itself to me now.

The first stone I pick up is too big. It might get overloaded and do some damage. I find a smaller rock and close my fist around it. Now, how to go about this? I close my eyes and give the stone a squeeze, wait for the bad energy to come coursing down my arm . . . I'm not sure if I can do this. First of all, I'm worried what might happen if somebody picks up this rock after I've downloaded all my anger into it. More importantly, I just seem to lack the conviction necessary for channelling and visualizing and all those other vigorous psychic exercises. Yet I think I can make this work on my own prosaic terms. Just having this stone in my hand can be a way to keep myself aware and questioning. Instead of an anger stone, then, it can be my thinking stone. And for that purpose, the one I have picked out should serve well. There's a seam that runs across it like a scar. It will wake up my fingertips when they touch it.

Matamoros

My mood has improved by the time I pull into Carrión de los Condes, that crazy mix of adobe stables and Romanesque churches. Part Wild West, part Middle Ages, its streets collide at odd angles, producing unintended plazas, as if the town had been built inwards from five directions without ever finding a centre. In the holiday-crowded bars, the TV sets are tuned to the fiestas. Apparently there's nothing Our Lady Pilar enjoys more than a good bullfight. At the refuge, the hospitalera tells me Linda was here last night, but today

she's off to Sahagún, forty kilometres on. Either she's overcome her antipathy to walking or she's desperate to get all
this over with.

Just off the main plaza, which tilts on its slope like a pie
plate on a rough sea, is the city museum, housed in the former
Church of Santiago. There I meet again with Raymond, the
cheerful little Frenchman who got to hear about my dream
this morning. He takes my arm and we pass wordlessly before
the assembled saints in painting, sculpture and tapestry, till
we come to one arresting statue. It is Saint James, rearing
back on his white steed, a bloodstained sword raised over his
head, a swarthy, turbaned, disembodied head at his feet.

"I detest this image," Raymond whispers.

The image that so repels him is a common one on the
Camino. It goes by the name of Santiago Matamoros—Saint
James the Moor-killer. The story of the Matamoros begins
in the days when the Spanish Christians were still leading a
hardscrabble life in the northern reaches of the country. For
years, the vicious Caliph of Cordoba required the tiny Christian fiefdom to pay an annual tribute of one hundred Spanish
damsels. Finally, the brave King Ramiro said no. He rode
against the gathered Muslim armies at Clavijo, accompanied
on the field of battle by Saint James himself. More than sixty
thousand of the infidel fell that day, the infamous tribute of
the damsels was ended and the Christian reconquest of Spain
was launched. In thanks to Saint James, King Ramiro decreed
that a tribute should be collected from every field in Spain to
enrich his shrine. This tax, the *voto de Santiago*, survived right
down to the nineteenth century.

It's a stirring tale, and almost entirely fictional. The tribute of the damsels, the battle of Clavijo and all the rest were
dreamed up some three hundred years after the supposed fact
by one Canon Pedro Marcio, a resourceful fundraiser on

the Cathedral of Santiago's building committee. We owe him thanks, for the document he forged of King Ramiro's fictional decree helped pay for the glorious Santiago de Compostela we see today.

In practice, of course, the question of whether the battle of Clavijo happened or not is academic. Santiago Matamoros answered a need. He was the divine general of the Christian cause, the counterweight to the Prophet of the adversary. Nor did his career end with the reconquest of Spain. Columbus, Cortés, Pizarro and all the rest of that company of adventurers won Spain's vast empire in the name of Matamoros. Under his banner the Camino was subdued, then Spain, then the Americas. I ask to hear more of Raymond's thoughts on Santiago Matamoros, but he only shakes his head in disgust.

He shows more tolerance later, accompanying me on a round of the town's restaurants as I check the blackboards for that big bowl of lentil soup I'm craving. As we sit over supper, he asks about Michiko. He's interested to know she is a shiatsu therapist. He's studied shiatsu himself, reiki too, and he's a black-belt judo instructor. He's also, he tells me, a Buddhist.

"How can you be a Buddhist and a Catholic? Isn't that a contradiction?"

"I feel no contradiction."

"But Christianity says that the 'I' you are now lives on after death, and Buddhism says the 'I' is an illusion that dies with you."

"Well, I'm on the side of Buddhism there. I don't believe that individual identity survives death. But I still believe in Jesus Christ. I know, I know. As far as the Church is concerned, I am a heretic. They would certainly have burned me in the Middle Ages. But Buddhism and Christianity are both religions of peace. All true religions are religions of peace. And that is the reason why I *cannot* accept the Matamoros."

I don't have an answer on the spot. I don't know if I have one now. I can only say that history has bequeathed us not one Saint James, but three: the martyr-Apostle, the pilgrim and the warrior. The first proclaims and dies for truth, the second seeks truth, the last fights and kills in its name. Raymond is not the only one who has trouble reconciling this trinity. To many, the Matamoros embodies the Spain of intolerance and Inquisition, the Spain that ejected its Jews and Muslims and would happily make a bonfire of many of today's good pilgrims. Yet the fact remains that the Camino was built not only on sweat, tears and faith, but also on rivalries, lies, greed, ambition, bigotry—and blood. Without the Matamoros, would there even be a Camino?

Isn't it better, in the end, to keep the facts in the open air where each may draw from them what lessons he will? For one, the Matamoros might be the avatar of a glorious past. For another, a sign that great good can come of evil. For another still, a harsh reminder of where we come from and a warning not to turn that way again. These differences of opinion are a part of the Camino's richness.

What do you say to that, Raymond?

Keep Our Love for Her in Front of Us

It's seventeen kilometres from Carrión de los Condes to Calzadilla de la Cueza. Four hours of stony fields, 360 degrees of level horizon. An eternity for the bashful pilgrim with a full bladder.

I think back to what Francisco told us that night in Tosantos: "At the start of the Camino, there is always something to look at. Your eyes and your mind are caught up in the beauty of the way. But on the *meseta*, where there is nothing to see but horizon, you begin to look into yourself." The theory is neat, but the reality, as usual, is not so tidy. I recognize now that in the first weeks of the Camino I always walked with at least half an eye on the ground, bearing in mind the wise words of Barbara Cappuccitti of the Little Company, "No stone is too small to break your leg." For much of the way from St-Jean to Castrojeriz, the path rises, falls, twists, narrows. There are roots and ruts to watch for. The only safe way to gaze at the beauty around you is from a full stop.

But here on the *meseta* the road is wide, smooth and straight. There's no need to look down when you walk. It takes a while for that fact to sink in. Through my first hours of *meseta* walking, my chin kept sinking when I lifted it, as if it were weighted. I didn't trust the earth not to throw something in my way. It's only today that the weight is gone and I can walk with my chin up and my eyes forward, following the racing clouds, observing how the tone of the sky is different in every direction, wondering if the three flickering pilgrim forms I have seen in the road ahead for the past hour belong to anyone I know. Far from looking inward, my eyes graze the surface of the world, while my mind grazes from thought to thought.

Yesterday's irascibility has given way to aimlessness. Snatches of songs and imaginary conversations flit through my brain. My thumb plays over the scar on my thinking stone. It only makes me aware how little thinking I'm doing. And then out of nowhere comes the prayer of the Irish woman that I read aloud in Tosantos. I stop in the road to find it in my little black book.

"Please pray for my mother who is slipping into the darkness of dementia. Give us the strength to be patient and understanding and keep our love for her in front of us."

Keep our love for her in front of us—as though the end of the journey were not Santiago, but love. Maybe in the end it's not a place we're walking towards, but a state of being—health, happiness, love, forgiveness, transcendence, peace—always discernible on the horizon, like the grain silos of these *meseta* towns.

At the end of the day, the village of Ledigos offers novelty in the form of a hill. From the top, where the church stands, a height of some thirty or forty metres, you look down on the terra-cotta shingles of the few dozen houses and stables, feeling you could cup them all in your hands. The whitewash has worn off the abandoned buildings near the church to reveal the local building materials—mud, straw and pebbles. The refuge is a wooden-beamed dorm in back of the bar. I look into the shady courtyard to see Big Bert and Little Oscar writing postcards. Bert is tall, broad-built, ponderous, Flemish. Oscar is short, slight, mercurial, French. They look like a comedy team. In fact, they are brothers-in-law, married to sisters, who set out from Antwerp almost three months ago, on July 25, Saint James's Day. For the first two months, they pitched their tent in farmers' fields. When it rained, they slept in the stables with the cows. In the towns, the people opened the public wash houses to them and they spread their sleeping bags on the floor. "For the first seven hundred kilometres," says Bert, "we didn't see another pilgrim or a refuge. We were thrilled the first time we got to a town with a place just for pilgrims."

The beds here are new and comfortable, and by nine o'clock they are already full of flaked-out pilgrims. In the bar, a soccer match rages on the tube—Spain 0, Lithuania 0. I have supper with Masa, a Japanese pilgrim who is doing the

Camino for the second year in a row. Last year, he started in France from Le Puy, this time from Arles, both 1,500-kilometre walks. Every day he takes dozens of digital photos. By night he uploads them to the notebook computer he carries in his king-sized backpack while pilgrims crowd around to see where they've been today. After the Camino, Masa will resume his English courses in Galway. It's all quite a departure for a man who spent the previous twenty years as a sales rep for a Japanese widget-maker.

I can't say for sure what Masa is walking towards, but I suspect it's his next meal. He's a joy to eat with. He loves Spanish food, French food, Irish food. Still, after so long away from home, it's Japanese food he craves. As we dine on juicy fried beef and pimientos, he quizzes me about Michiko. Where in Japan is she from? How old is she? How tall is she? Does she speak in dialect? We move on to dessert—rice pudding and flan—and a new set of questions. Can she cook this? Can she cook that? Does her mother cook well? What did we eat when we lived in Japan? From the way he savours my responses, I realize that I am channelling Michiko. Through me, Masa is talking to someone who can share his nostalgia for the taste of home.

Roberto the Magus

One hot day, upon one of these long, straight, lonely *meseta* roads, I met up with Roberto the Brazilian Magus. Roberto was one of the first and last companions of my original Camino, and the two of us had more in common than our names. We were both late risers. Hours after the keeners had evacuated the refuge, Roberto and I would be taking our pre-ambulatory *café con leche*. We both loved all the good things of the Camino, though Roberto expressed his appreciation more audibly, smacking his lips and intoning, *"Qué rico!"* when something pleased his palate. Both of us wore glasses and a pilgrim beard, mine trimmed close, his white, thick and bristly. We both had trouble with our legs. Roberto's knees gave him misery, and from the second day of the Camino they were already bound up in tensor bandages. We both left Roncesvalles on the same morning and arrived in Santiago on the same afternoon, though in between there were days at a time when we didn't see each other. And each of us got on the other's nerves.

We'd start out fine. When Roberto saw me, he would spread his arms wide and cry, *"Peregrinito!"* I don't know why I was his "little pilgrim," but that's the way it was. We would hug and slap each other on the back and moan about our legs. Often we'd pop into a bar together. But sooner or later, one of us would say the wrong thing and the chill would set in. At the base of our differences was the Brazilian author Paulo Coelho.

If you see a pilgrim reading a book on the Camino, chances are good it's Coelho's. The title in Portuguese, *Diário de um mago*, "Diary of a Wizard," gives a better sense of what it's all about than the all-purpose English title, *The Pilgrimage*, for Coelho's is a quest story about a wizard-in-training searching for his lost sword on the Camino de Santiago. Under the tutelage of a mysterious guide named Petrus, the narrator learns the secrets of the Camino while fending off demons and using spiritual exercises to access higher forces. In the end, he finds his sword in the church of O Cebreiro—thus saving himself the trouble of walking the last two hundred kilometres to Santiago.

It's not a book that would have inspired me to walk the Camino. Too much spiritual warfare. But what do I know? *The Pilgrimage* has set tens of thousands of pilgrims, from Brazil and all over the world, on the road to Santiago. Some turn sour on the book once they find that it's not a very accurate reflection of their experience. Blisters, weariness, heat and dirty laundry play no part in Coelho's Camino; there are weird inconsistencies of chronology and topography; and instead of the helpful locals that most of us meet, Coelho's Spaniards are like extras from *Deliverance*. These discrepancies can be explained to some extent by the fact that Coelho published his book in 1987. The Camino was still virtually unknown at the time, so he felt free to mould it to his story. How was he to know that, a few years down the road, pilgrims would be packing his book as a guide? Still, for every pilgrim who ends up disgruntled with *The Pilgrimage*, there are more who keep the faith, practising Coelho's spiritual exercises and seeing the Camino through his eyes. Roberto was one of these.

For all his enjoyment of the sensual Camino, Roberto saw himself walking another Camino as well, one that led to realms of secret wisdom. He did not hide his calling. The blue crystal ball mounted to the top of his staff was a giveaway, as was his way of announcing from time to time that he had to go and perform his "exercises." I wouldn't have minded any of this except that Roberto was a ball-breaker. Time after time, he would say things that he knew I would take issue with. When I did, he would call me a "materialist," which for him meant one of those stubborn people who, through blindness or plain malice, refuse to see the rivers of meaning that shimmer and rush beneath the world's dull surfaces. I would snort and mutter something about Paulo Coelho. And that would be it for our beautiful friendship, at least till the next time. Of course, our disagreements were less about the content of our beliefs than they were about being right and making the other admit it. They were as spiritual as arm wrestling.

Our encounter on the *meseta* was a strange one. I hadn't seen Roberto at all the day before, and suddenly here we were, together in the middle of nowhere. I was tempted to ask if he'd spent the night under the stars performing spiritual calisthenics, but I thought better of it. Instead, we fell into conversation about our lives. He was letting down his wizardly hair more than usual, talking about his kids, his breakup, his new woman. We walked slowly to keep our radiators from boiling dry, both of us trying a little harder than usual to find common ground on a day that was too hot for disagreeing. And then a gust of wind came and scattered all our good intentions. It rose from the east, sending a shiver through the grain that stood all around us. We stopped to admire the beauty of it.

Then Roberto cried, "The wheat is bowing to honour the pilgrims!"

I didn't have to say anything. Roberto heard me flinch.

"What?" he said. "Are you saying it's not possible? Do you think the world is not sentient? Everything is alive, my friend. Everything has mind. The wheat is alive. The earth is alive. There are rocks in the desert that move. They have been observed from satellites. Everything has awareness."

"I didn't say the world isn't alive. I just don't know why it would want to bow down to us."

"Because we are pilgrims, and pilgrims have walked through these fields for thousands of years. The land knows us. You underestimate the power of pilgrimage."

For someone else I would have conceded that the image of the bowing wheat was poetic or original or cute. I might even have given some thought to the proposition that the land felt our presence. But between Roberto and me there could be no quarter. We walked on in aggrieved silence for a few minutes. Then Roberto declared that the path was too hard on his knees, he'd rather walk on the shoulder of the road. He cut through the scrub and we followed our parallel paths all the way to the next village.

Timbuktu

I peer in the window of the tea shop in Sahagún to see the Weird Sisters sharing a British moment. I've never seen a tea shop anywhere else on the Camino, but it makes sense I'd see one here. Sahagún has a cosmopolitanism about it that goes back to the eleventh century, when this compact urban vessel sailing on a sea of wheat was chosen to be "the Spanish Cluny," the regional nerve centre of the French Benedictine order that dominated the Catholic Church. Wealth poured into the city, transforming it into the Camino's Timbuktu, a place of extraordinary churches and a thirst for high living symbolized by the legendary *cubo*, a wine vat (the property of the abbey, naturally) said to be the largest in Spain. The great churches still stand, in varying states of repair. The *cubo*, sadly, is no more. Its spirit lives on, however, in Sahagún's bright bars, fancy bakeries—and tea shop.

I don't plan to stay in Sahagún tonight. The refuge in the loft of the church of the Trinity is a nightmare thanks to the splendid acoustic qualities of the vaulted stone ceilings, which amplify and re-echo every creak, cough, drip, snore and tinkle. I will, however, stop in to use the free Internet. I am just settling down at a computer when I see Linda for the first time since Castrojeriz.

"I thought you were way ahead."

"I was, but I stopped here. This is my last day."

"You don't mean that."

"I've had enough of walking in the cold wind. And then you arrive at a dirty refuge where you can't get your clothes dry. Believe me, I'm at the point where it takes as much guts to quit as it does to go on. But it's the right thing to do."

We walk to the train station together.

"Will you come back?"

"We'll see. Maybe the Camino's one of those things that won't let you alone till you've finished it."

"Did you ever get to like the walking?"

"*Like* wouldn't be the word. But it got bearable. Once I got past the point where it just hurt all the time . . . Give Nuala and Kara my love," she says as the train to Burgos comes rumbling in, "and give Saint James a hug for me."

I haven't thought of Linda in days, but as I wave goodbye, I feel a loss. She's one of the people I wanted to see in Santiago. Still, the Camino never leaves you bereft for long. As I pace down the platform, an old man salutes me with his cane.

"Are you going to Santiago? If I was twenty years old, I'd do the same. Fifty years ago, I went to Covadonga on foot to fulfill a vow for my mother. One hundred and fifty kilometres I walked in six days. I crossed three mountain passes." He rhymes off their names. "Ah, what an adventure. I wish I could do it again. *Buen camino, chaval*. Remember me to Saint James."

As things turn out, I do spend the night in Sahagún, though not for its churches or its bars or its *pastelerías* or even its tea shop. I stay in Sahagún because, as I sit watching Masa take pictures of the magnificent, derelict church of the Peregrina, I feel the first stirrings of a tempest rising in my bowels. I learn later that I am not the only one—it must have been something we ate. For now, all I know is that I must find a restroom as quickly as possible, and not (please, God) in the echo chamber of the refuge. I commandeer a room at the nearest hotel and lock my door from the inside. Sahagún's urbane charms are wasted on me tonight.

The Pilgrim Uniform

While the storm in my digestive tract blows over, I dip into the dog-eared paperback that I picked up two weeks ago from the help-yourself shelf in Roncesvalles: Robert Ludlum's *The Prometheus Deception*. I'd heard that part of this thriller was set on the Camino, and it's true, give or take some poetic licence. To fit the pilgrimage to the plot, Ludlum has his pilgrims approach Santiago from the wrong direction. He lets them overrun the highway. He describes them as all being profoundly religious. But where his imagination really runs free is in his description of the pilgrims' clothing. When super-spy Bryson and femme fatale sidekick Layla get caught behind the pilgrim throng on the way to Santiago, they ditch their wheels, buy some duds from one of the numerous gypsy roadside vendors (!) and join the crowd.

Layla ends up in gaudy peasant rags, while for himself, Bryson selects a medieval monk's robe and a crook-handled staff. Thinking to conceal his face, he pulls up the hood of his cassock, but this only draws attention, as all the many similarly garbed pilgrims have their hoods down in the heat. Another pilgrim-monk pulls something from under his cassock that looks like a Bible but turns out to be—my goodness—a gun. Shots are fired blindly into the pilgrim crowd, chaos ensues . . . I can't wait to see the movie.

The pilgrim garb Ludlum describes is a funhouse reflection of a historical reality. In olden times, the holy brotherhood of pilgrims was premised on equality: rich and poor, all were humble sinners before the Lord. This equality was symbolized by the pilgrim uniform of staff, scrip, hat, cape, gourd and cockle shell. These items were both practical and significant. The staff (in Spanish, *palo* or *bordón*), essential as a support and a wolf-whacker, was also the pilgrim's "spiritual sword" against the Evil One and, as his "third foot," a symbol of his faith in the Holy Trinity. The scrip, a deerskin wallet for carrying food, money and papers, was small so that the pilgrim could carry little and would need to trust to charity, and had no string to tie it shut, tokening that a pilgrim must be as ready to give as to receive. At the outset of the pilgrimage, staff and scrip were blessed in a solemn ceremony. Father Wayne Manne of the Little Company still performs this service for departing members, though today it's mostly telescoping metal hiking poles and thirty-litre backpacks he blesses.

Other items of traditional pilgrim gear were the hollow, dried gourd, or *calabaza*, used to carry water or wine; the broad-brimmed felt hat, sometimes with a long scarf attached for extra protection from the elements; and some sort of coverall—either a long, coarse linen tunic or an *esclavina*, reminiscent of a friar's robe. Topping it all off was the scallop shell. Many pilgrims today pick one up before they begin, to wear as a badge on their backpack. The long-ago pilgrim acquired his at the end of the road, as a trophy. Just how the shell of Venus with its pagan fertility associations and whiff of the ocean shore became the symbol of the Camino is open to conjecture, but the link is long and strong. In the year

1200, the Archbishop of Santiago legislated to limit the number of shell merchants in the city to one hundred.

Today's pilgrims dress "sensibly," with an emphasis on light and quick-drying materials. Their only distinguishing features are their shells and sticks, and a worn-in quality to their clothes that wouldn't stand out in North America but looks dowdy in Spain. As for pilgrims dressed like Ludlum's, you can see them cast in bronze in the plazas of Camino towns (the "Unknown Pilgrim" has become a genre unto itself) or emerging from souvenir shops in Santiago (tourists in Santiago are easy to recognize: they're the ones dressed like pilgrims). Only once have I seen a pilgrim of old walking the roads. It was August 11, 1999, the final day of my first Camino, as I came down the hill to the city of the Apostle.

The pilgrim's *esclavina* was cinched around the waist with a rope. He wore sandals and a broad hat studded with shells. A gourd dangled from the red Templar cross atop his tall staff. He strode through the streets of the city, well aware that all eyes were on him. At the pilgrim office, where one goes to receive the Compostela, I found myself behind him in a line that snaked up the stairs to the upper floor.

One look and the journalists hanging around the foyer knew they had found their Camino human interest story for the day. And an uplifting story it was. The year before, this sixty-three-year-old pilgrim had undergone a life-or-death heart operation. Before going under the knife, he had promised Saint James that if he survived, he would walk to Santiago. His doctors had objected, but in the pilgrim's words, "You must do what you have promised." He had walked all the way from Barcelona in the apparel of a medieval pilgrim because this too was part of his vow. When his aunt called him crazy, he replied, "*Locos* also do pilgrimages." In the end, he covered the distance in twenty-five days, an average of twenty-four kilometres a day. He had never felt better, though his feet, he conceded, were destroyed. Now he would take some time to recover before his next pilgrimage, to Lourdes or Fatima.

His story made the paper the next day. That's me in the background of the photo, doing the math. I'm thinking to myself, *Twenty-five days at twenty-four kilometres per day doesn't get you halfway from Barcelona to Santiago. And where is his back-pack? And how did he walk all that way in those flimsy sandals? And why is he so clean?*

The journalists, however—like the journalists who inter-viewed José the sailor?—didn't delve too deeply. They ran off to file their story—but they only got half the scoop. For when we finally reached the office at the top of the stairs and the little pilgrim was asked to produce his credentials, it transpired that somehow, in all the miles between Barcelona and Santiago, he had not obtained a single stamp. The clerk pushed the credentials back across the desk with a shrug, and for all that the little pilgrim pounded the desk and threatened and cursed, he left the office that day without a Compostela.

Foundlings

Between Sahagún and Mansilla de las Mulas runs a thirty-two-kilometre track of compacted earth, laid down some years back by the local administration. Unfortunately, the trees planted along the path have never amounted to much. In summer, the poor, spindly things are blasted by the sun; on fall and winter days like this, the wind torments them. I've covered less than twenty kilometres from Sahagún, but walk-ing into the west wind today is like trying to open a door that someone very large is leaning against. After last night's adventures in digestion, I have no appetite for the struggle. I walk with Masa for a while, but conversation is impossible. When I see El Burgo Ranero ahead, I'm ready to pack it in.

Long ago, this stretch of the Camino was a dismal, dangerous, trackless marsh. When Brother Domenico Laffi and his companion passed through here one June afternoon in 1670, they saw a pack of wolves enjoying a meal. They ventured just close enough to ascertain that the special of the day was pilgrim, then hustled ahead to El Burgo Ranero, where they slept on the earth floor of a straw hut. It doesn't sound like a night to remember, but it is commemorated in the name of the refuge where we will bed down tonight: Albergue Domenico Laffi.

El Burgo Ranero retains a frontier feel—the bales of hay stacked to the sky, the sense of people huddled together against the emptiness. But it's no longer the bleak place Laffi knew. The refuge is cozy beyond a monk's most decadent dreams, and two taverns stand side by side, each with rooms to rent and identical pilgrim menus. On this Friday night, Bar Peregrino is packed with locals playing cards and pilgrims putting back an early supper. The Peregrino is a family business. Dad is a perky little bull who looks as if he keeps a rifle under the bar. Teenage daughter works the cash with the moral support of a half-dozen school friends. Little brother waits tables. At eight years old, he already plays the part of the jaded server to perfection, coolly scanning the room as he uncorks our wine bottle. When I ask what kind of *carne* I can expect in today's special, *carne estofado* (stewed meat), he replies with studied weariness: "*Carne es carne.*" Meat is meat. What are you, some kind of joker?

In 1999, I had a beer here with a young Irish pilgrim named Conor. He had lost all his money in some complicated circumstances and was now advancing as gradually as possible—eight or ten kilometres per day—so that he would not arrive in León before the bank draft he was expecting. In the meantime, he lived off the kindness of pilgrims and bar owners, sharing meals in refuges and cadging leftovers from kitchens. He told me, "I'm glad that things have worked out this way because it's actually helping me to achieve my goal on the Camino, which is to see God in each person. It's easier when they're all taking care of you."

We ambled back to the refuge to find a crowd gathered around some object. Squeezing our way in, we saw a cat in a cardboard box, a wretched, dirty, shivering thing with one leg that poked off at a right angle to its body. Two women, one French, the other Spanish, had rescued it from a ditch.

"The hospitalero told us there's a vet in Mansilla de las Mulas, so we're going to take it there tomorrow and see if he can do anything. If he can't help him, at least he can end his life without pain." Till then they were spoiling the animal with milk, love and canned herring by the spoonful. Conor seemed to take special satisfaction from the scene. He too was a foundling of the Camino.

Alguien Que Busca Algo

These *meseta* towns have a way of disappearing behind one. I'm twenty minutes out of El Burgo Ranero in the morning when it occurs to me to look back. I'm glad I do. The low, dark town silhouetted by the sunrise is as beautiful in its way as Venice rising from its lagoon. The true highlights of the Camino cannot be found in any guidebook.

The walking is tough again today, the wind still blowing hard from the west. I have a planned stop at Eva's bar, a refurbished tractor shed twelve kilometres up the road, in Reliegos. I ducked in there one morning on my first Camino to find Karl taking a morning beer. The Cat Ladies were there too; their little foundling was still in its cardboard box, looking as wretched as the day before. Eva, the keeper of the bar, was a sunny young housewife and mother of two who had been inspired by boredom and the need for pocket money to purchase this ramshackle building for three hundred dollars, run an electric wire in and slap a sign out front. She'd done a nice job inside, where the clunky antique farm implements that came with the shed now enjoyed a leisurely retirement as found art.

Eva brimmed with curiosity about the strangers from strange lands who passed through her door. Though she had only been in business for a few months, there were already postcards and snapshots on the walls from Switzerland, Holland, Brazil . . . She was also good-looking, twenty-three and blonde. Karl was in his element. "Karl is happy by Eva," he kept saying like a happy parrot as he slapped his bratwurst thighs. But there's no trace of Eva's anymore. The bartender at the big place in the centre of the village says, "Eva? Her husband got a job in Tarragona. She moved years ago."

So I trudge on to Mansilla de las Mulas, where John, Sandee, Bert and Oscar are already at the refuge fixing lunch. I remember Mansilla as an agreeable little town, but today, in spite of the good company, it strikes me as bleak beyond words. I'm too restless to stay here. My crossing of the *meseta* has been a choppy one. An irascible mood at the start, an unsettled stomach in the middle and then two days of gale force winds blowing the brim of my hat down over my eyes have kept me from achieving much in the way of introspection. It goes to show that you generalize about the Camino at your peril. "The *meseta*" is real as geography, but not as a state of mind, or not one you can expect to achieve in five days. So I push on into the wind, over the bluffs that rise like bookends at this western margin of the great plain, then down through the old Jewish quarter of Puente Castro to the city of León.

León today is just another busy, mid-sized regional capital without so much as a first division football team to its name, but for centuries it was a home to kings and dreams of empire. Among the legacies of those days are the stained glass jewel box of a Gothic cathedral and the frescoed Romanesque crypt of the basilica of Saint Isidore, the trophy saint whose desiccated remains the Leonese pilfered from Seville to provide their city with a patron worthy of its imperial aspirations. One senses that León, like other cities that have once known greatness, regards all history subsequent to her own golden age as a regrettable descent from the rightful state of affairs.

Tonight I will stay for the fourth time at the convent of the Sisters of Santa María de Carvajal in the heart of the old city. According to the register, I am the 21,699th guest of this Holy Year. In the lower 21,000s I spot some familiar names: Aaron, Maribel, Inácio, Tony Bush. They all seem impossibly far ahead, yet I could probably catch them in thirty minutes if I hopped on a bus. Of the hundred-odd pilgrims who are staying here tonight, I recognize only Masa's name. I discover him stretched face down on a mattress like a felled tree, still wearing his coat. Well, this is a sorry state of affairs: halfway through the Camino and surrounded by strangers.

I go down to the courtyard to find someone to talk to. The convent is a school by day; the yard is broad and paved with asphalt. I remember the first time I stayed here, a sultry night in July, when the whole area was a cat's cradle of clotheslines strung with pilgrims' hand-washed laundry. I had to duck and weave through the hanging socks and undies, encountering on the way the Cat Ladies, whom I now knew as Pilar and Hedwige.

"Ssh," said Hedwige as she lifted the lid of the cardboard box she held in her lap. The cat was sleeping peacefully inside. The vet in Mansilla de las Mulas had reset his leg, which was only sprained, not broken, and given him a bath, charging nothing for the services. Now the cat was as good as new and headed for Santiago.

"We've given him a name," said Pilar. "Peregrino."

I gave little Peregrino a stroke. He purred and stretched. For the next two weeks and three hundred kilometres, this box would be his mobile home. He had joined the pilgrim family.

Then I headed over to the big gates, where Karl was sitting with Marie-Annick and Yvonig, a couple from Brittany. I used to pass them every morning on the road, for though they started early, Yvonig's limp slowed them down. I assumed his problem was blisters till one day I asked. "It's not blisters," he replied. "It's my hip. I had it replaced two years ago. The doctor said that I'd probably never walk again without a cane." If we knew even half the stories that walk with us on the Camino.

When I saw Karl at the end of the day, it was usually as I had seen him the first time at El Lagar—a cigar in his left hand, a brandy in his right. This night, however, his right hand was empty. "Here is no wine, no brandy. *Katastroph!*" He puffed morosely on his Havana. On the other side of the walls, the rambling streets were suffused with the day's last light and the good burghers were musing over where to take their next pre-dinner drink, while here we were, sealed in our pilgrim bathyscaphe. But nothing could keep Karl down for long. All of a sudden, he was snorting with laughter.

"What is it, Karl?" asked Marie-Annick.

"My wife is working now," he said.

There's no Karl to make me laugh tonight, no kitchen or common room in this refuge, and León is not a two-tavern village where you can open a door and expect to find a friend. I'm wandering up in the direction of the cathedral, anticipating a solitary meal, when I see someone waving from the window of a restaurant. It's Alec, an affable, bearded Scotsman whom I met at the start of the *meseta*. I've seen him only sporadically since, because he and his friends are staying in hotels and private refuges. Now he introduces me to his wife, Milly, a woman with a generous laugh and a touch of the grand style, and Christopher, a ruddy-cheeked young priest from St. Louis. Milly and Christopher have been matching wits. She wants to know what her chances are, as an Anglican, of getting into heaven.

"I'd say that, as long as you behave yourself, you have nothing to worry about," Christopher replies. "You're misguided, but God won't hold that against you. The ones who need to worry are us Catholics, because we've been given the whole truth."

"How are the odds for non-believers?" I ask.

"Well, God in his mercy has the power to save anyone, so there's no reason why he can't save you. Look, God has shown us the straight and easy road. If you want to take a more difficult route, that's up to you. It doesn't mean you can't get to the same place in the end."

"So there's hope."

He casts a wise eye on me. "I realize you're being facetious. But then, can I ask what you're doing on the Camino? You might think it's all a lark, but how do you know God isn't reeling you in? You shouldn't put it past him."

Alec pipes up. "All right, you Aquinases, here's something for you to deliberate. I picked up a hitchhiker today. He was a pilgrim, and he said he had sore feet. Couldn't walk another step. Of course, I gave him the lift, but I couldn't help thinking he didn't look to be in such bad shape. I've certainly seen worse. And then I let him off at the refuge, which means he probably took some honest pilgrim's bed. So what's the verdict? Should I have left him by the side of the road?"

We agree without reservation that Alec did the right thing, but we also recognize that his question has a subtext. His group has been using a "support vehicle"—a car to haul their gear between towns. It's an arrangement made to accommodate Milly, who can't carry a pack for medical reasons. But a few days ago, two of the members started wearing their packs. I talked to them the other morning. "We decided that if we were going to do this pilgrimage, we should do it as pilgrims, and to us that means taking our things on our backs. We don't mean that as a judgment on the way anyone else does it, but we're afraid it's been taken as such."

It has indeed. Rightly or wrongly, Alec is smarting. "I guess what I'm asking ultimately is if there's some absolute criteria to define who's a pilgrim and who isn't. Must the pilgrimage be done in a certain way or is it enough to do it with a certain spirit? And who decides that? It's true that Milly and I take turns driving, and we don't carry our bags on our backs, but in the old days, didn't pilgrims of means use horses and pack animals? What's the difference?"

It's that question again of purity, orthodoxy. If there are good pilgrims, there must be bad ones; if there are great pilgrims, there must be lesser ones. Like all things human, pilgrimage breeds hierarchies and pecking orders. I'm sorry Alec feels he has been judged and must defend himself. I'm sorry, too, for the members of his group who want to do the

Camino in their own way. This is the kind of rift that makes you think twice about doing the Camino with anyone whose friendship you hope to retain. But there's no time to settle Alec's questions tonight. It's already time for me to get back to my nunnery.

One benefit of staying with the sisters is that you can join them for vespers. The second time I stopped here was a bitter November night when the six pilgrims sat among them in the choir, singing along from the sisters' hymn books. Tonight we are sixty, so we sit in the pews like an audience. The service is beautiful, swift and efficient. The nuns have been doing this for a long time and they'll be up early tomorrow to do it all again. When it's over, one stays behind to speak to us. I have listened before to this young, earnest woman, whose eyes glow with the light of a still inner fire. She speaks calmly, urging us to walk on with strength and to reflect always on our reasons for doing the Camino. And she has a beautiful answer to Alec's question, Who is a pilgrim? I wish he were here to hear it.

"*Un peregrino,*" she tells us, "*es alguien que busca algo.*"

A pilgrim is someone who is looking for something.

Does it need to be more complicated than that?

Three Marías and One Gran Vividor

At 7:30 a.m., laughing, singing crowds are spilling out of the discos and into the lamplit streets. A pilgrim's Sunday starts where a partier's Saturday ends. I might as well have been partying with them for all the sleep I got last night. I walk listlessly down the Avenida Suero de Quiñones to the Plaza

de San Marcos, where I see, at the foot of a stone cross, the very image of exhaustion: León's pilgrim statue. There are many statues of pilgrims along the Camino, realistic and abstract, humorous and heroic, moving and maudlin. A few depict pilgrims of today, with nylon packs and running shoes, but most are like this one, a figure of long ago decked out in the classic pilgrim ensemble. León's pilgrim is a weary figure. He has taken off his sandals and leans back against the cross as if to sleep. Before him is the Parador of San Marcos, a luxury hotel where he could never dream of staying. I sit down to keep him company for a while.

It's funny that in the old days, when pilgrims actually looked like this, there weren't any statues of pilgrims. The statues then were of Jesus Christ, Mary, James and the other saints. They were the heroes of the Camino. But the old heroes have retreated to the churches and the heavens. The hero of the Camino today—or so these statues suggest—is the pilgrim himself, the pilgrim of old, pictured always as humble, stoic, pure of heart, trusting, possessed of an unclouded faith that today's pilgrim can never hope to equal. "A pilgrim is someone who is looking for something," the sister told us last night, and the pilgrim of old knew just what he was looking for and just where to find it: at the tomb of Saint James in Santiago.

And what are you looking for, peregrino? the statue asks me.

I cast him a grouchy, early morning glance. "I don't know, but a coffee would be a good start." I bid the tired pilgrim *buen camino* and go looking for a bar that's open early. In the first one I come to, Javier is standing alone at the counter. He is a pilgrim in his thirties from the southwest of Spain who walks like a man who is counting his steps—or maybe it's just that his feet are killing him. I've spoken to him only once or twice since we first said hello in Boadilla del Camino, but I sense he's the right person to talk to on a morning like this.

"Tell me something, Javier, are you doing the Camino for any particular reason?"

He frowns as if it's something he's never thought about before. "No, no special reason."

"Is that right . . . What's that thing you're eating?"

"It's called a chocolate *caña*."

I ask for one of the messy cream-filled buns and dunk it into my coffee. "So you're not doing this for a vow or a challenge or an adventure or a penance . . .?"

"Well, I'm Catholic, I'm Spanish. Are those good reasons? But if you really want to know what I think, I'd say every person has many reasons for doing the Camino. More reasons than he knows. A guy might tell you, 'I'm doing the Camino to lose weight,' but if he only wanted to lose weight, he could go to a gym, couldn't he? Somebody else will say, 'I promised God I would do the Camino.' But there's lots of things you can promise God. You can promise to pray, or visit old people in rest homes, or flog yourself. God never said anyone had to walk across Spain to make him happy. So I think the Camino is something each person chooses to do. For whatever reason, they *want* to bang up their knees and hear old men snore all night. People do the Camino to do the Camino."

"And maybe they don't know why?"

"They know they want to do it. What other reason do they need?"

We walk out of the bar, and then out of León. As we go, Javier tells me about his town. It has a population of thirty thousand, which he judges to be the perfect size. "Big enough that you have everything you need, but small enough that you know everyone." Sounds like the Camino. Then he steps into a bar to say hello to some people he knows and that's the last I ever see of him.

But he's told me what I needed to hear today—that you don't have to know what you're looking for, as long as you're looking. He's awakened a bit of the old spirit of adventure in me. On previous Caminos, I have stuck to the straight, flat, drab path that runs alongside the highway from León to Hospital de Órbigo. But there is a road-less-travelled that cuts across the *páramo* of León, and I have heard that on this alternative route there lives an artist of some local fame, a man of talent and charm whose studio is always open to pilgrims. I'll take that road today.

My *Collins Pocket Dictionary* translates *páramo* as "bleak plateau," which doesn't sound too promising, but it proves to be just the thing for me. Scrubby, hilly, lonely, treeless, *wuthering*. A farmer's nightmare, a wanderer's delight. It's a step back in time; hard to believe that the highway and railway are just the other side of the hills. Today's wind is brisk but not aggressive, the sun is bright. A sudden vision of pale blue mountains ahead makes me catch my breath.

Along the way, a string of pretty villages, their names bigger than they are: Fresno del Camino, Aldea de la Valdoncina. At one o'clock in Chozas de Abajo ("the shacks down below"), the church bells are clanging and banging. Near the end of the village, a gracious house stands behind a yellow stucco wall. Set into the wall by the gate is a mosaic in the Romanesque style portraying a favourite theme of medieval art, the labours of the rural months: sowing, harvest, threshing, slaughter . . .

It's early afternoon when I reach Villar de Mazarife, where the painter has his studio. Sure enough, there is a stone building on the main road identified as the "museum" of the

painter Monseñor. The sign outside says *Pase sin llamar*—
"enter without knocking"—but the door is locked. I'll try
again later. In the meantime, I'll find somewhere to drop
my bag. A tangle of yellow arrows points the way to Villar
de Mazarife's three refuges. Two are private operations that
opened this summer, the third belongs to a local named Jesús,
who has opened his family's second house to pilgrims for
nine years now. The refuge is Jesús's gift to the Camino (on
the wall inside is a small donation box; pilgrims leave as much
as they like), and I would like to stay here out of respect for
what it represents, but I have a selfish desire tonight, and that
is for a good sleep. Seeing that the refuge of Jesús packs twelve
to a room, the odds are good that one will be a snorer. I'd like
to see first what the other refuges have to offer.

The next place is a bar that sleeps pilgrims upstairs. With
only four to a room, I like my chances of a quiet night. I stake
out a bed in the room at the very end of the hall, then settle
down at the bar with a glass of wine while I wait for the painter
to reopen his studio. I'm just thinking of doing some writing
when the Three Marías roll in, tall, well-constructed women
from Andorra with rolled-up wool socks, track pants and serious walking sticks. Accustomed to mountain hiking, they've
been leaving a cloud of dust behind them on the Camino,
though one María, to her vexation, has developed a blister.
"It's the flat roads. I walk twice this far in the Pyrenees without any trouble." But the Marías have only ten days to make
it to Santiago, so they're not going to be slowed down by a
mere flesh wound.

I call them the Three Marías on a whim. In fact, they are
only two Marías and a Nerea, but close enough. The original Three Marías, of course, were Mary Magdalene, Mary
Salome (the mother of Saint James) and the Virgin Mary, who
went together to Christ's tomb and found it empty. Spain and

the south of France have their own Three Marías: Mary Magdalene, Mary Salome and Mary Jacobe, who legend says sailed
from the Holy Land to the place called Saintes-Maries-de-
la-Mer in the Rhône estuary, where their relics are venerated
by the Roma to this day.

This is the second triad (or near-triad) of Marías I've met
on the Camino. The first were the ones I met outside the
refuge of Puente la Reina on the first morning of my Camino
last fall. They told me they wanted a picture, but when I
reached for their camera, they said no, they wanted a picture
with me. So I took my place between María Carmen of the
merry eyes and tall, self-possessed María José while petite
brunette María Consuelo, who would not allow her picture to
be taken under any circumstances, handled the pointing and
clicking. Then we all went to a nearby bar to fortify ourselves
with *café* and fresh-baked cream, apple, nut and honey pastries. The people in the bar were Spanish, and the Marías were
Spanish, so naturally they talked intently and at great length
about everything in general, and food in particular. More pilgrims arrived, and they also were Spanish, so it was necessary
to exchange addresses and invitations, which Spanish pilgrims
swap as readily as nods. By 9:30 a.m., I had covered a full one
hundred metres of road, but I had met twenty people and I was
with the Three Marías. What better way to start a Camino?

When at last we set out for Estella, the Marías made good
time, singing pop and folk songs in Castilian, Galician and
Basque as they walked. Then they put me on the spot by
insisting I sing "something Canadian." I could think of nothing more Canadian than Gordon Lightfoot, but that wasn't
what they had in mind. "Come on, sing something by Leonard
Cohen!" How European.

When I say they made good time, I mean *between* the villages, for in the villages it was necessary for us to kick out our

legs and drink or eat whatever the Marías said was the correct thing to drink or eat in that place at that moment, and talk to whoever was there to be talked to. By the end of the day, we had sampled pan-fried garlic shrimp, pimientos, tortillas, olives, blood sausage and cured ham, and knew the locals as well as if we'd grown up with them. We ended the evening with a trot back to the refuge fifteen minutes past curfew. No worries: when the Marías knocked, doors opened. A pilgrimage with the Three Marías was no act of penance.

In another country it might be strange to meet three women with the same name, but in Spain it's almost unusual for a woman not to be called by the name of the Virgin or one of her double-barrelled avocations—María Belén, María Dolores, María Mercedes and all the rest. It might have been remarkable till recently, however, to meet three Marías walking the Camino together. For long centuries, the Camino's model of womanhood was not the bold, venturing Magdalene but the stay-at-home Virgin. The women who did make the pilgrimage in the old days would mainly have gone in the company of men. But all this has changed, as more and more women take the road, many on their own. In the early nineties, women represented about one-third of the total pilgrim body. Through the decade the percentage climbed to forty, and 2004 shows a remarkable leap. More women than men will receive the Compostela this year. The Marías have found their legs, and their feminine energies are transforming the old macho way of Saint James.

As the three Andorran women prepare to go out and demolish another twenty kilometres of trail, I remark that if Nerea were a María, they would be the Three Marías.

"But I am," says Nerea. "I was born under Franco, when Basque names were forbidden. Since my parents couldn't call me Nerea, they called me María instead. After Franco died,

I started using Nerea. But on my identity card I'll always be María."

The Marías are gone and I'm ready to go looking for the painter when the Weird Sisters come waltzing in. Back at the start of the *meseta*, when the weather changed, they stuffed their ghostly white frocks into their backpacks and became (for me at least) just plain Helen and Hayley. I get the feeling they're listening to the Camino more now, not trying to impose ideas on it. "We're not so sure about our project anymore," says Hayley. "We'll figure it out when we get to Finisterre." Just like the rest of us. I ask if they know about the painter and they tell me they tried his door too and it was still locked.

A few minutes later, in comes Rhoda, a girl I took for Japanese when I first saw her, but who is actually a native of my country's northland. Naturally, it's on the Camino that I meet my first Inuk. After working for a couple of years as a legal secretary on a sub-Arctic circuit court, Rhoda came to ramble around Europe. It was only after she got here that she heard about the Camino and thought it sounded like a good way to stretch her travel dollar. She's no fan of churches or religion. Over the past three generations, Christian missionaries have scrubbed away almost all of her people's traditional beliefs and culture. But Rhoda has no axe to grind. She's out to meet the world.

Vivian from Germany is next to join the party. When I ask why she's doing the Camino, she explains that her parents wanted her to go to university, but she wasn't sure that's what she wanted for herself. So she spent a year in Paris, learning French and caring for disabled children, then set out on the Camino to have some space and solitude to think things over. "I was disappointed at first at how many people there were, but I've changed my mind. Meeting and talking to different people has given me so many ideas."

But it's not all serious talk at our table. Mostly we're goofing around, swapping stories about other pilgrims. Our tablecloth is a sheet of paper, and Hayley doodles a running commentary to the conversation. Somewhere along the way, the subject of birthdays comes up, and I discover that the four women at the table are all twenty years old. I marvel at their élan. I had enough trouble coping with the Camino at thirty-six.

The day drifts along like a paper boat on a stream of wine. At some point I give Michiko a call. Of course, she asks about her stick. Yes, I'm taking very good care of it (I don't mention the dream). Then she asks if I'll do something for her. Last week some pigeons built a nest on our balcony and laid two eggs in it. She moved the nest to a tree by the parking lot, hoping the parents would find it, but a squirrel got there first. Now she wants me to say a prayer in Santiago for the unborn chicks.

And there it is. My reason for doing the Camino.

Suppertime brings more pilgrims. It's a private refuge, so no curfew. The party goes on past midnight, an outrageous hour by pilgrim standards. In the end, I teeter upstairs to my room at the end of the hall, anticipating the sleep to end all sleeps. But after a day illuminated by the women of the new Camino, an enduring masculine reality awaits me. Andreas from Leipzig, an epic snorer with a long Sunday's drinking behind him, has occupied the other bed and he's already thundering away. We always find the things we run from. I make my bed, once again, on the hall floor.

It's not till next morning, when I skulk downstairs for my coffee, that I remember the painter. The owner of the bar is a sociable middle-aged woman, a transplant from Asturias (only a hundred kilometres away, though when she talks about it, it sounds like some lost Atlantis). When I ask about the painter, she shakes her head.

"Monseñor is sick. Leukemia. He's in hospital, hooked up to oxygen and shot full of morphine. He won't be coming back. It's a shame, only sixty-five and so much talent. I have one of his paintings, the labours of the months."

"I saw a painting like that yesterday outside a house in Chozas de Abajo."

"That's his house. He lived there and had his studio here. He could have had houses everywhere if he'd wanted. He made millions on his paintings, and he spent every cent living it up. Only the best food, the best wine, always travelling. And the women . . . so many women. He was *un gran vividor*—a great liver." She says it with profound admiration.

The Six Ingredients

The wind that has blown in my face for a week has stopped dead. Is this cause for celebration? "No, it just means it's going to rain," says the bartender in Villar.

Thirty minutes out, I feel in my pocket for my thinking stone. It isn't there. I can now choose between two narratives. In the first, I return to reclaim my stone, showing a quirky loyalty but adding an hour to my walk. In the second, I return to Villar years from now and find my stone on the windowsill where I left it. I take a look around me. Lots of stones in this flinty land. The second story sounds just fine.

I try out stones Goldilocks-style. "Too big . . . too small . . . too smooth . . . Just right!" I've found the perfect stone in no time. But then it troubles me that I am so easily satisfied. Shouldn't I shop around? I let the stone fall from my hand and pick up another. And another. And another. Till soon it's clear that the one I left behind really was "just right." Now, how's that for a life lesson? So what's the chance of finding that stone again? I retrace my steps, scanning the rocky road for a particular dark brown, flattish, ovaly, river-smoothed yet pockmarked, palm-fitting stone. I snatch up and toss away a half-dozen before I find the right one. How do I know it's the right one? The warmth of my hand is still in it.

Hospital de Órbigo is renowned for its bridge, where in 1434 the knight Don Suero de Quiñones challenged all comers to joust in the name of his lady. He thrashed 166 knights, killing one, then declared himself free of the bonds of love and ready to complete his pilgrimage to Santiago. This piece of Renaissance showmanship went down in Camino legend, though I don't see what it proves except that, with the days of fighting to defend the pilgrimage over, the knightly class had too much time on its hands.

I arrive in Hospital before noon with a dozen kilometres' walking behind me. A paltry effort, but the clouds are ganging up and it looks like a good day for typing. You can buy computer time by the hour at the new private refuge, so I park myself in front of a screen and get to work. I have ten days' notes to catch up on. Outside, the rain has started to come down. Faces peek around the door, wondering how long I'll be. "Just a few minutes," I tell them. By the time I dash out in the rain for some supper, it's nine.

I'm halfway across the historic bridge when two pilgrim forms loom up like tugboats from the mist. "Bobby!" exclaims one.

Nuala and Kara have had, not surprisingly, an eventful time since we last saw each other in Castrojeriz, a hundred years ago.

"We walked all night to Frómista . . ."

"We slept in a doorway . . ."

"It was freaky. We were hallucinating."

"Thank God Saffron was there."

They've come all the way from León today, thirty-two kilometres, mostly in the pelting rain. October 30 and the party in Finisterre is getting closer and closer. They need to make up some days.

"We got off kind of late today . . ."

"About one."

"But we made good time."

"I should say we made very good time. Are you going to eat, Bob?"

I am, and in a few minutes the three of us are sitting down with a pitcher of *tinto*, scanning the menu for something that isn't meat, just like old times.

There's another refuge in Hospital de Órbigo that I think of as the refuge of the Persuasive Dutchman because of a story I heard from Isolde, a pixieish pilgrim from Austria. She told me she showed up there once with nasty blisters, which the Dutch hospitalero treated by piercing each one with a needle and drawing a thread through. The idea is that the thread keeps the blister open and allows it to drain, and it's a method many pilgrims swear by (they're the ones with feet that look like shag rugs), though it carries a risk of infection. Isolde was not keen on the procedure at all, "but that Dutchman was very persuasive." I've thought since that the Persuasive Dutchman would make a fine name for a pub.

Like many refuges, the Dutchman's was open all day to anyone who wanted to come in to fill their water bottle, take a break in the tranquil courtyard and even snatch a nap in one of the beds. I found Karl there one afternoon, hiding from the heat. The burly Bavarian was still smitten with his Eva. He sighed and joked that he had to finish the Camino so that he could hurry back and see her. Then our talk turned from bartenders to bars, and soon we were hatching schemes to find ourselves some busted-up shed and turn it into a pilgrim oasis. In the bruising heat of that August afternoon, we could think of no nobler project. Then Karl leaned back and closed his eyes and I went for a stroll in the courtyard. I saw a page pinned to a bulletin board, a photocopy of a photocopy of something written by a Spanish priest. I read it, and read it again. Then I copied it out, word for word.

Walking the Camino de Santiago:
Six Essential Ingredients, Plus One

SILENCE: The Camino is not a place to talk, but to listen. To listen to your interior voice, to all of the creation that surrounds us, to God. Even if you walk with a partner, agree to walk in silence.

SLOWNESS: Along the Camino we find plenty of evidence that the world does not believe in God, that it has no experience of the Sacred, simply because it can't keep quiet and it's always in a hurry. Let us approach the Mystery step by step, without haste, on foot, at a human rhythm.

SOLITUDE: You alone, in your sole and unique selfhood, before the sky, before the earth and, in the end, before the sea. Before God.

EFFORT: Walk, walk. In tribute to true and diligent pilgrims, let us not make the Camino too comfortable. It is very good to get lost in the mountains and to sleep on the earth. The spirit is refined by effort and rude lodgings.

SOBRIETY: Don't eat too much, it is good to experience hunger and thirst. This is not masochism, but command of the spirit.

GIFTS FREELY GIVEN: Refuge gratis, smiles gratis, the sun gratis. God and life gratis. There is a richness in the Camino that we cannot lose.

THE ROMANESQUE: Art as symbol and expression of another reality. Not "rational," but sacred art. Like the liturgy. We mustn't over-polish it, for if we wash it too much, we will wash away the prayers and the grief of those who have prayed and wept upon these stones.

I thought then that this was the perfect description of how to walk the Camino. I still think it's *almost* perfect. As I read it, I feel what it describes: the silence, slowness, and solitude of a lone pilgrim, crossing the *meseta* in the arid heat of August, smelling the grapes in La Rioja's air at harvest time, rounding the mountain to El Acebo in a whistling blizzard, listening to the waves crash on the rocky beach at Finisterre. Some might find it strange that a so-Christian document would resonate with a non-believer. I can only say that for God's name I substituted "the Sacred, the Mysterious, the that-which-is-bigger-than-we-are," and the framework held up fine.

Not to say that I had no reservations. Given a choice, I preferred not to get lost in the mountains or sleep on the earth, and as far as sobriety was concerned, I didn't see any harm in treating myself to a pilgrim special and a bottle of wine after a hard day's walking. In other words, even as I took the "six ingredients" to heart, I exempted myself from the clauses that didn't suit me.

I translated "the ingredients" for Karl and he approved, especially the one about slowness. He could have taught me a lesson in it if I had been content to stay in the cool of the Dutchman's courtyard that day, but for no discernible reason I was in a hurry to get to Astorga. So while Karl took it easy, I put on my backpack and got ready to go. The two of us agreed that when we saw each other again, we would talk some more about our pilgrim bar. But as things turned out, I never did see Karl again.

That, too, is Camino.

PART IV

All the Good Pilgrims

ASTORGA TO SANTIAGO - 260 KM.

GALICIA

Montes de Galicia

LEÓN

Santiago de Compostela

Arca

Melide

Arzúa Ribadiso

Palas de Rei

Portomarín

Sarria

Triacastela

O Cebreiro

Ruitelán

Villafranca del Bierzo

Montes de León

Cacabelos

Ponferrada

EL BIERZO

Molinaseca

El Acebo

Manjarín

Foncebadón

Rabanal del Camino

Astorga

N

0 km   20   40

Map Area

Romería

After Hospital de Órbigo, there is a hill. On the other side of the hill, a shallow valley where a village nestles. Then there is another hill, and another. You feel a spring in your step that's been missing since the start of the *meseta*, the spring that comes from knowing there's something ahead that you can't see yet. The dirt road winds, climbs and loses itself in groves of oak. Then the mountains of León appear ahead, not the pale blue dream of yesterday, but solid green and brown, mottled with bald patches and shadows. An hour's walk takes you to the edge of an upland from where you see the next two days' walking and the noble twin spires of Astorga's cathedral rising from the basin.

Astorga was where my first Camino started to go off the rails. The day I left Karl in the courtyard of the Dutchman, I arrived here to find the refuge full. That was fine. There was a campground, and camping has its benefits: no curfew, no one to chase you out in the morning. The "six ingredients" were fresh in my mind, and camping seemed like the next most virtuous thing to sleeping on the ground. But Astorga's campground was far bigger than any I had seen to that point, a real tent city. And its population was all dressed in freshly pressed clothes. Surely they couldn't be pilgrims? I squeezed into a tent with five Spanish university students, who grudgingly shifted their gear for me, then I went for a look around. Everywhere there were cars and caravans. At the neighbouring site, some folks from Madrid were unloading a barbecue from their trunk. They stoked it up and started laying on slabs of meat. Soon a gang from Valencia with a boom box had joined them.

At two in the morning, the party was still in full swing, not just next door but through the whole tent city. Then the ground beneath my sleeping bag started to shake with the thud of fireworks, and suddenly it all came clear to me. This was Sunday, August 1, the beginning of the Spanish month of holidays, and 1999 was a Holy Year to Saint James. The entire Spanish nation had just joined me on pilgrimage.

On the road the next morning, before and behind me as far as I could see, there was nothing but pilgrims. They rushed out of Astorga like a river—a noisy, chattering river. They talked much and loudly of family, school, friends, work, TV, soccer . . . Only their feet were on the Camino; their heads were still back home. And they had no sense of the ways of the road. For hundreds of kilometres, I had greeted and been greeted by every pilgrim I met on the way with *"Hola"* or *"Buen camino,"* but the newcomers barged by without a nod or a word. They had brought the city with them to the Camino.

At noon, I arrived in Rabanal del Camino to find several dozen pilgrims waiting in line for the doors of the refuge to open. At first I didn't know what to do, but then I saw a ray of hope. Maybe they would *all* stay here. So I kept walking. I climbed the brambly paths above Rabanal for an hour or more, past the lonely farms and the broken village of Foncebadón, until the only sound was the flat clank of cowbells floating up through the stillness like a Zen gamelan. Only then did I dare to look back. There was no one else in sight. The Camino was mine again, all mine—at least for the rest of that day. But this was stolen time, and I knew it. The mob was only a half day behind. The flood waters were rising. The *romería* had begun.

A *romería* is a characteristically Mediterranean form of pilgrimage, a communal walk in the country to a sacred grove or spring, a picnic and a procession rolled into one. There is song, music, *alegría*, contests, wine, and heaps of food cooked on open fires. While the *romeros* celebrate, the flower-bedecked image of the local saint or Madonna smiles over them like an indulgent grandparent. The aim of a *romería* is to renew the sacred bonds of community, family and deity, and the time-honoured way to achieve this is with laughter, food and drink. Silence, solitude, sobriety and the rest of the "six ingredients" (except maybe slowness) are not invited.

Of course, the Camino is not a *romería*, but Spanish pilgrims tend to treat it as one. I spoke once to a pilgrim who did the Camino with a group of five thousand from the diocese of Madrid. The thing he remembered was the sound and the feel of five thousand voices singing. The point of the pilgrimage was not solitude but solidarity. And there's nothing wrong with that. The pilgrim path of joyous fellowship has a lineage just as long and noble as the path of silence and sobriety. In fact, it is in many ways more authentic. Solitude held little allure for Camino pilgrims in the days of wolves, bandits, snowstorms and raging rivers. Safety in numbers was the way to go, and those numbers sang and told stories as they went. Think of *The Canterbury Tales*.

Of course, all this is clear and reasonable in hindsight. But you would have wasted your breath trying to convince me on that August 1 morning that the Camino as "*Canterbury Tales* with mobile phones" was a valid expression of the pilgrim spirit. These people, to me, were not pilgrims. They were locusts.

To Rabanal

The view of Astorga from the uplands, with the mountains of León as backdrop, is for me a landscape of conflicting desires. I feel the pull of the distant hills even as I long to wander the winding streets of the city. Every city is a tangle in the Ariadne's thread of the Camino, but here the contrast between the stretched-taut pilgrimage road and the loose urban ball of twine is laid out for the eyes to see. Maybe this is why Astorga is the Labyrinth in Father Ojeda's Goose Game.

It's a labyrinth worth losing yourself in, from the magnificent cathedral to the art deco, toy castle bishop's palace, one of the rare commissions to lure the eccentric genius Gaudí from his native Catalonia. The restaurants dole out mountains of *cocido Maragato*, a medley of meats and garbanzo beans, the local pastries and chocolates are legendary, and there is one especially bright and gracious bar that lingers in my memory.

The rain is starting as I hit town, and I take shelter in the Café Gaudí. From my seat by the window, I look up from my notebook to see pilgrims trotting across the plaza, yanking up their hoods. I don't like walking in the rain. I have heard there is a comfy new refuge in town with a kitchen. Why would I want to be anywhere else?

I cradle my empty espresso cup a minute. Then I close my notebook, put on my coat, pull up the hood, strap on my backpack. I pause in the doorway, hoping something will happen to keep me here. Nothing does, and soon I'm following the yellow arrows out of town. Why can't I sit still? I don't need to be out here. Before I've reached the bottom of the hill out of town, the rain is already wearing down my shoes' resistance. I curse as I walk, but I keep on walking. "I'll stop at the next town," I lie to myself. There are several places to stay in the twenty kilometres between Astorga and Rabanal del Camino, tiny, picturesque flint villages with refuges and bars where I could listen to the rain on the roof. One by one, I find them wanting and squelch on. Something inside me has decided that tonight I will sleep in Rabanal del Camino, and I might as well get used to it.

My object, Rabanal, is not the most accessible place. I once asked the girl in the bar what time the bus left for Astorga. "Saturday," she told me. But the proud houses in the Calle Mayor, and the twelfth-century church and hospital show that it was once an important stop on the Camino, important enough to justify a squadron of Templar knights. The road through Rabanal was the most direct way to Santiago, so that was the way pilgrims took, disregarding the perils of the stormy mountain pass above. When the pilgrims stopped coming, it became a backwater. By the time writer-pilgrim Laurie Dennett spent a night here in 1986, sleeping—or trying to sleep—on the floor of the windowless schoolhouse in the dust and the bat droppings, the population had dwindled to seventeen.

It must have been fond memories of that night that brought Dennett back to Rabanal three years later. The newly formed Confraternity of St. James had decided to add a British island to the Camino's archipelago of refuges, and when initial plans to build in Foncebadón proved impracticable, Rabanal's long-disused parish house provided a viable second choice. In 1990, after extensive rebuilding, it opened its doors as the refuge of San Gaucelmo. In its first year, the refuge sheltered 1,913 pilgrims; by 1999, the number had climbed to over 9,000. But this was only the start of Rabanal's renaissance. Several years ago, three Benedictine monks started up a monastery in the former pilgrim hospital next door to San Gaucelmo, offering guided spiritual retreats for pilgrims. The monks have also provided Rabanal with a new pièce de résistance: twice-daily Gregorian chants.

Night is falling; the rain drifts in sheets; my feet are soaked. The only thing keeping me warm is the thought of the reception I will receive at San Gaucelmo. First, some jovial Brit hospitalero will insist on taking my bags upstairs. I'll warm up by the fire for a while, hang my clothes to dry. Then, when everything's in order, I'll be off with the other pilgrims for a glass of mulled wine and a nightcap of Gregorian chants. I realize that it is the promise of contrasts that has kept me walking tonight: dark to light, wet to dry, cold to warm, hungry to full, alone to embraced.

But from the moment I arrive at San Gaucelmo, I can tell that things will not go as planned. My first hint is that the hospitalero is not British. "We're full," he declares with a far too cheery German accent. "Been full since four-thirty. It's terrific. Haven't seen a crowd like this in weeks. You should try Pilar's refuge. Maybe they have a bed."

Maybe?

Pilar's is a private refuge with the feel of a holiday resort. I elbow my way through the throng at the outdoor bar and locate the manager. There is one bed left. In the long, narrow dorm, lined on either side with bunks, there is nowhere to hang my wet clothes, no heat source to dry them at. They'll have to go out on the covered patio, where they'll be as soggy tomorrow morning as they are now. But that's no disaster, I still have a dry change of clothes. I unzip my bag, shake my things out onto the bed. Surprise! The rain has found its way through the stitching. I usually take care to double-pack my things in a green garbage bag, but it seems this morning I was negligent. My clothes, while not quite wet, are dewy; my sleeping bag is slick and slippery to the touch. But the real fun is still to come. The lining of my "waterproof" jacket has been infiltrated, the moisture has found my precious note-book. While the pilgrims at the bar outside toss back their wine, I kneel on the mucky floor between the bunks blowing long, dry breaths on my humid words, like a lifeguard giving mouth-to-mouth resuscitation.

There are other wet papers: passport, money, maps. These I arrange under the bed in hopes they'll dry. By now the Gregorian chants are over, the happy pilgrims are coming home to bed. I have just enough time to grab a sandwich. My night of contrasts has come out half baked. Instead of wet to dry, I have to settle for wet to damp, cold to chilly, hungry to half full, alone to . . .

Where *have* all these pilgrims come from? I count back on my fingers. It must have started three nights ago, on that busy Saturday in León. I stepped out of the flow when I took the road through Villar de Mazarife then stopped early in Hospital de Órbigo, but I've caught up with the crowd now. Counting forward, I see that the weekend after next is the November 1 holiday. So these new pilgrims are aiming to hit Santiago on the long weekend. From here on in, there'll only be more and more of them. Good grief, not another *romería*!

Long after midnight, the revellers are sloshing in and out, laughing and slamming doors. At least my body heat has dried out my sleeping bag. I pull my jacket over my head and find solace in the thought that twenty years ago in Rabanal I would have had the refuge all to myself. But I would have been sleeping on a mattress of bat turds.

A Sharing of Misery

The rain has been banging on the roof all night. From six-thirty, the pilgrims are marching out with an air of "We who are about to die salute thee." I wish them all the best. It's quiet at last. My bedding is warm and dry. It's not till eight that I open an eye. The first thing to check is the papers beneath the bed. They'll never be crisp again, but they've survived the crisis. My shoes are soaked, but I have sandals for backup. The rain has stopped and a cloudless cobalt sky is waking into day. I mosey to the bar for coffee and lunch provisions. Slowness, one ingredient of a perfect Camino.

The cold, dry wind blowing down from the hills has painted a skin of ice on the puddles. By the roadside just above the village, I stop at a tiny white cross, a handmade thing adorned with wildflowers and the faded, pen-scrawled inscription *"la 22 de julio 1998 murió un peregrino suizo aquí"*— a Swiss pilgrim died here. I heard his story—which had the ring of a parable—from my friend, *peregrina* Barbara Overby, who was the hospitalera in Rabanal that month of July 1998. The pilgrim suffered a heart attack shortly after he and his wife left the refuge in the morning. By a stroke of good fortune, or so it seemed at the time, the first two pilgrims to reach the scene were a nurse and a heart specialist. Alas, their skills were of no avail. The only pilgrim who got to ply her trade that day was the third to arrive, a grief counsellor.

Stunted conifers by the roadside, wildflowers, thistles, ferns. And everywhere fragments of shale, slate, quartz, like hard candy smashed with a hammer. The road ahead, with its abandoned stone villages, its cross of iron, its rain, snow and thunder, is one of the most haunting stretches of the Camino, a place where fantasies become real, where pilgrims lose and find themselves. In terms of spiritual topography, this is where the third stage of the Camino, the ascent to the next level of meaning, begins.

I've just come in sight of the ruined village of Fonce-badón when a few drops of rain fall from the blue sky. I pause and take out my now-dry notebook to record the event. A few more drops fall. Looking up, I see a cloud like a massive bruise drifting in front of the sun. The note-taking will have to wait. Before I know it, I'm running flat out through the teeming rain for the nearest shelter, a roadside restaurant known as La Taberna de Gaia. I can't complain about my luck. There are only three places of shelter (three *ocas*!) in the eighteen kilometres between Rabanal and El Acebo. This is the first.

There's already a young Spanish pilgrim standing outside the restaurant, talking on his mobile phone. I duck in to join him. The sign says the restaurant is only open Saturdays during the off-season, but the roof jutting over the doorway provides shelter. The Spanish pilgrim puts away his phone. "*Es muy malo,*" I offer. He doesn't reply. That's fine. We'll commiserate in silence. I note for the first time the components of the word *commiserate*. *Co* plus *misery*. A sharing of misery. How apt. A few minutes later, a taxi rolls up. Without a glance my way, the Spanish boy tosses his pack in the back and climbs in. So much for sharing misery.

Foncebadón, the village where I find myself, and where I will continue to find myself till the rain lets up, was once a farming village with a monastery and a pilgrim hospital. By the 1980s, however, there was nothing left but a street of tumbledown houses and an ancient female Boo Radley, who lived among the ruins with a pack of surly dogs. Presumably it was these canines that inspired Paulo Coelho to set here the climactic scene of *The Pilgrimage*, in which the Brazilian drops on all fours to fight the coal-black demon-mastiff that has been tracking him across Spain. Rumours of devil dogs reached the ears of Shirley MacLaine too. She was sent tearing out of town by the mere sight of a couple of mangy curs. So are legends of the Camino born. When I passed through Foncebadón in 2000, its ghost-town days were numbered. La Taberna de Gaia had opened its doors, and everywhere was a whir and gnaw of electrical tools, a kind of reverse termite life that was not devouring the old buildings but restoring them. Today there is a German-run refuge, a refurbished church, and a bar with beds for pilgrims.

Two dripping Danish girls join me in the doorway. They are followed by four Spanish women who have done the Camino they-don't-know-how-many times. "This always happens to us here. It will pass." And then, improbably, a car pulls up and the owner of the tavern jumps out. This isn't Saturday, so it must be providence that brings him here. "No, I got a call to say there were some pilgrims outside my place, and I didn't want you to drown." I ask if he lives nearby. "I guess forty kilometres is nearby if you have a car." He is a bear of a man with a shovel beard and a gruff manner, but right now he is stoking the wood stove for us, turning on the music and heating up the coffee maker, so he can be as gruff as he likes. The Danish girls string a clothesline in front of the wood stove. The Spanish women light up smokes. I squat, back to the heat, my damp jacket sending up clouds of vapour. Come back in a few minutes and you can fold me up and put me in a drawer. It occurs to me that I'm enjoying now some of the contrasts I had looked forward to last night; they've just been deferred.

The ceiling of the restaurant is cloudy Plexiglas, so when the rain stops and the sun reappears, we are suddenly bathed in brilliance. We peek outside. The skies are high, blue, amnesiac, retaining no memory of clouds. Sunlight glistens on grass and quartz. We thank the keeper of the tavern and pack up our clothes. Up past the town I stop, as I have stopped before, to listen. Minutes go by with only stray sounds to let me know I have not gone deaf—a whistle of wind, a cowbell, a bird call. Then a dog comes loping across the fields in my direction. Not a black hell-hound, just an old ginger cattle herder with a job to do. He sits down ten metres in front of me. "*Bouff . . . bouff . . . bouff . . . bouff . . .*" he says patiently, till I get up and move along.

Now the rain has stopped, but the wind is strong enough to blow you off your feet. They go in for excess up here. Ten kilometres from Rabanal stands the famous cross of iron, where pilgrims leave a stone of remembrance. I grabbed one on the way up—I'm not parting with my thinking stone— and now I'm trying to fill its lithic memory with prayers and good thoughts. This business of piling up rocks is rooted somewhere deep in the psyche. There are stone mounds— waymarks, cairns, creations of whimsy—all along the road to Santiago. Just how long pilgrims have been leaving stones at the base of the tall iron cross at the pass of Irago is anybody's guess, but today it is the done thing for pilgrims to bring a stone from their country. The monks of Rabanal will even bless it. My inner curmudgeon smells an instant tradition, but I suppose every tradition has to start somewhere.

Just as I'm approaching the cross, the rain comes rushing back as if it's forgotten something. But my luck is really in today, for I have reached the second place of shelter, the Hermitage of Santiago. A team of Italian bicycle pilgrims joins me by the leeward wall, and we laugh as the hurricane blows by. Ten blustery minutes later, the sun is back at his desk and it's time to do what pilgrims do here. I root myself at the base of the cross of iron, take my stone from my pocket and pitch it onto the pile. Then I close my eyes, join my hands at chest level as I have seen Michiko do before Shinto shrines, and let the faces run across my mind's eye. Family, friends, pilgrims I have known. Pepe, wherever he may be. Tony Bush and Harry Kimpton. Kara, Nuala, Saffron, Linda. Julio, Paco, Maite. Montse, Karl and German John. I think of the Irish woman whose prayer fell to my lot in Tosantos. Of José the sailor, and Roberto the Magus, and Del the optimist. And I think: It has been good to walk with you all, to have shared even a kilometre of the way with you. May your roads be long and full of discoveries. *Buen camino.*

The Enchanted Castle

In 1986, Tomás Martinez de Paz found his destiny in the forgotten village of Manjarín. He was rolling out his sleeping bag for a night under the stars when a passerby spotted his lantern and cried, *"Una luz en el Camino!"* Tomás heard those words as a calling. He would be "a light in the Camino." Specifically, he would take up the old mission of the medieval Templar knights, to guard and guide the pilgrim. Seven years after that first journey, he left family and city life behind him and returned to this desolate, beautiful middle-of-nowhere at the height of the pass of Irago to restore the abandoned stone house that serves today as his home, a refuge for pilgrims and the headquarters of the Order of the Resurgent Temple, Tomás's self-founded knightly order. Since then, Tomás the Templar has become a legend of the Camino. For some pilgrims, the goal is not Santiago but Manjarín.

This stretch of the Camino—from Rabanal, once home to a Templar garrison, to Ponferrada, whose massive Templar castle was the symbol of the Order's dominion over the west of Spain—is prime Templar real estate. So who were the Templars? The Knights of the Order of the Temple of Solomon started out as a small band of crusaders dedicated to keeping the routes to the Holy Land safe for pilgrims. But the Templars soon grew far beyond their humble origins, becoming the bankers of Europe and one of the most powerful corporate bodies in Christendom. In Spain, they were charged to settle and govern the western frontier. So adept were they at amassing power and wealth that it was said they practised black arts learned from the infidel. King Philip of France made use of this popular belief when, looking for a quick way to erase his enormous Templar debt, he levelled charges of witchcraft against the Order. Confessions were extracted, the head Templars burnt at the stake, and in short order the whole Templar edifice of power was brought to the ground. And that should have been the end of them.

But it wasn't. Something about the Templars—their ringing name, the fiery sword-cross that was their emblem, their brimstone aura of power, mystery and secret wisdom—kept them alive in the European imagination. For centuries they were cast as the dark force in a host of conspiracy theories. It's only recently that the bright side of the Templar legacy has been rehabilitated, their mission as guardians of the pilgrim path. As with all things esoteric on the Camino, Paulo Coelho can claim much of the credit for the revival of interest in the Templars. But it is Tomás of Manjarín who actually took up the old gauntlet and declared himself a defender of the Camino.

Tomás's refuge is the third *oca* on the road to El Acebo. The yard looks like a petting farm. There are dogs, cats, chickens, a mule and, naturally, a goose. The howling wind blows me through the ever-open door. The Spanish ladies from the Taberna de Gaia are already in the kitchen, helping themselves to *caldo*, a broth of potato and cabbage. I've enjoyed Tomás's rustic hospitality before. The last time I crossed the pass of Irago, it was into the teeth of a November blizzard. Tomás's solar panel battery was depleted and the weak light from outside expired on its way through the deep window wells, so we ate our soup in darkness. Today the sun is bright and the electric lights are working, so I can see the big mural of knights going into battle, the photos of Tomás and his acolytes in Templar regalia, the images of Isis, the Virgin Mary and the archangels in the candlelit prayer alcove. The house is snug and cozy, and it must be even warmer in the loft, where the pilgrims sleep. I've never stayed in Manjarín, never witnessed Tomás's famous Templar morning rites. Could this be my chance?

The girl tending the kitchen, a slight thing in her twenties from Germany, shakes her head. "Sorry, we're not allowed to take pilgrims in winter. It's the regulation."

"Are you the hospitalera?"

"Yes, and also I am training to be a Templar knight." It comes out matter-of-factly. Training to be a Templar knight. As one does.

"And why are you . . . doing that?"

"I stayed in Manjarín when I did the Camino last year, and I knew then that I would come back. This place has an energy I've felt nowhere else. Mind you, it's not easy living here. It's very lonely sometimes, and the wind never stops. But I like the quiet, and Tomás is a very special man."

"He's not around today?"

"He went away in the car this morning. He didn't say when he'll be back."

I'm not surprised. On three previous visits to Manjarín, I have never managed to exchange more than a passing word with Tomás. It puzzles me. Sure, the man is a hermit, but he's not a clam. I've heard him talk at length with other pilgrims on everything from reincarnation to weather conditions. Why not me? Maybe I've never caught him at the right moment or asked the right questions, but I have a sneaking feeling that I am not meant to know Tomás. Roberto the Magus would say it's because I'm a materialist. Maybe he'd be right.

My first hint of all this came on a roasting hot day in June 2000, another time when I had it in mind to spend a night in Manjarín. A harried and paint-splattered Tomás met me in the doorway. "Sorry, we can't take pilgrims now, the house is too hot, it's a stone house, a mountain house, the roof is slate and the sun heats the roof all day, it's unbearable upstairs, you'd die if you tried to sleep there."

"Can I get some lunch?"

"*Hombre*, I see you're hungry, I wish I could feed you, but there isn't any food, the kitchen is closed, wait a minute and I'll give you some bread, that's all I have." Through the open door, I caught a glimpse of something that looked like the prop room for *Camelot*. The place was strewn with flags and banners, swords and breastplates. Tomás was back in a minute, followed by a young woman in a sundress with a can of whitewash in her hand.

"Tomás, this shit won't stay on. There's not enough lime in it."

"Well, *coño*, put more in," Tomás grumbled.

"I don't know where it is."

Just then a muscular young man in briefs sauntered over from the yard. "What the hell, aren't you finished yet? I need help here."

"Screw you, you're the one who didn't put enough lime in the whitewash."

"Yeah, everything's my fault."

Why there was such a rush on to paint Tomás's hovel, I couldn't guess. Tempers were flaring and I just wanted to get out of the line of fire. I thanked Tomás for the bread and hurried on. The next day, I met an Italian pilgrim who said he had stayed the night in Manjarín.

"Tomás told me it was closed."

"Tomás is cool. You just have to keep working on him. But you won't believe who was there yesterday afternoon. Paulo Coelho. He's making a show about the Camino and he drove up with this TV crew from Brazil. Tomás and his knights were all dressed up with their Templar robes and swords and they did this ceremony . . . What a production!"

And when did this happen? An hour after I was there. Which confirms, to me at least, that Manjarín is one of those enchanted castles, like the ones Don Quixote knew, visible only to those with eyes to see.

The Baseball Cap

From Manjarín, the road climbs and winds until across the way new mountains appear, with forests and pastures hugging their muscular shoulders like a green wool sweater. Then the view opens up, you see the fertile valley of El Bierzo and the city of Ponferrada below, and the Montes de León are behind you. Half an hour later, you're looking down the steep path onto the thirty grey slate roofs of El Acebo coiled around the village church with the land falling away at either hand.

One of the things that brought me back to the Camino last fall was a dream that came again and again for I can't say how long, because even the first time it seemed I had dreamed it before. In the dream, I stood on a hilltop at the end of a long day's walk looking down at the town where I would stay that night. I would think of the meal that was waiting for me, the friends I would see at the refuge, the familiar bars and fountains, the bustling twilit streets . . . Usually the dream ended there and I would wake tingling with the anticipation of arrival. Sometimes, though, I took the path down to the town—where invariably I would lose my way, or find the refuge full, or realize that my flight home was tomorrow and I had to get back to Madrid at once. It was as if even in my dreams, the arrival could never live up to the expectation.

And which of all the towns and villages of the Camino was the one I dreamed of? It was, as I knew in the moment of waking, no town on the Camino de Santiago, or anywhere else in the world except my dreaming mind. Still, if there is any view on the Camino that matches the view from the hilltop of my dreams, it is this one of El Acebo, stone village in the clouds. So I sit for a while in the sun-dried grass and think of the day behind me and the evening ahead, and then settle into the warm, windy, silent *now* that lies between. When my arrival has been deferred long enough, I skip and crab-walk down the steep, rocky path till it crosses the two-lane highway and becomes the cobblestone street of the village. Where at once I hear my name called, as if I'd been expected.

"*Bobito!*"

The girls set out this morning from ten kilometres behind me and still beat me here.

"We've found this fantastic place for tonight . . ."

"It found us, actually."

"Yeah, the guy came up and asked if we needed somewhere to stay. It's twenty euros, but that includes a *vegetarian* dinner . . ."

"The other room's still free. Why don't you come and stay. It'll be fun!"

I'd love to, I tell them, but I already have plans. They exchange a look. Then Nuala says, "Well, actually, we were kind of hoping you would stay, because as it is we're alone, and the bloke who runs the place . . ."

"He's kind of . . ."

"*Witchy*. You know? He's just got this *witchy* vibe."

I don't want the girls to be turned into lizards or thrown into the tofu pot, so I agree to come and inspect. But a Spanish family has taken the other room in the meantime, so they won't be alone. I wait for them to get settled, then we all head together to Mesón El Acebo. This is where I have stayed every time I have walked the Camino, and every time has been memorable, from that first day in the heat of August when I was running away from the *romería* to the last time, when I came in from a blizzard. The police had closed the highway, so the family was not expecting a pilgrim that night, but they installed me at once beside the wood stove with a bottle of wine and a platter of pig flesh while the manager wrote a commemorative message on my credentials and signed it *Gumersindo*.

"Gumersindo?"

"It's a Visigoth name, the longest name in Spanish with no repeated letters."

I reported this event in my book *Virgin Trails*, and today I mean to show Gumersindo the ten unrepeating letters of his name in print. I have invited Kara and Nuala to come and watch the fun (we reckon there could be a bottle of *tinto* in it for us). Big G is behind the bar when we come in. "Gumersindo!" My smiling hello evokes no flicker of recognition. I ask if he remembers the *canadiense*. He shakes his head. I remind him of my heroic winter mountain crossing. He's too honest to flatter me.

"I'm sorry, I really don't remember."

The moment is deflated, but I pump some air back into it by breaking out the book. "See, here. I wrote about you." There are a few other patrons in the bar, and the book goes from hand to hand to a round of *aaah*s. It doesn't matter that no one reads English, they can see the words *El Acebo* and *Gumersindo*; they'll take my word for the rest. The hoped-for *tinto* materializes and soon everyone is laughing. Then Kara and Nuala go off to their broccoli and aubergines while I tuck into a mountainous *botillo*, the smoked pork plate that is the regional affront to vegetarians. A pilgrim from Avignon comes to join me. She was impressed by today's wind.

"It's very windy in Avignon too, you know. Often as much as 120 kilometres. What did you think today? I would say 130."

"Oh, 130 at least," I assure her.

The first time I ate at Mesón El Acebo, my dinner companion was also a French woman. Her name was Bénédicte, and she seemed to have a nasty streak, for not only did she require me to speak her language—which comes out of my mouth like an *éclair* from a meat grinder—she expected me to carry the conversation. I tried to play the ball into her court by asking why she was doing the Camino, but even that evoked only a listless shrug.

"How do I know? It wasn't my idea."

"Ah. So whose idea was it?"

"My sister's."

"And is your sister here?" I hoped she was, and that she spoke English.

"I have no idea where my sister is. She talked me into coming because she didn't want to be alone, and then she vanished."

"When was the last time you saw her?"

"A week, maybe."

"Are you worried?"

"Not really. It's the kind of thing my sister does."

"So what happened?"

"Well, I'm always up before her in the morning, so we agree where to meet and I go ahead. But this one day she didn't show up. I slowed down the next day to let her catch up, but it didn't work. Now I think I'll have to wait for her in Ponferrada."

I knew by then how stories and rumours raced up and down the Camino on a kind of telegraph, as some pilgrims moved ahead and others fell behind, so I thought it was worth asking if she had spoken to other people.

"Well, I was talking to a French boy the other day, and when I described my sister to him, he told me some crazy story about two women with a cat in a box."

"Then your sister's name would be Hedwige?"

The pilgrim telegraph: rudimentary but effective.

After supper, Gumersindo comes to join me for a drink. He feels bad that he doesn't remember me.

"There are so many faces and they pass so quickly. People arrive in a hurry, they leave in a hurry, as soon as they get here they all want to know, 'Where is my bed? Where is the shower? When can I eat?' So I appreciate it when someone like you stops and notices the place, and even comes back. I've seen so many people walk right through this town with their heads down. People forget that this is a pilgrimage, not a race. They don't take their time. They bring their stress with them. Sometimes it kills them."

The words come out in a rush. This stuff troubles him. For him, El Acebo is a little Shangri-La. A place where people should stop, and look around, and breathe the air.

He pulls out his wallet. "There was a man who stayed with us last year, a Belgian pilgrim, a very nice man. I have his address here. Another pilgrim just wrote me to say he died of a heart attack. He was only fifty. He had this baseball cap with pins of all the places he had been on the Camino. They buried it with him."

Europe on Ten Litres a Day

At eight in the morning, I lean out the door of Mesón El Acebo and blow. My breath makes fluffy cloudlets. The blind old German shepherd lying by the Coke machine lifts his head with a snort. *At least you got to sleep inside.*

Gumersindo's dad is manning the espresso machine this morning. Gumersindo doesn't live in El Acebo anymore. When I ask Señor Florez how many people do, he counts them off on his fingers. "Eleven." He remembers when there were 270, enough to support a school, a post office, a pharmacy, a church. "Everyone moved to the city. They only come back in August." On Saturdays, he and his wife take the bus down to Molinaseca to shop. They're usually the only ones on it. Yet the empty houses are neat and well kept, the shutters drawn as though the owners were out for the day. I ask Señor Florez if any of the out-of-towners would consider renting their houses during the eleven months they're not here. He doesn't think so.

The way down from El Acebo is one long, steep scramble, much of it over rock-strewn dry stream beds. People have the funny idea that going down is easier than going up. If you have sore joints and tendons, or blisters that get jammed into the toe of your shoe with every step, or you're slipping and sliding on damp stones, you know it isn't so. My shoes are still wet from my walk to Rabanal, so again I am wearing my sandals. For the first hour or so, my bare toes are numb with the cold. Then the sun peeks over the mountains and suddenly it's something it hasn't been in a month: warm. Not blustery or rainy or blistering hot or icy cold. Just warm. This is the valley of El Bierzo, between the mountains of León and the mountains of Galicia, where the earth is good and the growing season long.

Halfway down to Molinaseca, the path levels out for a few hundred metres. In a sunny grove, a couple in their seventies are stuffing sacks with windfall chestnuts.

"Lots of chestnuts," I say cheerfully.

"Not lots," the woman protests. "*Pocas.*" She points to the hill behind the grove. "There was a fire this summer. July 25, St. James's day. Somebody in Molinaseca was having a barbecue, one tree caught fire and *puff*, everything went up in flames. It's a disgrace. We've gathered chestnuts here for sixty years."

The trunks of some of the chestnut trees are scorched. It's not clear yet whether the wounds are fatal. The unhappy couple insist that I take as many chestnuts as I can carry in both hands, and I continue down the fire-scarred hillside. It's a depressing prospect, so I'm glad when I see another pilgrim ahead. He's shuffling along at a turtle's pace and I gain on him quickly. From behind, he looks to be about sixty. Pale, skinny knees showing between short pants and white sneakers. German or Dutch, I would guess.

"Good morning," I venture.

"What's good about it?" he fires back with an Aussie twang. "I'm ready to pack it in. These bloody shoes. Got 'em in Istanbul. Made in Thailand by monkeys and sold at European prices. Somebody's makin' a pretty penny there, I reckon."

I've undershot on the age. You couldn't etch the smile wrinkles around Alan's blue eyes in less than seventy years.

"What am I doing on the Camino? I ask myself that every day. Read about it on the Internet. The first sites I looked at were Spanish sites. They said thirty-two days. I thought, 'Well, that's not much of a pilgrimage, is it? That's just a little stroll across Spain.' So I looked into it some more and decided I'd start back in France, at Le Puy. I'm sorry I did now."

Seems he managed all right through the first sixty days, till his ankle started to give him grief. Now he plans to walk the sixteen kilometres from El Acebo to Ponferrada in two days. "Slow and steady. Don't want to bugger up the ankle any worse than it is, not when I'm this close to Santiago."

I'm itching to walk and Alan's pace is painfully slow. But every time I start to say my see-you-laters, he snags me with another story about his travels. At last I conclude that he really doesn't want to be left alone on this mountain, and who can blame him? So we take our time, as pilgrims should, and by the time we get to the refuge in Molinaseca, I'm starting to find his pace quite comfortable after all. We pick up a loaf of bread, some *jamón* and a litre of the local *tinto* and settle in on the porch of the refuge. We've almost drained the red when Alan cocks an eye at me. "So what's your angle?"

"I'm doing some writing."

"Suspected as much." He splashes out more wine. "Good stuff, this. And since you asked, I'm doing the same. Rough Guide, updates for the next edition. I send 'em in whenever I can find a computer. But maybe you know my book." He fishes a card from his pocket and I learn that I have been lunching with no less an eminence than Alan Hickey, author of *Europe on Ten Litres a Day*. "My idea was to write something for the young traveller, especially the young American traveller, who doesn't know any better and is touring around Europe drinking Heineken. The book aims to direct her to two pubs in every city where she can drink a beer that she'll remember for the rest of her life."

Alan says he'll Google me, I promise to get a copy of his bar-hopper's Baedeker, and it really is time to totter on.

"Been good knowing you," says Alan.

"I'll see you up ahead."

"Not bloody likely," he chuckles. "I ain't never seen nobody twice, 'cept this one girl—and when I saw her the second time, she was on her way back."

I'm almost out of earshot when I hear him yelling after me: *"Don't spell my name wrong!"*

I haven't, Alan.

Here and There

Five years ago, I stopped in Molinaseca with Bénédicte, the Cat Lady's sister, at an elegant little café-*pensión*. When the owner heard Bénédicte speaking French, he came to our table to tell his story.

Once, not so many years ago, when Europe was still waking from the nightmare of war, a pilgrim sat on the front steps of a ruined house in a Spanish village. Pilgrims were rare in those days, and this one had walked all the way from France, searching for sense in a senseless world. As he sat, his eyes lingered on the pilgrim cross that stood in the little plaza before him. It was a cross of the sort that stands all along the Camino, a waymark and station for prayer, showing on one face Christ crucified, on the other his sorrowing mother.

As the pilgrim contemplated the cross, he felt that Christ grieved. He grieved for the world, and for humanity, and for his Camino, which men had forgotten. Specifically, he grieved to see the house before him falling to ruin. The ruined house was the symbol of a ruined world. In that insight, the pilgrim found his task in life. He would repair the broken house, making it something good for the Lord to behold. It would be a humble act, but maybe through a million humble acts the world could be rebuilt. He vowed at the foot of the cross to come back when his Camino was done, and he kept his promise. Now Bénédicte and I were sitting in his *pensión*, looking across the neat patio at the pilgrim cross, listening to him tell his story.

I imagined that he told this story almost every day. It was *his* story, the story of how he had become who he was. Different listeners would take different things from it, but what stuck with me was that this Frenchman had found his life story in Spain. God knows there was no lack of ruins in France after the war. But for some reason this man couldn't find his answers at home. He could only find them *here*, the place where all things are possible.

It's mid-afternoon when I arrive in the city of Ponferrada. For the first time, I see it not looking like a war zone. The construction work that filled the old centre with squeals and thuds for five years is finally over, and with the hoardings and gangplanks gone and the holes in the pavement filled in, it's not a bad-looking place. At the refuge, John from Derry says there's a spot for me in his four-bed room. "You'll sleep well with us. Me, Bert and Oscar, three men over fifty and not one of us a snorer. Will wonders never cease?"

John's just come in on the bus from Astorga. He's having leg problems. He's been having leg problems since the day I met him. First it was the knees, now it's shin splints, or so he fears. He's a healthy, active man, and it's getting him down. Sandee and Chris, his walking partners, are somewhere back in the mountains with leg issues of their own. They're all supposed to meet here at noon tomorrow, but who knows?

"The girls were looking for you, Bob. I said I'd keep them company till you showed up, but they weren't interested. You've cast a spell on them."

Last night I told Kara and Nuala to meet me downtown at Bar Central, the place where years ago I met a friendly young English-speaking bartender named Mino. I was his only customer that day, and he served me beer on the house and talked about his *there*.

"America, man. As soon as I get the money together. Spain has nothing for young people. *There*, they're open to new ideas."

Echoes of the painter Alberdi, except that Mino's land of dreams was not the green prairies of Saskatchewan but the emerald city of New York. And not the New York of the Statue of Liberty; no, Mino's icons of America were the lonely gas pumps and all-night diners of Edward Hopper's Camino to nowhere.

"I love *Hop-pair*. He's cool. There's no one like him in Spain." He pointed to one of the paintings on the wall. "Do you see that? I want to be in New York City at four a.m. in *that* diner."

I feel a kinship with the Minos of the world, and with the French pilgrims whom Christ calls to build guest houses on the Camino. Here I am looking for "material" in Spain as if there were nothing to write about at home. Here we all are, looking for wisdom on the Camino that we might acquire with much less effort and expense by talking to the person beside us on the bus, or sitting quietly in a room for an hour. But we have to do what we have to do in the way we have to do it.

Mino said he'd call me when he got to New York, but I never heard from him. Now I'm curious to know if he ever made it. I walk up past the Templar castle to the old town, peering in the windows of bars till I recognize the telltale Hoppers. The place is bustling today, not with bohos and beatniks, but with cliques of housewives with baby carriages. A middle-aged woman is rinsing glasses behind the bar. Mino's mom?

"Mino? I've been here two years and I've never heard of any Mino."

The picture of *that* diner is still on the wall. Could it be he's sitting there now, chasing a hangover with a cup of thin American coffee and loving where he is, or hating it, or not even remembering that things were ever different from how they are? Only two things are sure: he isn't here, and the manager should get some new pictures. Without Mino, the Hoppers are meaningless, like family portraits left by a former tenant.

I finish my beer—this time I have to pay for it—then go out to look for Kara and Nuala. They won't be able to find me at Bar Central for the very good reason that there's no such place. It's Bar Principal, always was. Ponferrada suffers from no bar shortage, so it takes me a while to find the one where the girls are. Nuala is bursting to tell me the latest.

"We've had the most amazing day . . ."

"We took a wrong turn and got *totally* lost."

"We saw a fox and a wolf . . ."

"*She* saw what she *thought* was a wolf track," Kara qualifies.

". . . and we went right to the tippy-top of a mountain. We were looking right down on Molinaseca, we just couldn't figure out how to get there. And I'm sure that was a wolf track. It was enormous."

"How did you get lost?" I ask when I can slip a word in edgewise.

"We just did what you told me last night," says Nuala without a hint of reproach. "We took the left-hand road after El Acebo."

"Oh, no! I meant the left-hand road *before Ponferrada*."

"Give *me* the directions next time," says Kara drily.

Poor Kara's tendons have seized up on her and she can hardly walk back to the refuge. Still, the two of them are hell-bent on making it to Finisterre for the thirtieth. "No worries," says Kara. "The last time my ankle was like this, I did thirty k's. Of course, I was laid up for the next three days . . ."

With the exception of Nuala the indestructible, my friends keep coming up lame and halt. And the road out of Ponferrada tomorrow won't help. Nothing but pavement for twenty kilometres, the last thing crippled feet need.

Ave Fénix

In a little park at the edge of Camponaraya, a wiry man with a red bandana sits strumming a guitar. It's Charley the photographer.

"Hey, man, I haven't seen you in weeks. Remember when I played my guitar in the church in Irache? That's still the most beautiful church I have seen on the Camino. But I have been to an even more spiritual place since then. Did you stay with Tomás the Templar at Manjarín? There was just three of us, we slept up under the roof, and Tomás made supper and told us all about the Templar knights . . ."

Could it be clearer I'm not meant to see that place?

Charley has been taking it slow for a couple of days, timing things to meet his wife in Villafranca del Bierzo, which is why I've caught up with him. I haven't heard his story before, but he tells me on the way to Cacabelos. Till two years ago, he was a self-made businessman with a stake in the generic pharmaceuticals firm he had founded. Then he decided he wanted something different from life.

"It was hard. Just when I was ready to get out, I was offered a chance to buy the other eighty percent of the firm. I could have flipped it for a big profit, but that would have meant spending another year or more in the business, and I didn't want to do that. I passed up the opportunity, and for the next two months all I could think about was the money I hadn't made. After I got over that, I knew for sure I was doing the right thing. You see, I had become addicted to money."

Since then, he has taken up photography, learned the guitar and set three goals for the next ten years: to walk the

Camino, motorbike the Americas and climb Mount Everest. The Camino is first up.

I leave him to photograph a church in Cacabelos and go strolling through the narrow medieval streets of the village. There is a new refuge in town at the church of Our Lady of the Seven Sorrows. On my first Camino, I shared a room in the old refuge with the Seven Beautiful French Bike Pilgrims. The one in the bunk below me was an agriculture student who had spent a year on a farm in Canada. She embraced me like a soulmate. Canada, Canada, how she longed for Canada, how good it was to find someone who could feel her longing. I asked her where in Canada she had lived.

"Saskatchewan," she said.

Oh, Saskatchewan, land of dreams. Toronto is as far from Saskatchewan as Paris from the Ukraine, but what did that matter to either of us? She led me down to the courtyard of the refuge and introduced me to her companions. Then they all took out guitars and sang songs about Jesus. At lights-out, I thought I heard a catch in her voice when she told me she and her friends would be away before dawn, so we would not see each other again. We bid each other a tender *bon chemin*, then she threw her body on the sagging mattress and snored all night like a saint in glory.

The pilgrim enters Villafranca del Bierzo by the back door, on an old trail through the vineyards called *el camino de la Virgen*. You round the hill and suddenly the town is there, sloping down either side of the valley. First you pass the Church of Santiago, where by ancient dispensation the sick, the weary, the lame—any who cannot take another step—are permitted to pass through the Door of Pardon and receive all the blessings of a pilgrim who has walked to Santiago. After it is the place where I will stay tonight: Ave Fénix.

Twenty years ago, Jesús Jato started building his refuge here on the site of a medieval pilgrim hospital. Jato envisioned his project as a phoenix, a new life not only for the refuge but for the Camino's spirit of sharing and giving. Passing pilgrims lent their skills and their sweat to its construction after the manner of the medieval pilgrims who built the Camino as they walked it. Many stayed for days or weeks to help. But the phoenix image proved prophetic in ways that Jato never intended. Twice his refuge has gone up in flames; twice Jato has spit on his hands and made it rise again.

It is easy for a layman to mistake Ave Fénix for an ancient structure. Each stone is carefully set in place, and the gaps are filled with plaster, not concrete. No nails are used; the beams and planks are fitted together. The ceiling timbers with their blackened-by-centuries-of-woodsmoke look are in fact former telegraph poles. The friend of Jato who points out these features to me defends the old building methods with vigour. "Look around Villafranca at the renovations. They're spending millions to keep things from falling down, but it's always the new buildings. The old ones, built with the materials of the region using the traditional methods, are solid."

I haven't seen many "new buildings" in Villafranca. Which ones does he mean?

"The eighteenth-century ones."

At eight, we gather to eat in the spacious yet cozy foyer, with its floor mosaic of a goose. María Jato brings in platters of soup, salad and tortilla from the kitchen. We're a nice-sized group tonight, fewer than twenty of us, including Helen, Hayley and several friends of Jato who seem almost residents. The only one missing is Jato himself. He is not well tonight, says María, and won't be joining us. First Tomás, now Jato. My run continues.

Hours after supper, I wake to see the moon shining through the skylight above my bed. I come down the spiral stairway to the wooden porch. The sky is deepest blue, the air chill with the moisture of the surrounding forests. Mounted on the wall is a wooden plaque carved with the Japanese characters *Santiago junrei no michi*—"Santiago's pilgrim road." I could be in Kyoto. A wood chime hangs from the rafters. No wind tonight, so I reach out and give the chimes a shake. And as if I have summoned a friendly spirit, the door of the refuge opens and out comes Jato. He is talking to a pilgrim from Brazil. I watch as they cross slowly to the far wing of the refuge. Jato is known as a mystic and esoteric thinker—Paulo Coelho has cited him as an inspiration—and he is expounding on a familiar theme. The words are not intended for me, but I hear them all the same.

"*Peregrino*, you have reached the last and most important part of the Camino. You have surmounted the physical stage. You have practised introspection on the *meseta*. Now you embark on the mystical Camino, whose true end is not Santiago, but Finisterre and mother ocean. In the days of the Celts, Druids came all the way from Ireland and Charlemagne's court in Aachen to be baptized at sunset at Finisterre. There they died with the sun, like Jesus, sinking into the waters of death, only to be born again when they emerged. They took on new robes, new names. That is why pilgrims burn their clothes at Finisterre. Their old self must die before the new can rise from the ashes . . ."

The climb from Villafranca del Bierzo is so steep that a rope ladder would come in handy. From the top, Villafranca really does resemble a French *ville*, with its château and churches on the high places, the houses rolling and tumbling down to the river. I spare a thought for the walking wounded. John, who stayed behind in Ponferrada yesterday. Kara and Nuala, who must have stopped in Cacabelos. I wonder how Tony Bush is getting along, and Inácio. And out of who knows where, my memory fetches up a memory from three weeks ago in Puente la Reina: María of the bundle buggy. The thought of that sweet old Argentinian woman lugging her cart up this slope with a smile on her face almost makes me laugh out loud. Not that she would come by this route. Luckily for her and others like her, there is now a paved path along the valley bottom on the shoulder of the old N6. It's no treat to walk, but climbing is not required.

The path skirts the hillside for a while, then plunges into a vast grove. Cars are parked everywhere. It's chestnut season. Bloated sacks slump at the feet of trees like sleeping farmers. A donkey stands patiently swishing its tail. "Is that your burro?" I call to the old man scavenging nearby.

"That's my taxi," he replies.

Then a phoenix memory leaps like a flame from the dead leaves. The very first time I passed this way, an August afternoon when the chestnuts were green on the trees. It was the third day since the beginning of the *romería*. My third day of racing to stay ahead of the pack, of losing touch with the slowness of the Camino. I was hurrying through this grove when something orange and slender shot up from the grass. It was Montse.

"*Peregrino!*"

"*Peregrina!*"

I hadn't seen her in three long weeks, not since the morning in Puente la Reina when she drowned the tick on my knee with olive oil. Now here she was, running towards me like a Renoir study in light. She kissed my cheeks, took my hands and stood back to look me over with her great soulful eyes.

"How have you been I haven't seen you for ages I'm sorry I don't remember your name what happened about that tick?"

As she spoke, she dragged me over to where her walking companions of the day lazed in a disarray of wine bottles and cheese rinds. Andrew from Canada proved to be a trove of pilgrim gossip, a regular switching station on the Camino telegraph. Renan from Brittany insisted I finish off the wine. For the first time in days, I relaxed. Montse and I got caught up on our news, not that there was much to tell. She had been walking the Camino and I had been walking the Camino and wasn't that wonderful?

Then we all went traipsing in the shade of the chestnut trees down to the village of Trabadelo. We stopped at a shop whose patio was peopled by Snow White, Venus on the half shell, a menagerie of stone lions, eagles, roosters, frogs, and a pair of guitar-strumming dwarves. Looking right at home amidst the lawn ornaments were more long-lost friends, John Kennedy and Matt from Long Island and long-legged Richard from Paris. At first, the elderly shopkeeper was overwhelmed by our orders. His shelves were randomly stocked with individual items—one can of beans, one packet of biscuits, one bottle of beer—but somehow, in the fullness of time, he managed to scrape together enough meat, bread and liquid to satisfy us all. Then, for a precious hour or two, we waited out the heat together, snoozing under the watchful gaze of Snow White.

What memories. But today, Snow White's patio is strewn with rotting apples. The dwarves and the lions are faded or defaced. It looks as if no one has sat here for years.

"Is the shop still open?" I ask a passing couple.

"The shop is closed, but the people still live there. Can we call them for you?"

"That's okay. Tell them a pilgrim said hello."

Leaving my stick and backpack on the melancholy patio, I go to refill my water bottle at the village fountain. I come back to find Nino being put to novel use. An elderly Italian pilgrim is batting apples off the tree with him, catching them with his free hand. I have just sunk my teeth into one when I look up the highway and see a familiar figure trundling towards us. She is wearing a blue raincoat and white sneakers, and she is pulling a bundle buggy.

"María! I swear, I was thinking of you just an hour ago."

She doesn't look in the least surprised. "Yes, people are always thinking of me. I'm lucky that way."

As we walk the quiet road to Vega del Valcarce, she tells me of other travels with her bundle buggy, to Rome and Jerusalem, and of the wonderful time she's been having the past few weeks on the road to Santiago. "Oh, people are funny. They look at me, then they look at my buggy, then they look at me again, and they say, 'You are walking with *that*?' 'Well, I couldn't walk without it,' I tell them. 'How else am I to manage, a woman of my age?' Then they all want to help me, and they won't take no for an answer. 'Don't worry about me,' I say, 'worry about yourself. I can do fine on my own.'"

But María is never really on her own. In Vega, an elegantly bearded French gentleman pops out of a bar.

"María, María," he cries, spreading his arms operatically, "we missed you this morning. Where have you been?"

Where do I know this man from? The face, the voice . . . Of course! He's my favourite actor, Alan Rickman. Or at least he would be, if he weren't who he is: a Frenchman in his sixties with moist, shining eyes. And now out of the bar behind Monsieur Rickman comes Charley the photographer. "María, we've been waiting for you. Come in and have a beer with us. Bob, you too."

I'm glad to see that Our Lady of the Bundle Buggy's angels are watching over her, and I'd love to join them. But right now I have a date with a massage.

Monsieur Rickman

The day I met Montse again, we walked the river valley to Ruitelán beneath a dime-sized moon, groping for something to talk about. I had never been alone with the Catalana for so long before and I hoped this time we would make a connection. But our conversation was composed, as usual, of awkward questions, encouraging silences and lame non sequiturs, as if we were tossing a Frisbee that, the harder we aimed, the more it went sailing over the other's head and into the river. Still, we kept tossing for the sake of the odd catch.

We were walking towards the great hill—or small mountain—that was the last thing now between us and Galicia. "El Cebrero"—*ehl theh-breh-roh*—in the harsh, lisping Castilian tongue; "O Cebreiro"—*oo se-braay-roo*—in the soft, rounded speech of the Galicians. However you call it, it is the Camino's mountain of miracles, from the olden-days miracle that occurred in the tiny village chapel, when the sacred bread and wine changed to real flesh and blood in the middle of Mass, to the more recent miracle of a simple parish priest, Padre Elías Valiña Sampedro, who coordinated the great task of painting the yellow arrows across Spain to Santiago.

The refuge in Ruitelán, called Little Potala after the palace of the Dalai Lama, is a sort of base camp at the foot of the mountain. Each time I have walked the Camino, I have spent the night there. I know it now as a homey place with a madcap manager who whips up magnificent communal (vegetarian) suppers. But that night when I walked in the twilight with Montse, all I knew about Ruitelán was that you could get a shiatsu massage treatment there. For weeks I had been seeing the notices in refuges, and the prospect of a full-on professional foot and leg massage had sustained me through many trials. I was to be disappointed, however. Carlos and Juan were already booked solid. And that was only the first in a string of disappointments, for in my two visits to Ruitelán since, despite all my best efforts, I have never shown up in time for a treatment. Which is why today I passed on Charley's lunch invitation. And here I am at Ruitelán at one. Plenty early, I'd say. I can almost feel those fingers going to work . . .

"Sorry. No massages today."

This time it has nothing to do with the hour. Carlos is just too busy. Juan has gone away for the week, leaving him with one helper to handle the cleaning up, checking in and cooking for sixteen. If anyone needs a massage, it's Carlos. I feel for him, but as a frequent guest I think I've also earned the right to wheedle.

"Carlos, you remember me, this is my fourth time. I came early just for a massage."

Carlos would sooner strangle me. And he could—his arms look like they came off a lathe. He's not in the greatest mood, either. The reason he and Juan came out here in the first place was to get away from it all. They were optimistic enough to call the place Potala, maybe with the idea that they would win merit by helping pilgrims for a few hours every day and have the rest of the time to themselves to read, meditate, relax. And here they are instead, in the "off-season" no less, scrambling to keep doors shut and floors dry, answering the unending questions about phones and laundry, cooking for a multitude, and dealing with wheedlers such as my good self.

"Look, I can give you twenty minutes. Right before supper. I'll call you, okay?"

In the end, I get better than I deserve. Carlos tries not to race through the massage, but his mind is in the kitchen and the treatment is cursory. He applies a method I've never encountered before that mostly involves blowing lightly on the skin. Refreshing, but miles from my craving for strong fingers kneading tired muscles. Juan, it turns out, is the shiatsu specialist. But do I complain? Never. *El turista exige, el peregrino agradece.* "The tourist makes demands, the pilgrim gives thanks." Besides, Carlos could crush me like a peanut.

Carlos's cooking, at least, does not disappoint. The food, the company, the music, the wine, the laughs at the end of the day—this is Camino. We are seated around two big tables, Helen and Hayley, María of the bundle buggy, Charley, Monsieur Rickman, and a host of new and goodly faces: Mario, a young painter from Portugal, who has already walked to Santiago this year from Oporto and liked it so much that he's trying again from a different direction; Georges from France, a stocky, good-natured man in his sixties who first walked the Camino in 1999, the same year I did; Marina from Brazil, a work psychologist who is upgrading her skills in Barcelona. She tells me her project keeps her at a desk fourteen hours a day, then follows her home at night. "I have not been 'off' in nine months. The only thing I want from the Camino is to disconnect. No alarm clocks, no deadlines, no mobile phones, no email."

We're finding plenty of things to talk about, but Monsieur Rickman, who has been thoroughly enjoying the local wine, decrees that each of us must sing a song from our country. We make it through Germany, Ireland and Portugal all right (I'm getting worried that I'll be called on to summon up some Leonard Cohen), but the game ends with France.

Monsieur Rickman has a fine, deep voice, and he treats us to a whole songbook of *chansons* to which only he, and sometimes Georges, knows the words. It's not bedtime yet, but Carlos looks at his watch and decides it is. We all say, "Ohhh!" and get up from the table. I'm on my way out the door when I feel a gentle hand on my arm. It is Monsieur Rickman.

"Excuse me, Georges tells me you wrote a book about the Blessed Virgin and the Camino."

"Yes, I did."

"How fascinating. Perhaps you can explain to me what connection you discovered between them." His tone is light. His eyebrows bristle with amusement.

"Connection? Well, every church along the Camino has an image of the Virgin. Many of them are famous, miracles are attributed to them. Of course, the Camino is the way of Saint James, but in a sense you could also say it's the way of the Virgin."

Monsieur Rickman takes this in, then replies in a voice that is suddenly clipped and precise, "I'm afraid I cannot agree. There is the way of Saint James and there is the way of the Virgin Mary, but there is *not* the way of Saint James which is also through some obscure logic the way of the Virgin Mary. The distinction is clear."

"Well, of course it's not the way of the Virgin in the sense that, say, Lourdes is—"

"It is not the way of the Virgin in any sense at all. If that is something you cannot grasp, then perhaps it is something you should not write about."

This is a moment I have always dreaded yet never encountered: to be told, simply and clearly, that I am writing on holy ground. My response is unequivocal. I rally my troops and beat a full, craven retreat.

"I'm sorry, it was not my intention at all to . . . if I said anything that was in any way . . . I'm really truly very . . ." There's no way I'm going to argue with someone who holds a twin home-field advantage: his religion and his language. Luckily for me, we're standing in the doorway and, before the debacle can go any further, Carlos has bundled us off to our beds.

The Magic Mountain

The climbing of O Cebreiro is the Camino's biggest fish story, a morning's walk up a big hill that rumour has turned into an assault on Everest. If O Cebreiro is an adventure, it's not for the steepness of the slope but for the fickleness of the weather. This morning is no exception. Just like the first time, when I walked this way with Montse, the limpid blue skies of evening have given way by morning to dismal, pelting rain. I follow the road, head bowed, through unwaking hamlets, then up into thick forest by earth paths and stone steps. I catch up with Marina from Brazil, who teaches me songs from her country as we climb. The first images of Jobim's song "Aguas de Março"—a stick, a stone, the end of the road—are a perfect fit for the Camino. Marina is a wisp of a woman with springs for legs and soon we have overtaken most of last night's party, including Monsieur Rickman, who warbles like a bird as he walks, and waves us hello. To my relief, he seems oblivious to last night's unpleasantness.

At eleven, we hit the open slopes and the rain stops. Mist lifts like a curtain to reveal near-vertical hills across the way, a patchwork of forests, pastures and farms. Then the long climb to the village, which we enter over the back wall of the churchyard. And we are there, in O Cebreiro's single street of low shops and bars, all alone—except for the several bus-loads of day trippers who have come to savour the tranquility of an unspoiled Galician village.

This warren of ancient stone buildings has always been for me a place of strong impressions and vivid encounters. The first time I came here, I had just read Thomas Mann's tale of an ingenuous young man who spends seven years in a mountaintop sanatorium, taking the imprints of the characters who live there. When I came to O Cebreiro, I felt that I had found my own Magic Mountain—and not just on this hilltop. The Camino itself was a Magic Mountain hammered flat, thin and long enough to stretch across a country. I can't wait for tonight, when last night's crowd from Ruitelán will gather once more, this time around a roaring fire.

Marina and I elbow our way into a packed, smoky pub and warm ourselves with *caldo gallego*, the Galician soup of kale and potatoes. While we eat, Marina tells me more about her project. She's developing questionnaires to determine what is important to workers in their workplace. This has proved more complicated than she expected, for she has found that workers only consider something important when they don't have it. Thus, if everyone is bickering, "harmony in the workplace" becomes a top priority. But if everyone is getting along fine, it doesn't crack the top ten.

"How do you interpret that?" I ask her. "Is it that people only appreciate good things when they don't have them?"

"That's one possibility. Or else the things that people consider important are the ones they complain about."

A sudden *thap thap thap* on the windows tells us the rain is back. Good thing we're inside, cozy and warm. I go to the bar for a glass of mulled wine. When I come back, Marina is putting on her rain gear.

"Where are you going?"

"It's too early to stop walking."

"This is O Cebreiro. Stay."

"I've got too much energy still."

"It's pouring out there."

She laughs. "Bob, the place in Brazil where my family comes from is dry. Really dry. When I went to stay with my grandparents when I was a kid, my dad would drive me to the end of the dirt road, fifteen kilometres from the house, and my grandfather and I would walk all the way through sand up to our knees. So there is nothing that makes me happier than walking in the rain."

I wish I could find such romance in this rotten weather, but it's beyond me. Before Marina leaves, she takes my hand. "I think you're under stress. You seem very tired. Look, I brought these pills to help me sleep, but I haven't needed them. I'm going to give you a couple, okay?" She places the whole bottle on the table and wades out into the storm. Thanks, Marina.

The rain keeps coming, harder and faster. Last night's pilgrims keep straggling in. Helen and Hayley. Georges and Mario. Surely they're staying tonight? No. Too soon to stop. They wring out their clothes and splursh off through the rain and the muck. Another pilgrim from last night, Philomena from Ireland, looks in. She's not staying either. She's used to those tough Irish pilgrimages.

"The whole time, barefoot and sleep deprived. Nothing but black tea and bread. Makes the Camino look like a picnic. One time I opened a book and the priest took it away from me. He said, 'You're not on holiday, you know!'"

Will no one share O Cebreiro with me tonight? The noise and smoke of the bar are getting to me, so I step out to find some quiet in the tiny church. A bundle buggy is parked at the door. Inside, María is alone, kneeling before the crucifix, her head tilted a little to one side like the statue of Our Lady of O Cebreiro. At dinner last night, someone asked her why she was doing the Camino. "For peace," she said.

When she has finished her prayers, she turns and smiles, coming back from some great distance. "How are you? I had a wonderful walk today. Just me and the sky! It's very lovely here, isn't it? I got here and I knew I had to stay."

So at least one pilgrim will be sharing the magic of O Cebreiro with me tonight. I'm glad María has found a little of what she was looking for. I also feel a little better knowing that I'm not going to be outstripped by a sixty-five-year-old woman pulling a shopping cart.

Orphans of the Camino

At the refuge, Monsieur Rickman is lying on a lower bunk, eyes closed. I pass on cat's feet.

"May I have a word with you?" Sepulchral, that voice of his. He wasn't sleeping, he was lying in wait. "I have been reflecting upon our discussion last night. Forgive me, but I am a person who thinks a good deal about words and what they signify." He forms a little steeple above his chest with his fingers. "This is because I believe that words have the power to change thoughts. Therefore, they must be used judiciously."

And with that he commences his exegesis on why the way of Saint James is most emphatically not the way of the Virgin. Clearly he has devoted considerable mental energy to the subject. I dare say he's been formulating it all day. It's unfortunate that I am in no mood to hear him out. "Please, monsieur, that's not what I meant to say."

"But did you not write that the way of Saint James is the way of the Virgin?"

"Yes, sort of, not exactly . . ."

"Are they or are they not the words you used?"

Maybe Marina's right. Maybe I am stressed. Because what I mean to say next is, "My French is not adequate to explain," but what comes out instead is, "I'm sorry, I don't speak French."

The important thing is, it works. While the flabbergasted Monsieur Rickman gasps for air, I seize my chance and scurry away.

The rain has stopped. I stand for a while at the head of the valley, hoping I'll see Kara and Nuala coming to my rescue. Then I try one more round of the bars, looking for a friendly face. In one of them, Monsieur Rickman sits alone with a rum and Coke, his toque pulled down so low on his forehead that it traps his bristly eyebrows. He's at loose ends, just like me. Last night he was the life of the party, today he's alone in the crowd. We hook eyes, nod, I walk on.

My thinking stone finds my fingers. *Why are you being unkind to that man? He means no harm, he's just a bit of a pain. Go and speak to him. In French if need be.* I return to the bar, fetch a glass of wine for strength and sit down across from my tormentor. He gets out his digital camera to show me the pictures he took today. Something easy to share. When the show is over, I say, "Tell me again what you were telling me before, but keep it simple."

This is like tying his hands and telling him to play the piano. It pains him. And truly, he looks as if his hands are tied, for as he speaks, his fingers grow extra joints. They twine around each other like tendrils while he searches for the *mot simple* that must stand in place of the *mot juste* for my uncultured ears.

"*Saint Jacques*. Cousin of Christ. *Sainte Marie*. Mother of Christ. Same family. Same doctrine. Same destination. But the way, the *chemin*, no. The *chemin* is not the same." He extricates his right hand from his left, dips a finger into his rum and Coke, then draws a line of liquid on the table. "We, all of us, walk the *chemin de Saint Jacques*"—he two-finger walks the line—"until we reach the end. And there we are. We are finished, and . . . and what? What is next? The Camino has cared for us. We have been its children. Now we are its orphans. The orphans of the Camino."

He looks up to see if I'm following. I notice again how moist his eyes are, not in a rheumy but a dewy way.

"Go on."

He wets his fingertip again and this time traces a circle around the line. "In the end, on the last day of our long walk, we find that we have come all this way *only to return to ourselves*. Yes? We walk until we meet ourselves. Then we see that the rest was all illusion. And this, *this* . . . is the way of Saint Jacques. A going out, but a coming home. A voyage that leads us to where we already were, where we have always been." He pauses to let the poetry of the thing sink in, then dips his finger once more and retraces the line—"A going out"—and the circle—"and a coming home. Do you see?"

I do. I don't. I don't know if I don't or I do. I am entranced by Monsieur Rickman's delight in his own analogy. He has an eloquent soul, though his eloquence usually flows in fine words. With that valve closed, the eloquence leaks from his hands, his eyes, the angle of his head. His eyebrows leak eloquence. I want to push his toque up to liberate them.

And most eloquent of all is his tone of voice. He is a singer, though I like him better when he doesn't sing.

"Now the way of the Virgin—"

"Excuse me . . ."

I should not have interrupted him. Now I will never know how he meant to show me the way of the Virgin in rum and Coke. But it has become clear to me that our discussion since last night has proceeded from a false premise, and it would be cruel to let him continue.

"Excuse me, monsieur, but you think I am Catholic, don't you?" His look answers my question. "You misunderstand. I am not Catholic, not a believer. And my book is not a book of theology. It is a travel book."

He sits back, joins his fingers once more in a steeple and smiles gently. "Ah!" he says. "Ah. Then none of this makes any difference to you."

"Well, it's very interesting . . ."

He thinks a little while. Then his fingers start working again. "You will forgive me for saying so, but it is still the responsibility of a writer to write with wisdom."

"I understand that, and I agree, but if we waited to write only what we knew, then very little would get written. Can't writing be a way of learning?"

"Good writing comes when the journey has been made."

It's only a table between us, but it might as well be a valley. We gaze across at each other, wondering if our voices are being heard on the other side. Then Monsieur Rickman finishes his rum and Coke. He won't need it for any more diagrams. "I must get back to the refuge and see how María is doing." He offers his hand. "I'm glad we spoke."

"I'm glad too."

"Good night."

Monsieur Rickman leaves me alone in the crowded bar. Marina was right, I *am* tired. This talk has made me even more tired. Suddenly everything feels old and stale. Nothing on the menu looks good. When some minstrels come in with pipes and tambours and start in on the Celtic music, it all seems forced. What am I doing here?

I look around at the other tables of pilgrims. I could easily go join them. As Monsieur Rickman says, we're all the Camino's children. But I'm weighed down with what else he said. That the others will fall away, and at the end of the road there will be no one waiting to greet us but ourselves. In the end, we are all orphans of the Camino.

The Rain in Spain

Georges blows into the bar in Alto del Poio next morning waving a glossy brochure. "I'm famous! I'm famous! I am the most famous pilgrim on the Camino!" It's a pamphlet printed by the government of Galicia to promote its twenty-four-hour pilgrim helpline. On the cover is a photo of a pilgrim with all the dressings: gourd, staff, shell, grizzled white beard. Georges! "This is me doing the Camino in 1999. You can tell by the hat."

"Are you going to sue them for using your picture?"

"No, but I think they owe me a T-shirt."

Soon Helen and Hayley join us, then Mario and Marina.

"You can have these back," I tell Marina, handing her the sleeping pills.

"Did they help?"

"I didn't need them."

I did something last night that I've never done before: I went back to the refuge at nine o'clock without eating supper, climbed into bed and slept. At six-thirty this morning, I was out walking the highway in the dark, saluting the cars as they passed with a flicker of their high beams. With a week to go before Santiago, there's still time to be happy. I'm not an orphan yet. The others stayed last night at Hospital da Condesa, five kilometres from O Cebreiro, and I'm sorry now that my fixation on reliving past glories kept me from joining them. While I moped on my mountaintop, they were enjoying supper in a restaurant with a big fireplace and, according to Marina, an outstandingly attractive waitress. My one consolation is that I got things sorted out with Monsieur Rickman.

There is a fireplace in this bar too, around which four college students in tartan kilts are toasting their kneecaps. The kilts are for the Celts, for we are now in Galicia, Spain's Celtic corner. Like Ireland, Wales, Highland Scotland, Brittany— all the redoubts of the Celtic tribes before the conquering Romans—Galicia is green, rainy, Atlantic. And like them, it is a land of mist, magic and blarney, a "thin place," where little divides this world from the next. Despite all the best efforts of missionaries, the Christians of Galicia could never bring themselves to abandon their sacred springs and holy stones, their tales of giants and witches. Under Franco, Galicia's culture, language and aspirations to self-government were suppressed (ironic, in that Franco was an arch-*gallego*), but recent years have seen a reflowering of the region's rich traditions of music, literature, art and folklore. Just for the record, however, there's no evidence that the Celts of Galicia ever wore kilts.

None of us is in a hurry to leave the bar this morning. The rain was just starting when we came in, and the last time anyone checked, it showed no sign of letting up soon, or even today. Shaw had it wrong: the rain in Spain falls mainly on Galicia. But the time comes when we must move on. We adjust our rain gear, pull up our hoods—and step out into a new day, where the air is warm and sunlight glints off the greens of the valley. No wonder the Galicians believe in magic. The turn in the weather determines my plans for the day. It's over thirty kilometres to Sarria, but I'll go for it if this weather holds. In Galicia, you don't squander sunshine.

I walk with Evaristo, a burly man with a bad cough. He's from Galicia, but not the Galicia of kale and cattle, the Galicia by the ocean. His family has always lived by and from the sea. He went out with the fishing boats himself when he was young, before the industry went into free fall. He lost his management job last year, and now at age fifty he's taking a retraining course in marine maintenance. He sculpts and paints, too; his dream is to paint the sailor's life "before it vanishes." In ten days he will reach the front door of his home at the edge of the boundless blue. Till then, he's walking through green Galicia, where the horizon is always the next hill.

It takes the morning to come down from O Cebreiro, with pastoral vistas all the way. From Triacastela, at the foot of the mountain, there are two roads to Sarria. The left offers shelter halfway at the ancient monastery of Samos (handy in case of rain); the right rambles over the hills. The first time I came this way, I went right. The last two times, it was left. Looks like it's right's turn today. If the weather turns, I'll be as exposed as the cows in the fields.

For the first hour, the path is sheltered by oak trees with boles like monstrous goitres. The banks on either side are a green cascade of tendrils, ferns and mosses. My footsteps are cushioned by a carpet of crushed chestnuts, parasol mushrooms, slippery black leaves. Then I reach the wide open heights of the Alto de Riocabo. The river valley below is dotted with farms. The ancient monastery of Samos perches on the opposite slope, five kilometres distant. The only sounds are a dog barking—and thunder. A kilometre before me and behind me, Galicia's eternal rains are falling. I walk in the slim interval of sunlight between.

Just before Sarria, a white van pulls over and a sixtyish man jumps out. "Are you staying in Sarria tonight? My son has a refuge. Just opened this summer. Internet, hot shower, hot supper. I'm the cook. I used to work on fishing boats. You're from Canada? I love Canadians. I knew lots of them when I was a fisherman." I rejoice to hear it. A few years ago, there was little love lost for Canada in Galicia, after the Canadian navy seized a Spanish boat accused of poaching in Canadian waters. The incident was immortalized in Canada as "the turbot war"; in Spain, *"la guerra del fletán."* Since then, however, the Galician fishing industry has moved on to worse crises. The *fletán* business pales beside the disastrous wreck of the oil freighter *Prestige* in 2002, which coated hundreds of kilometres of shoreline in a deadly black muck.

"Can I give you a drive into town?" asks the man with the van. "No? Of course, I understand. But take my son's card."

When I arrive in Sarria (on foot) a few minutes later, the card comes in handy. The municipal refuge is packed to the rafters. This is not a total surprise, for Sarria, at 112 kilometres from Santiago, lies just over the minimum distance a pilgrim must walk to receive the Compostela. The upshot of this accident of geography is that Sarria is up there with St-Jean and Roncesvalles among the most popular places to begin the Camino. Luckily, there are still a few beds at my fisherman friend's place.

And here is Masa. We haven't seen each other in over a week. We round up Georges and head out for supper. After my solitary night in O Cebreiro, it's good to be back with friends.

The Camino Will Make You Think Differently

My map shows twenty-three place names in the twenty-one kilometres between Sarria and Portomarín. When I catch up with Eileen and Julie around ten-thirty, we've passed through nine of them. Julie can't believe it: "I must have blinked."

"I kind of remember one place," says Eileen. "There was a refuge and a postbox."

Before I came to Galicia for the first time, I would look at maps and marvel at all the villages, my mind picturing one idyllic node of humanity after another, each with its own plaza, fountain, church and amenities. How would I ever walk twenty kilometres a day with so many bars to stop at? I was extrapolating, of course, from Navarra and La Rioja, where the towns are strung along the road like pearls on a necklace. But the "towns" of Galicia often proved to be no more than a handful of slate houses, or a few big farmhouses barely within shouting distance of each other, and bare of urban furniture: no plazas, benches, shops, fountains, or even (could this be Spain?) bars. As for street life, it was mainly bovine.

How to account for this difference? Part of it is that Navarra and Castilla-León have had livelier histories than Galicia. For centuries they were war zones, and the human settlements that grew up in them were complete in themselves, as armed camps must be. But the fundamental reason is water. Over much of the Camino, water is scarce. Where a source is found, people crowd around it. In Galicia—*ojalá!*—if only there were a shortage of water! In Galicia, water roars down ditches, drips off leaves, weeps from the heavens. With so much water, people don't need to crowd around a well. On the contrary, the conditions are just right for small farmers and cow herders, people who want to have some distance from their neighbours. As for the fine Spanish custom of living in public, most of its attractions are washed away by the rain. It wasn't till my November Camino that I started to appreciate how Galician life centres not around the well but the hearth. When you do find a bar in rural Galicia, you can be sure there will be a fireplace, and the wetter you are, the gladder you are for it.

I hike on through more invisible villages with Eileen and Julie. They are flight attendants for Qantas and good company. Julie is a skeptic, Eileen a believing, if not frequently practising, Catholic. She was turned on to the Camino by Shirley MacLaine's book, which she regards with fascinated ambivalence: "It's ridiculous. I've read it twice." In Morgade, we duck into one of those toasty Galician bars just as the rain blows in. A few minutes ago we passed the stone marker telling us that we are a hundred kilometres from Santiago. It has focused our minds.

"So, Bob," ventures Julie, "you've spent a bit of time on the Camino. Any *spiritual* experiences you can share with us?"

We've been talking about Shirley MacLaine, so I know what she means: time travel, out-of-body experiences, waking dreams, déjà vu felt not in flashes but as a normal state of being. On the Camino, Shirley—when she wasn't fleeing the paparazzi—relived the spicier moments of her past life as Charlemagne's Moorish concubine, engaged in learned debate with the medieval philosopher John the Scot and discovered the true end of her pilgrimage in the lost city of Atlantis. Julie's just asking if I've experienced anything similar.

"Well, no. A few funny coincidences, too-good-to-be-true sort of things. But nothing exactly . . ."

"Earth-shattering."

"No."

"So maybe in the end it's all just a long walk," says Eileen. "Maybe."

Should we be disappointed or relieved? Do we really want our earth shattered? We're all of us modern, rational, basically secular; not really believers in magic or miracles. Yet it's hard for us to accept that the Camino is just a long walk, from here to there, without mystery or meaning. Deep inside, we were hoping for something more. Now, ninety-nine kilometres from Santiago, we sit listening to the rain split and splat on the windows, wondering if that's all there is.

After a long moment, Eileen says, "I have to admit, I love the refuges. I've never known anything like them before. Just being together with all those strange people and yet feeling at home, like you can be yourself . . ."

Julie laughs. "You can complain to a complete stranger about the smell of the toilets. That's what I call intimacy."

"What I'll remember is the meals, when everyone helps out and you all eat together."

"And the way you treat everyone like a friend. At home, if you met a stranger on a trail, you wouldn't look him in the eye, much less say hello."

Then they tell me about a Spanish couple they met walking the Camino. The husband invited them to Burgos for a weekend to meet his family. "His wife had tears in her eyes because she was going to be seeing her father-in-law—I mean, not even her father, her *father-in-law*! She kept telling us what a wonderful man he was and it had been, I don't know, *weeks* since the last time she'd seen him. Then we got there and he started crying too. Everyone was just tearing up . . ."

"They couldn't keep walking, but they send us text messages every day to see where we are. It's like they've adopted us. They're always giving us advice, making sure we're okay. They're so sweet."

At first, they're laughing. Then Eileen takes on a thoughtful look. "Our friend's father-in-law, he was a very kind man, and I think a very wise man. And he had just one thing to say about the Camino: that after we did it, we'd think differently. He wouldn't get any more specific than that. After the Camino, we'd think differently."

We pause to weigh this modest consideration against the miracles and epiphanies of the Shirleys and the Paulo Coelhos. When Julie speaks, she speaks for all of us. "Well, if the Camino can really make you think differently, I reckon it's worth it."

Dining with the Enemy

The Camino has made me think differently about many things. That's one of its specialties. Lining up your prejudices, fears, illusions, then picking them off one at a time, sometimes with indifference, sometimes with kindness, often with the sort of deft irony it showed in Portomarín five years ago, the night I dined with the enemy.

You can smell the colour of the air in Portomarín. It's freshwater blue. Even in the handsome main street with its white-stuccoed, arcaded buildings, you can sense the nearness of *the lake*. It is a stupendous thing, after the long parch of the Camino, to look down from the bridge into its great blueness and see the houses of the drowned city. The water is low this fall, leaving the foundations visible on the banks like memories, submerged but never lost. Until 1962, the houses of Portomarín faced each other from either bank of the river Miño. Then Francisco Franco decreed that Spain needed more lakes (and really, who could disagree?) and Portomarín disappeared beneath the waters. Only the church of Saint Nicholas was saved, disassembled brick by brick, with a number painted on each one so that Humpty could be put back together again.

The municipal refuge has been refurbished since my last time here. Sparkling showers, a lavish kitchen, high ceilings, spacious lounging areas with leather couches—and fifty bunk beds crammed into two long, airless dorms. Can they not get this right? But things have been worse—five years ago when I and several hundred other pilgrims shared the floor of the public gym.

Almost from the moment I entered Galicia in that summer of 1999, my Camino turned sour. I had raced from Astorga to Ruitelán under the illusion that I could keep ahead of the crowd. In the end, I only butted up against a whole new crowd. Every day brought thousands more pilgrims to the road to Santiago. Galicia was experiencing the rainiest August in its whole rainy recorded history, making things even more interesting. My mind was tied up in angry, self-righteous knots. My silent, slow, solitary pilgrimage had been overwhelmed by a hustling, bustling, roaring one that I refused to adapt to. The new pilgrims were too many, too noisy, too regardless of the Camino. They could do no right in my eyes. But where did my anger really well from? Wasn't part of it that I didn't feel invited to this party? I consoled myself by saying that I didn't want to be.

My Camino scraped bottom the night before Portomarín, when I bedded down like a dog under the kitchen table of the refuge of Calvor. The kitchen was packed till the wee hours with carousers, and from my hiding place I snarled at them in my thoughts, saving, I recall, a special growl for the loud, tarty blonde in the skin-tight Lycra top with the boyfriend who looked like a cop. *Nice way to dress for a pilgrimage*, I thought. If I'd been in the mood for irony, I could have savoured that moment. I was experiencing exactly what I had feared before I started the Camino, the loneliness of being alone in a crowd. But the cause of my loneliness was not that the other pilgrims were holier-than-me; it was I who was too pure for them.

The next day brought new monsoons. I washed up at the crowded public gym in Portomarín foul-tempered and dripping, staked out my three metres square of floor space and sulked off to the nearest restaurant. There were already twenty parties waiting to grab one of the six tables. I didn't stand a chance. Well, that was fine, I'd go sit in the plaza and dine on the injustice of it all. I had turned to leave when I felt a hand on my shoulder. It was the pilgrim from Calvor who looked like a cop, the one with the tarty girlfriend.

"Hey, we saw you last night. Where are you from, anyway?"

"Canada."

"*Joder*. Where did you start the Camino?"

"St-Jean-Pied-de-Port."

"*Hostia.*" He called a friend over. "Javier, this guy's from *Canadá*. He's walked all the way from France."

"What's he drinking?"

There was a beer in my hand and I was being steered across the floor. "Patricia, Ana. This is Bob from Canada. He's walked all the way from France."

There were five of them, two couples and a single woman who had come to the Camino as separate entities then joined forces in O Cebreiro. Sonia (whom I had to stop thinking of as "the tart") was brash, raspy-voiced, funny and a furious chain-smoker. Marco (who was in fact a cop) was the quiet, manly sort, happy to leave the talking to Sonia. Javi had done the Camino before and loved to toss out nuggets of wisdom. Patricia's eyes sparkled with warm intelligence as she matched Sonia smoke for smoke. Ana had fair skin, sad eyes, a long, fine nose and dark, curly hair, that special Spanish blend of Jewish, Arab and Visigoth good looks. When the waitress came to tell them their table for five was ready, there was no hesitation.

"Can you get us another chair?"

The fun my supper companions were having on the Camino stood in inverse proportion to my misery. They were exactly the noisy, party-making pilgrims I had been running from, and holding in contempt, for a week. But that evening, as they plied me with food and jokes, I forgot how much and with what justice I despised them. I forgot about being a virtuous pilgrim and settled for being a happy one. These were smart, inquisitive, thoughtful people, and it was clear they were all looking for something, and getting something, from the Camino, even if they didn't go about it in a "six ingredients" way. Mostly they were walking the Camino of joyous fellowship, deepening and broadening their circle of compassion (Einstein would have approved) and giving thanks every step of the way for the good things of this earth—especially the food.

Ah, the food. We ate for hours, and all the while my friends, for so I already considered them, talked of food. As if the meal before us were not enough (the platters that kept arriving, the pitchers that were never empty), they recreated other meals, eaten on past trips to Madrid, Catalonia, Murcia, Asturias. They conjured up cheeses, smoked meats, mushrooms, paellas, soups and seafood; and then bottles of *orujo*, *licor de hierbas* and *patxaran* to wash them down. By the time dessert and coffee came around, I felt as if I had eaten a dozen meals.

It was well past midnight, but my friends had made arrangements with the janitor to keep the door of the refuge ajar. They invited me to join them in a further survey of Portomarín's nightlife, but I had already had more fun than I deserved. I thanked them, and went back to my air mattress on the gym floor, where I stretched out with that line from *Twelfth Night* twinkling in my brain: "Dost thou think, because thou art virtuous, there shall be no more cakes and ale?" There would be more cakes and ale, more tortilla and *tinto*, too. And there would be silence and solitude besides. Each in its season. The Camino would provide.

As I lay there, I reconsidered the "six ingredients." For the first time, I noticed one missing: the people. There was no doing the Camino on your own; that was an optical illusion of the consciousness. The Camino was people, and the only way to take people was as they were. I went to sleep feeling full, content and just a little loved.

Jean-Yves the Penitent

The way out of anywhere in Galicia is up a hill. This morning, coming out of Portomarín, it's a slippery, muddy one. Up ahead, something that looks like a blue box-van tilts and teeters through the muck. It turns out to be a sturdy Frenchwoman in her sixties with a backpack as big as a house draped in a vinyl rain sheet.

"*Every* morning on the Camino is like this. Climbing, always climbing. How have I sinned to deserve this? I swear, when this is over, I will never climb a hill again. And this morning we have this horrible mud to make it worse. Please don't slow down, I'll still be climbing this hill tonight. I'll see you in Santiago if these hills don't kill me first." I wish her *bon chemin* and walk ahead, but I'm still within hearing distance when the next pilgrim catches up with her and the complaining resumes. "*Every* morning on the Camino is like this. Climbing, always climbing . . ."

In a few minutes, the man at the receiving end of the latest lament overtakes me. "That woman never changes," he laughs. "'Oh, I cannot take another step. I shall lie down right here and die.' Do you know when the first time was I met her? Six weeks ago, in France, climbing up the hill to the church in Figeac. And she said exactly the same thing then. She is an original, that one."

I know how she feels. My pack weighs a ton this morning. Last night the snorers were in full voice. And all these new pilgrims who started in Sarria, full of beginner's pep—I'd like to wring their peppy necks sometimes. Fortunately, this hasn't shaped up to be the *romería* that I feared, but it's still much busier than I expected for this time of year. The trick is to feed off the energy of the newcomers rather than let them sap mine. Last night a new group from England joined the pilgrimage, two dozen public school students with half again as many adult chaperones. They were all singing "Jerusalem" when I got to the refuge, and I joined in. Since then, every time our paths cross, they break into a rousing chorus: *"And did those feet, in ancient time, walk upon England's mountains green?"* I tell them I doubt it. And then there is the enormous French family: parents, half a dozen children below the age of twelve—one in a baby carriage, one with Down's syndrome—cousins, friends from California, Finland . . . They have been walking the Camino for seven years, a week each year, and this week they will finally arrive. There's enough joy radiating off that bunch to dry wet clothes.

Bert and Oscar set a good example for me. They haven't lost their high spirits in the 1,600 kilometres they've walked from Belgium. Little Oscar tells me he was troubled by snorers last night too. "I got out of bed and gave this fellow a shove, but he was the wrong one. So I shoved someone else, and *he* was the wrong one. I couldn't tell where the noise was coming from, it seemed to be everywhere. I shoved one more, and it was still the wrong one, so I went back to bed."

The hours pass, a step at a time, the stone markers reminding us that we are half a kilometre closer to the end of the road. I would soon lose my sense of distance without them, for among the hills and forests of Galicia there are no distant targets to aim for. You look ahead without seeing where the road is taking you, and back without seeing where you have been. The rain holds off, and it's warm enough to sit outside for lunch, though when a cloud passes in front of the sun, I can see my breath.

I stop to peer into the locked sports complex on the outskirts of Palas de Rei, another of the floors I slept on five summers ago. The gym is closed today, which is unfortunate, not because I have a deep nostalgic yearning to go inside, but because the heavens, which have been storing up rain all day, have split open like a ruptured bladder. It's a ten-minute sprint to the refuge, where I arrive soaked. No more beds? What a shame. I have *no choice* but to take a private room tonight. But my heart goes out to the enormous French family, who are draped all over the reception area of the refuge wondering what to do next.

My rented room comes with ensuite shower and a radiator by which to hang my dripping clothes. There will be no snoring here. I'd say that was worth getting cold and wet for. I put on dry clothes and step outside to find the sun shining and the pilgrims promenading. I stop in for a drink at Bar

Albariño, where five years ago I dined with Jean-Yves, the penitent legionnaire.

Suffering is a thing we almost play at on the Camino these days—walking an extra kilometre on our blistered feet, braving the wind and rain—knowing full well that at the end of the day we will have a dry place to sleep and a hot meal. But there was a time when pilgrims walked the Camino with the intention of bringing suffering upon themselves, the more the better, in hope of redeeming their sins. Some were even sentenced by law to make a pilgrimage of penitence for a year, or a lifetime. Jean-Yves was, to some degree, a throwback to those days.

I first met him over dinner one night on the *meseta*, a wiry man in his forties with a high, balding forehead, a gentle manner and a wise laugh. He introduced himself as a former member of the French Foreign Legion. I guess I didn't take him quite seriously, for I said, "So you used to destabilize democratically elected governments for a living?"

To which he placidly replied, "Well, yes, there was a certain amount of that."

For Jean-Yves, the Camino was a time to think out his future. He had retired on full pension. He had a new name, a new identity, a new history. He was still young enough to chart out a second life. "I have a resumé," he said, "a detailed and very impressive resumé of the imaginary places where I have worked. If anyone calls a phone number on the resumé, someone in an office somewhere will answer and tell them what a splendid employee I was." He was thinking of starting a counselling service for others in his circumstances. There were a lot of them, he said, and many had trouble adapting to dull civilian life.

In most respects, Jean-Yves was a thoroughly modern pilgrim. But he was also something older: a penitent. "There

are things I have done that I don't feel good about," was how
he put it. His was not a rigorous penance of the sort pre-
scribed by tenth-century English canon law: "that a man lay
aside his weapons and travel far barefoot, and nowhere pass a
second night, and fast, and pray fervently, and be so squalid
that iron come not on hair or on nail." Jean-Yves wore good
European walking shoes, prayed with moderation, ate and
slept well, and kept his nails trimmed. Yet he *had* laid aside
his weapons, and on his pilgrimage he travelled far.

In the weeks after our first meeting, we saw each other
often but seldom spoke. His regime was not mine. He would
set out quietly before daybreak, walking swiftly and alone.
In the afternoon he would rest at the refuge before evening
Mass. By the time I came back from dinner, he would already
be sleeping. It wasn't till Palas de Rei that both of us went
looking for a quiet place away from the crowded gymnasium
floor and ended up at the same table in Bar Albariño.

After a glass of wine or two, I told Jean-Yves, "These
crowds are wearing me out. Sometimes I almost wish the
Camino was over."

He replied in the placid tone of one who knows things
you don't. "If you wish the Camino was over, keep walking.
You can walk in your sleep, you know. I've done it a few
times, in Africa. You just hold on to the belt of the one walking in front of you and you can actually fall asleep. Only for
some steps, of course, but a few seconds' sleep can go a long
way in extreme circumstances."

"How far do you think I could cover in one go?"

"With the right incentive, you can easily walk sixty to
seventy kilometres in a day, even carrying a heavy pack."

"So I could be in Santiago tomorrow night?"

"Without doubt. We put artificial limitations on ourselves. We look at our watch and say, 'Oh! It's time to stop.'

But we can keep going. Humans are more resilient than they know." He speared a chunk of octopus with his toothpick, swished it in olive oil and popped it into his mouth. "Walking, in fact, is an underappreciated strategy. Especially when you are in the jungle, where aircraft can't spot you. In one night an army can shift fifty kilometres. They just disappear, without a sound, without a trace. And then they show up somewhere no one expects them to be." I envisioned a massive nocturnal deployment of pilgrims to the gates of Santiago.

All that night, and the next in Arzúa, Jean-Yves spun me tales of that strange ex-job of his: fighting guerrilla wars in Africa, keeping Arafat's bed warm the night he was spirited from Lebanon, swimming at the atoll of Mururoa before the atomic tests. He could talk about it now, or most of it, and he did, unburdening himself to a stranger in precise English, smiling all the while the mild, ironic smile of a man who knows he has done wrong but can't bring himself entirely to regret it.

"Do you think your life will be boring now?"

"Yes, but that is probably a good thing. I still have some years to atone for my sins. Maybe someday I will retire to Addis Ababa. Have you been there? Fascinating place. Lots of old spies. There was one time in Lebanon when I had a gunfight with a Mossad agent. We were not trying to kill each other. You understand that sometimes you shoot at someone without meaning to hit him—though of course things don't always work out as you intend. Anyway, several years later I was in Addis Ababa, reading the newspaper in a café, when I looked up and there he was, sitting at the table across from me, the same Mossad agent. I wasn't sure if he had noticed me or not, so I waited till I caught his eye and then I smiled. And he smiled. And I went on reading my newspaper and he went on drinking his coffee. It was very curious."

As we walked back to the refuge in Arzúa, he started talking about doing bayonet practice on dummies and how, even though the dummies were given synthetic ribs and spines to make the exercise more realistic, it still wasn't the same as the real thing. Then his voice trailed off. That was one story that stayed between him and God.

Where Seldom Is Heard a Discouraging Word . . .

I'm meeting Masa for lunch in Melide. Melide, where great vats of octopus bubble on the street. *Pulpo a feira*—octopus boiled, hacked up and served on a wooden platter with a drizzling of olive oil, a dash of paprika, a fistful of sea salt and a homely side dish of potatoes—is the Galician national dish, and Casa Ezequiel is the most famous local purveyor. It's an unpretentious place that had been dishing up octopus to locals for thirty years before it was "discovered" and proclaimed the Camino's best *pulpería*. Now it is a mandatory stop on *el Camino gastronomico*. A platter of fatty octopus isn't the ideal dish for the midpoint of a day's walk, but I want to see the smile on Masa's face. Octopus is a Japanese favourite, and Masa's tone is reverent when he speaks of *pulpo gallego*.

Ezequiel's house has prospered since I was here last, with a new annex to seat the pilgrim hordes. Masa is waiting for me at one of the long benches. In the seats adjacent, a pilgrim couple with whom I exchanged a few words last night have just finished lunch. Elaine is awfully tall and angular; Dennis taller still, with calm eyes and a manly reserve. They are a handsome couple in their stylish matching leather coats, and apparently in love. They hold hands and share quiet jokes like actors in a commercial for diamond rings.

"Sleep well last night?" I ask.

Dennis smiles. "We did for the first hour or so, until they turned off the heat. But that's about what you can expect in Spain."

"Well, this lunch should warm you up. I see you're drinking red wine. You should try the white with the *pulpo*."

Elaine responds sweetly, "You know, we started with the white, and it was somewhere between vinegar and cider. So then we ordered red, but we couldn't decide if it was more like grape juice or Coke. So finally we just asked for a cup of tea. They managed to get that one right, didn't they, dear?" Dennis caresses her hand. They are united in suffering.

This is not going well. I try another tack. "So tell me about your Camino. Where did you start?"

"We started in September, back in Le Puy," says Elaine.

"You're fast walkers."

"We *are* pretty fast, but we also skipped the *meseta*. Took the bus from Burgos to León. Not that I imagine we missed much." They look at each other and chuckle.

I should know better, but they have poked a stick in my cage. "I'm sorry to hear you say that. I mean, it's true that there's not much to see on the *meseta* in conventional terms, but . . ." They are kind enough to let me maunder on until I'm finished, then Dennis leans across the table and speaks sadly but wisely, laying out his words like well-polished cutlery.

"I'm sure, as you say, that there are nice things to see on the *meseta*. It's just that they are nice by *Spanish* standards, and there is simply nothing in Spain to match the road through France. The food here is horrible. Every day, the same fish soup, the same cutlet, the same bread, the same wine. The refuges are pathetic, dirty, crowded. We've stopped using them altogether—not that the hotels are a great improvement. The churches in Spain are always closed. In France, you can go into any church anytime and sit as long as you like. Here you can only imagine what would happen if they were left open. There would be graffiti everywhere. The Spanish have no respect for their holy places. Or the environment. The garbage by the paths is a disgrace . . ."

There is more, all equally depressing. Elaine corroborates his testimony now and then with a sigh or a shake of her lovely head. They are both very sad that Spain is such a dreadful place. Very disappointed. I'd like to say a word in the nation's defence, but I know it will only prolong the agony. Eventually Dennis is done. He drains the dregs of his awful Spanish wine and sits back, looking relieved but not happy, like someone who has just had a painful bowel movement.

I feel sorry for the two of them. If they hate what they're doing so much, why don't they do something else? At the same time, I can see that they're happy to have something to complain about. They have brought the habits of a culture of complaint with them and, travelling together as they are, they have been too insulated from the Camino to lose them. The worst thing about their negativity is that it's infectious. Listening to them bitch makes me want to bitch too. My head feels as if it's full of wasps. Just in time, the wooden platters of *pulpo* arrive, glowing with olive oil, and the basket of fresh bread and the earthenware pitcher of young wine.

Dennis and Elaine have been distracting me from Masa, but now I catch the look on his face as the plates hit the table. His eyes are seeing the glory. The wasps are swept out of my head by a gust of gratefulness, for Masa's smile, for this gorgeous meal, and—why not?—for Dennis and Elaine, who have reminded me that for the past four weeks I have scarcely heard anyone complain. I have been in the company of people who give thanks for small comforts and laugh when things don't go their way. Masa and I click cups to the Camino.

The Stick That Spoke

After lunch, I call Michiko from the refuge in Melide, putting Masa on the line for a minute so that he can have the pleasure of speaking his own language. Then he toddles off for a nap. Heavy with octopus, I'd happily do the same, but the sky is clear and I don't want to miss out on any good walking. I have stayed in Melide before, anyway, the second time I did the Camino, when I met the False Templar and my stick spoke to me.

There are true Templars out there, but the one I met in Palas de Rei was a false one. I was napping on a top bunk when he walked over and rested his elbows on the mattress. He was lean and well muscled, bearded, in his late twenties. He told me he had been walking for five months on a pilgrimage for world peace. He had a large blue album in which he was collecting signatures. So far, 442 people had signed— would I like to be number 443? I have nothing against world peace, so I jotted down my name and a note of encouragement and hoped he would go away. Something about him made me squirm.

"Thanks," he said. "When I get to Santiago, I'm going to call up the Archbishop and say, 'Hey, José Luis,' and he'll say, 'Don't call me José Luis,' because that's the kind of jerk he is.

But when I show him this album, he'll change his tune. He'll say a Mass for everyone who's signed it. It'll be in the media as well. This is an important movement."

He produced his pilgrim's passport and pointed to a smudge on the first page. "Do you see this? It certifies that I am a Templar of the Order of Ponferrada. That means I'm a defender of the Camino and the pilgrims on it. Here"—he drew a wooden tau from under his collar—"this is my Templar's Cross."

It was an Antonian cross and I told him so. He shrugged. "The Antonians were Templars too. All defenders of the Camino are one. Listen, friend, can you lend me some money to buy a sandwich? I need support to continue my pilgrimage of peace."

I forked over a couple of hundred pesetas and he joined his hands in thanks. "You are a friend of peace. Let me give you my energy." He closed his eyes and laid a cold, inert hand on my chest. After a minute he tugged it away and gave it a shake. "I'd better quit now or I won't have any left. You're draining me." He went back to his bed and turned on his radio.

The next day, I walked hard to get to Melide in time for lunch at Casa Ezequiel. I stopped off first at the refuge, where already a tinny radio was filling the dorm with noise. The Templar was lying on his back in bed, candles at either hand as at the tomb of a saint. I had left him looking exactly like this in Palas de Rei in the morning, and he hadn't passed me on the road. Had the angels of peace flown him here, mattress and all?

"I don't like walking on days like this," he informed me. It sounded like the preface to something I wasn't in the mood to hear. I found a bunk in a part of the room where the Templar wasn't and dumped my backpack on it. Then I stood my stick at the head of the bed and hung my hat off its forked handle. This was the stick that Little Miguel had found for me on the way down from Roncesvalles, the one I called my goose-footed stick for the way it branched at the top like a *pata de oca*, and it had been in my hand for four weeks.

"Are you going out?" asked the Templar. "I'll watch your things."

My things were not worth stealing; no one had ever volunteered to watch them before. I guessed it came with defending the Camino.

"I'd appreciate that. See you later."

"May peace be with you."

I arrived at Casa Ezequiel late for lunch and early for supper. But Señor Ezequiel didn't shoo me away. He limped over on his bad leg and administered the sacraments: wine, bread, soup and *pulpo*. My appetite gratified him, and he kept coming back with more bread and wine. Everything he laid before me went down my throat till I was full to the brim. Then I sat back, closed my eyes and let myself drift. I was just on the verge of sleep when a voice came swimming up like an octopus from the murky waters of my consciousness:

Don't forget your stick!

There was no need to think of my stick just then; I wasn't going anywhere. I yawned and laid my head on my arms, but the words floated up once more. *Your stick. Don't forget your stick.* I tried to ignore them, but they kept on prodding. I sat up, shook the sleep out of my head—and realized that there was nothing to worry about. I hadn't even brought my stick with me. I had left it at the refuge, standing by my bed, under the eye of the Templar. But I had been stirred from my torpor, so I offered my compliments to Señor Ezequiel and weaved my way home. My bag was on the bed where I'd left it, my hat was on top. I stuffed them both under the bed and went off to sleep.

Several hours later, I woke with a start. The dorm was dark and still, everyone else was sleeping. I reached for my stick, knowing already I wouldn't find it. I ran my mind back to midday, saw myself standing the stick by the bed and hanging my hat off it. But when I came back from Casa Ezequiel, my hat had been on my backpack. What had happened to my stick? I dropped to the floor and felt beneath the bed. I padded between the rows of sleepers, peeking under bunks, poking toes into corners, hoping no one would wake. (At three in the morning, who would believe I was looking for a stick?) I searched the common room and the washroom. Nothing. I would have to wait till morning.

I was up at first light, prowling around. Then I realized there was one place I hadn't looked. The refuge had an upstairs. It was supposed to be closed for the winter, but it wouldn't hurt to check. I slipped up the stairs, snooped around the dorm, peeked into the bathroom . . . and there it was, my stick, tucked into the corner behind the door. My fingers closed around it with relief and anger. I could understand someone stealing credit cards, a passport, a watch—but a stick? What kind of monster would steal a pilgrim's stick?

The Templar was standing on the porch when I came down, waiting for the rain to start. "Ah, you found it. You know, if I were you, I'd put it back and wait to see who walked out with it."

I thanked him for the suggestion, wished him all the best on his pilgrimage of peace and took off before he could hit me up for bus fare.

All the way to Arca, my stick ran ahead of me like a dog on the trail. I watched it with new eyes. Had this piece of wood spoken to me? Yesterday, as I floated in a soup of octopus and wine, had I heard a voice I usually screened out? Maybe the world was more full of wonders than I gave it credit for. I thought of Roberto the Magus, with his bowing wheat and moving rocks, and wished he were there so he could have the satisfaction of saying "I told you so."

I walked by myself that day, but I wasn't alone. My stick was with me, and so was the man or woman who carved it and left it by the path, and Little Miguel who gave it to me. The trees were with me too; the birds, the rain, the sky; the pulsing, breathing, pensive earth.

A Town Called Wisdom

I open my eyes. The stars above me are fading. How did I get here? Then it all comes back. The Spanish man in the next bunk snoring like a motorboat ("I could feel his breath on my face," a Frenchwoman tells me later), the midnight trot through the rain to the gazebo, where I fitted two benches together to make a base for my foam mattress, cocooning in my sleeping bag against the cold . . . The rain has stopped now, but I hear the rush of the river by the refuge of Ribadiso, the sweet sound that persuaded me to stay here last night instead of continuing to Arzúa. "This looks like a place where a pilgrim could get a good night's sleep," I thought, forgetting the fundamental truth that on the Camino a good night's sleep is not a matter of where, but with whom.

In the town of Arzúa there is a place where I can check my email. It's not open till ten and I don't like to cool my heels when the skies are clear, but I have a feeling someone wants to talk to me. Sure enough, there is a message from Nuala. The girls made it as far as Sarria before Kara's tendons gave out. But the party in Finisterre is still on and, perfect hostesses that they are, they will be there, Saffron too. They're busing to Finisterre today, and they'll go back to Sarria next week to pick up the walking. Why don't I join their party at the end of the world? Then we can all finish the Camino together.

"Have a great time. See you next week in Santiago," I write. It takes me a minute to hit SEND.

There's another message in my box. It's from Mathilde the potato thief. I contacted her a few months ago and got a message back about her post-Camino adventures. When she arrived in Santiago last fall, she saw a flyer for a local theatre school. She had always dreamed of studying music and dance; now she was happily enrolled in her second year. In today's message she says: "So you're back in Spain. Call me when you get to Santiago. One more thing, you said you didn't know why you keep coming back to the Camino. Is it perhaps because the Camino wants to teach you something and you have to repeat it till you learn it? Couldn't that be right? Well, keep going, keep writing, keep walking."

There is a breeze stirring and enough warmth from the sun to dry yesterday's wet clothes. The backpacks ahead of me are festooned with socks, shirts and undies, fluttering like hands in a car window—*We're going to Santiago!* From Arzúa to Santiago is about forty kilometres, a longish walk, though Jean-Yves the legionnaire would say you could do it in your sleep. Most pilgrims stop partway—in Arca, or Monte de Gozo—so that they can arrive in the city early and catch the midday pilgrim Mass. Five years ago, I nearly walked right to the end.

In the days after I had been befriended in Portomarín, my gloom lifted. I started talking to, instead of sneering at, the happy pilgrims, and when I wanted to be alone, it only took a little patience; there was always space between the walkers if you waited for it. But while I had recovered my equilibrium,

I had lost my Spanish friends. It happened the morning after we met. We were walking together from Portomarín when the rain began to pour down. I ran ahead to a bar, where I stopped to wait for them. They never arrived. The Camino had swallowed them up.

On the second-last day of my Camino, I woke on the gym floor in Arzúa. My stick and my bag were beside me, my only companions. I scanned the bleachers just in case my Spanish friends had arrived in the night; they had not. I looked for Jean-Yves, but he was already out walking. And then I made up my mind. Over the previous five weeks I had had the experience of a lifetime. There was no need to draw it out for another day. I was one long walk from Santiago. If it came down to choosing between another night on a gym floor or pushing on to the end of the road, I knew what I would do.

I covered the nineteen kilometres to Arca as fast as my sore feet would carry me, sensing all along that it was a futile gesture. Why should Arca be different from any of the places since O Cebreiro? It would be packed, noisy, festive and lonely. Full of people I didn't know, nice people to be sure, but it was too late in the game to be making new starts. Sure enough, when I got to Arca, the line of pilgrims already ran from the front door of the refuge up the hill to the highway. In an hour they would pour in and fill every space except the one under the kitchen table. The question had been settled for me. I turned and kept walking.

Then I heard someone call my name. I looked back and saw Patricia running after me. "Where are you going?"

"Santiago."

"Forget it, you're staying with us."

The rest of my Spanish friends were waving from the head of the line. Patricia dragged me back to them. There were kisses and hugs, and then the three women marched me up to the door of the refuge. They banged till a sheepish hospitalero stuck his head out.

"This guy has walked from France," said Sonia. "Let him in."

"Unless he walked from France this morning, he can wait like everybody else," said the hospitalero. "Don't worry, we always save beds for pilgrims who come from Roncesvalles."

As we waited for the doors to open, Sonia and Patricia threw together some lunch for me and got me caught up on what had happened since we had seen each other last.

"Oh, Bob, we've eaten so well. In Palas de Rei we had this *pulpo* you wouldn't believe, and last night in Ribadiso, what a feast . . ."

"What happened to you that morning after Portomarín?"

"Well, you ran ahead when the rain started, but we kept on walking. Then this little van pulled over and offered us a ride. The people owned a country inn, and they invited us to stay that night. It was fantastic. They dried our clothes by the fire and fed us till we couldn't eat any more. We were up all night with them, talking and drinking. We kept saying, 'If only Bob were here.' Next morning they drove us back to where they picked us up and we started walking again."

At one, the doors of the refuge opened. The hospitalero smiled as he stamped my credentials. "So you're the one who walked from France in one day. We've got a bed for you in the no-snoring section. Come on."

But the women had a hold of me. "He's coming with us. We have a place for him upstairs." One took my backpack, another my stick, and they swept me up to a cozy white alcove. In that moment, Arca became my ark. A little home floating on a foreign sea. I didn't know how to thank my friends for what they had given me. Tears would have been excessive, so I showed my appreciation in the way that seemed most appropriate: I climbed up onto my bunk, pulled back the crisp sheets and fell fast asleep.

Hours later, over dinner, Javi laid out the plans for next day. We would be out before six in order to reach Santiago in time for Mass. At night we would stop for one drink at every bar in the Rùa do Franco, from the Café de Paris to the Bar Dakar: "the Paris–Dakar." And then we began to talk about a rumour that had been buzzing along the pilgrim telegraph about what else tomorrow might bring. Earlier that summer, the couturier Paco Rabanne had published a book predicting the end of the world. According to his reading of Nostradamus, the space station Mir was even at that moment hurtling through space on a crash course with Paris, where it would explode with the impact of a million Hiroshima bombs. It gave us one more reason to get up early. If the world was going to end tomorrow, we wanted to see Santiago first.

Arca, the ark, is my destination today. I have no thought of going farther. The day passes in a blur of meetings and partings. The rain comes and goes. These last forty or fifty kilometres before Santiago are the Camino's most featureless, as if everything were now being saved for the end. I measure my steps, trying to live each one, so it's almost dark as I reach Arca. A last cloudburst hits ten minutes before the refuge, and I step in the door dripping and laughing. "It's me, I'm back!"

It is dangerous returning to places where we have been happy once. Today's hospitalero is not cheerful and welcoming like the one who greeted me five years ago. He's a churl, shouting at the children of the enormous French family for getting the floor wet. I won't let him bring me down. I turn and head upstairs to look for my warm, bright corner. But the upstairs alcove, so white in my memory, has turned black with mildew. The place feels cold, damp, unclean. How has this happened?

I know that things don't stay as we left them, that nothing is immune to time. But does the Camino have to rub it in? Especially on the last night . . . I look around and see no one I know, no one I can explain to. I turn and go back down the stairs. A hundred metres down the highway, there is a bar with rooms to rent. Maybe I'll be alone there, but I'll be alone with my white memories.

I lock the door of my private room. I'm sulking, being ridiculous. But it's the end of the road; I don't care. I seek comfort in the physical amenities of twenty-first-century pilgrimage: a shower, a shave, heat from a radiator, a lie-down on a freshly turned bed. Then, feeling somewhat composed, I step down to the bar for a quiet drink. Who knows, maybe someone will come and keep me company.

And who is there but Raymond, my little French Buddhist. How long since we've seen each other? Was it really the *meseta*? We embrace and he tells me in a hoarse voice that he's been down with bronchitis, resting on doctor's orders. The quiet woman with him is a pilgrim I have been nodding to for several days, thinking, "It's too late to be making new starts." Soon we're deep in a discussion of that topic that never gets old, Why Are You Doing the Camino? I'm sorry that I didn't make the effort to talk to her sooner. I'm glad to have the chance now. Next come Eduardo and Manuela from Barcelona, another couple I haven't really talked to. Tonight I'll have supper with them. Soon Georges pops in, Big Bert and Little Oscar in matching sweaters, Eileen and Julie, Marina. It is the last night of the Camino; there is still time to celebrate.

At 4:30 a.m., I am suddenly awake, seeing the world with that diamond clarity that it sometimes has when we're still this close to dreaming. It's something from Mathilde's email: "Perhaps the Camino wants to teach you something and you have to repeat it till you learn it? Couldn't that be right?" Yes, of course that's right. That's why I'm here. To repeat until I learn. I forget so quickly the lessons the Camino teaches me, but it is a patient teacher. It keeps calling me back in the hope that next time I will learn a little better, remember a little longer. And then I see what I've been walking towards all along. It's that little town called Wisdom, the place where you live by what you've learned.

One More Hill to Climb, One More Bridge to Cross

Pilgrims out walking before dawn with flashlights, fireflies in the eucalyptus. Everyone is alert, laughing. Almost there, almost there. Some drops of rain, then a rumble in the mist, not thunder but a plane landing at Lavacolla airport—Lavacolla, where in the days before hot showers, pilgrims washed (*lavar*) their privates (*colla*) before presenting themselves to the Apostle. And there's Charley the photographer, waist-deep in the frigid river, one hand down his shorts, doing it right. Outside the last bar before Santiago, the English public school students are lying in wait for me: *God save our gracious Queen* . . . There will always be an England. Inside, I meet a Bostonian who doesn't know the Red Sox have won the Series. Oh, world of wonders.

Then one last hill, Monte de Gozo, *mons gaudii*, the mount of Joy, from whose summit the pilgrim at last sees Santiago. I think of old María, maybe tomorrow or the next day, hauling her bundle buggy up while Monsieur Rickman sings pilgrim hymns in his warm baritone. In the old days, they say, pilgrims raced to be first to the top. Then, when they saw the cathedral below, almost close enough to touch, they would fall to the ground, weeping, praying, praising God. There'll be no such performances this morning. The mountain of joy is completely fogged in.

Well, there's no point waiting for the mist to clear. I know the way from here. Down through the sprawling campus of the Monte de Gozo refuge, big enough to hold a thousand pilgrims. I find most of last night's crowd taking a last breather at the big cafeteria. The moment is upon us, though Georges plans to drain it to the lees. "I will stay here tonight, then go down to Santiago at eight in the morning, when the church bells are ringing, and have the cathedral all to myself." Only Eileen displays anything like medieval-style emotions. "I really didn't expect to feel this," she gasps between flash floods of tears. Then one and two at a time, for the last time, we gather our things and step into the day. The fog has lifted, the sun is shining, the freshly washed city of the Apostle glints below.

At the base of Monte de Gozo there is a bridge. No river runs under it; it's just a highway overpass that you'd cross without noticing if it weren't for the sign in the middle that says *Santiago*. And here I stand for the third time in my life, feeling, I can't deny, a twinge of sadness to be crossing it alone. Every time I've crossed it alone. That has been my choice, or my destiny, or the way things have worked out.

Five years ago I should have crossed it with my Spanish friends. We set out early from Arca as planned, tromping through corridors of dappled light. Then, just before Monte de Gozo, I started to walk ahead. In the old pilgrim style, I wanted to be first to the top, waiting for them when they got there so I could point at Santiago and say, "Look!" as if it were something of mine that I could share with them. So I raced to the top and I waited. Half an hour later, I was still waiting. I walked back a ways to look, but I couldn't find them. Once more, the Camino had swallowed them. When I could wait no longer, I walked down the hill beneath glorious, high white clouds and—on a day when the world did not end—crossed the bridge to the city of the Apostle alone.

The second time too, I was alone. That time it seemed natural. I came late in the year and there were many days when I didn't see another pilgrim. The last day was no different.

But now, for a third time . . . Well, it's not a big deal, this bridge. You've still got a distance to walk when you hit the other side, it's not like you've *arrived*. And what does Santiago mean to me, anyway? Isn't it just the excuse for the journey? Still, there's that sign . . . I'll tap it with my stick when I pass, like the other times, and think of some pilgrims I'd like to cross this bridge with. Karl, Pepe, Kara and Nuala, German John, Jean-Yves, Michiko. Someday. Next time. Not today.

I have leisure to entertain these thoughts because right now I am stuck behind a pilgrim bottleneck. The enormous French family is preparing to cross the bridge. After seven summers of walking, they are on the verge of arriving, and they want Santiago to know it. Mother stands at the head of the procession. She has made a cross from two sticks and twined it round with flowers. Now she raises it high for all to see and begins to sing a song of joy. Children and adults join hands and all together they set out across the bridge. It's only a highway that flows below them, but to hear them singing you'd think it was the river Jordan.

I watch them clear to the other side, my stick clutched to my chest, my feet rooted. Where have they come from, these tears? What is this thing splitting my chest? Is it joy or pain?

Sorrow or relief that this all must end? It is all these things. Just when you think you know the Camino, it pulls one more surprise for you. I stand like a child, not knowing how to put one foot in front of the other. And then I think of them, all the pilgrims who have passed this way. They tell me, "You're not alone. We're here with you. We've been here all along. Take our hands now and we'll cross together. It's time."

The End of the Road

What can I say about the city of Santiago that hasn't been said before and better? Maybe I should just go along with the German scribe Schaseck, who described it as "a small town of moderate size and not too large." Schaseck's Santiago was surrounded by a narrow moat and a single wall with square towers on whose ramparts grew great quantities of yellow violets and ivy. Today the violets, the towers, the ramparts are gone and the city is wrapped around by motorways. If you are the rare pilgrim whose critical faculties have not dissolved in the emotions of this moment, you are braced for a letdown. What city could live up to all those expectations? But then you pass through the city walls and enter the narrow, climbing, winding, car-free streets, clamorous with pilgrims, and catch your first glimpse of the cathedral's spires against the sky . . .

If any city can repay the toil, the blisters, the nights of snoring, it is Santiago. If it's only the excuse for the journey, it's a good excuse. More beauty, joy, devotion, tears, humanity, love and, yes, gold have been packed into this small circle than it could ever possibly hold. It is a place of overabundance. At its centre is the symbol of what Santiago is and has been, the Plaza de Obradoiro, welcoming, intimate, yet grand enough to hold a million pilgrims, and at its head the glorious Cathedral of Santiago—aspiring, intricate, its towers and pinnacles alive with lichen, clover and blotchy spores that make it shine orange and green in the sunlight like some North Atlantic Angkor Wat.

All roads in Santiago lead to the cathedral. In Holy Years, you can enter at the back, by the *puerta santa*, a door that is walled up the rest of the time—though it escapes me why anyone would want to enter by any way except the front doors, through the medieval sculptural ensemble of angels and Apostles known as the *pórtico de la gloria*, where a pacific Saint James waits to welcome you home. You place your fingers in the grooves worn into the Tree of Jesse by millions of pilgrim fingers, then head up the aisle for the *abrazo*, the embrace of the statue of the Apostle. On weekends like this, pilgrims line up for hours to climb to the high altar of the cathedral, put their arms around James's shoulders and murmur a prayer in his ear. After, they stay for Mass, where the new arrivals sit in a designated area as the priest calls out welcomes to "ten pilgrims from France, four from Germany, one from Canada . . ." before everyone sits back to gasp at the cannonball flight of the *botafumeiro*, the massive silver-plated censer that hurtles on its chain like a rocket-powered pendulum to the heights of the transept, then swoops back low enough to ruffle the hair on pilgrims' heads.

Once the ancient rituals have been performed and the Compostela obtained, there is no end of things to do in Santiago. There are museums, galleries, churches and historic buildings, indoor and outdoor concerts, street performers, restaurants, shops, bars and even a 3-D show, *El Camino Virtual*, that lets you walk the Camino without taking a step. The city itself is an endless source of wonder, a labyrinth where you sometimes run into yourself walking down the same street you walked up ten minutes before. But the real pleasure of Santiago for the pilgrim is waiting for the chickens (or the geese?) to come home to roost. In Santiago, we catch up with the pilgrims who got here before us and wait for the ones who are yet to arrive. Mysteries are solved and storylines tied up. My first time, I met up again with Hedwige the Cat Lady and Bénédicte, sisters reunited at last. (Peregrino the pussycat had traded in his cardboard box for a comfy carrying case and was on his way to France.) I saw Montse too, Roberto the Magus, my Spanish friends (who explained that Ana had come down with a charley horse at the foot of Monte de Gozo) and others. This time, there's my Inuk friend Rhoda, Helen and Hayley, María of the bundle buggy. Charley the photographer plays "The Sound of Silence" at pilgrim Mass in the cathedral. John from Derry accosts me in a bar and says, "For God's sake, Bob, don't put me in your book. I've got a family, man." I'll see Kara, Nuala and Saffron next week after I come back from Finisterre. Pepe and Masa, alas, remain unaccounted for.

Yet with all this to be happy for, Santiago is also a place of sadness. It is the great orphanage at the end of the road where the children of the Camino gather one last time before they scatter like dandelion seeds to their own countries, their old lives. There is no next refuge to walk to, no next horizon to aim for. And no number of Masses, *abrazos* and last suppers with friends can fill the gap in our hearts or our days.

I spend three days in Santiago. Luisa Rubines's wonderful photo exhibition on the Goose Game is on display at the

Museum of Pilgrimages. There are backlit photos on the walls of the darkened gallery, and on the floor a spiral game board lit from below. There are big cushiony dice to roll. While I'm there, a group from a local elementary school walks the Camino of mystery. I spend a day with Mathilde the potato thief, hearing all about her happy life in Santiago. At first she paid her expenses by waitressing, but now she's found the ideal part-time job, helping out on a farm. I ask if she remembers Maite, Paco and Julio.

"The man in the wheelchair? I saw him last fall in Santiago. The others weren't with him, but his wife was. I think they went together for the last part. She was a nice woman and they looked very happy together. He was quiet with her, a different person."

One day, as I stand transported by the cacophony of the cathedral bells in the Plaza de Obradoiro, Big Bert and Little Oscar join me. "Can you believe this racket?" asks Oscar, who plays the church organ back in Antwerp. "It's like a cook with a big spoon banging his pots and pans." To each his own.

I remember to say a prayer at the high altar of the cathedral for two pigeon eggs in a motherless nest.

And one night, over supper at Casa Manolo, I listen as a passionate French-Canadian man tells the table, "If there was one thing about the Camino that I will always remember, it was meeting a sailor named José, a remarkable man who has walked *everywhere*. What an inspiration it was to . . ." Somehow I hold my tongue.

Then it is time to go, because for a pilgrim Santiago is not a home, it is a goal. There was a man I met once coming back on the overnight bus, Ramón, a security guard from Madrid. "The thing I love best about Santiago," he told me, "is arriving. I've done the Camino several times, and I always make sure that I have time to finish. There are some people who, one year they'll go from Roncesvalles to Burgos, the next year from Burgos to Léon . . . Me, if I have four days to walk, I start in Sarria. If I have two weeks, I start in León. But I always arrive."

Maybe that is the way. To be always arriving.

PART V

To Finisterre

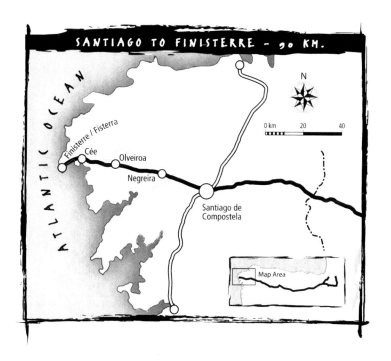

Last Word

In Luisa Rubines's photo exhibition of the Goose Game, the sixty-third and final square does not show Santiago, but the beach at Finisterre. The eye of the camera looks into a bonfire and sees, through the flames and smoke and heat haze, a naked woman walking to the ocean. She has left her old life behind—the clothes burning on the beach. Now she goes to drown and be reborn. There *is* one horizon beyond Santiago. *Finis terrae*, "the end of land," where the brown-green earth meets the cold blue element.

The pilgrimage to Finisterre is not a New Age innovation. Pilgrims have been going the extra hundred kilometres since at least the early 1100s, "officially" to see the miraculous Christ of Finisterre, unofficially to gaze at the mighty Atlantic. It may be they have been going for much longer; the symbol of the Camino is a scallop shell, after all. For many pilgrims, the trip to the ocean is more than just a coda to their Camino. The Cathedral of Santiago, though it welcomes all, will always be first a Spanish, Catholic place. The ocean belongs to no people, no creed, no time. In the cathedral of sea and sky, we are all free to worship in our own way.

On previous Caminos, I have gone to Finisterre by bus. The time has come for me to walk. I start on November 1, *el día de los difuntos*, when the souls of the departed return to the earth. It doesn't sound like a propitious day to start a journey, but this is the road to the west, to the sunset and the world's imagined end. German pilgrims of old had their own fanciful etymology for the name Finisterre: *finster Stern*, they called it, "dark star." I bid goodbye to the Cathedral of Santiago, the place I have walked so far to reach. It has ceased to be a destination and become a point of departure. The journey begins once more.

It is a hundred kilometres to Finisterre—three days of villages, farms, rolling hills, forests and rivers. Horses and ponies stand on the hillsides. In the morning, women wait in doorways for the bread truck to come. There are windmills, oak groves, wizened peasants pushing wheelbarrows piled with vegetables. And a sense of freedom. There are fewer than twenty of us now, including Charley and Raymond. The silence, the green hills, the road are all ours. On the third day, just as the rain lets up, I reach the deepwater inlet of Cée, with its smell of ocean. The path rises to trace the headland. Tantalizing glimpses of blue flash through the trees. And then I see it, the cape of Finisterre, that great surge of land, with the lighthouse at its tip. The path falls to sea level and ahead there is only miles of white sand, shingle and scallop shells by the bucket.

The refuge in the village of Finisterre ("Fisterra" in *gallego*) is not open to pilgrims who arrive by bus. The Finisterrans are proud of their pilgrimage, even issuing their own certificate, the Fisterrana. The hospitalera checks my credentials for the stamps of Negreira and Olveiroa, the refuges after Santiago, then runs a Fisterrana off the printer for me. Technology in the service of tradition. She points the way to La Galería, Roberto's bar, where I mean to collect the drink he promised

me three weeks back in San Juan de Ortega. Opening the
doors on the long, narrow room with the French windows
at the back overlooking the harbour, I have my final déjà vu
of this Camino. This is the bar where I stopped at the end of
my first Camino, the place where my first book began.

Roberto is alone, reading. *"Peregrino!"* He pours me a
beer and tells me about his Camino in that singsong Galician
accent that leaves me always a few words behind the meaning. I learn that just a few days ago La Galería served as the
venue for Kara and Nuala's end-of-the-world party. I am
honoured to hear that my name was mentioned in the course
of a "Whatever happened to . . .?" conversation, when an
Australian pilgrim named Aaron recalled a Canadian fellow
he had met way back when. Then I tell Roberto that not only
have I been to his bar before, I've written about it.

"It's amazing that I couldn't remember when you asked
me. I loved this place. But I didn't see you that time. There
was a different guy, tall and skinny."

"Luis," Roberto confirms. "There's a photo of him on the
corkboard over there."

"Yes, that's him." It's easy to pick him out, with his high
forehead and prominent Adam's apple. "The thing I remember is that it was lunchtime, and he opened the windows and
leaned out and made this incredible *Aaaooooooooo* sound, like
an air-raid siren, and then he called out in this megaphone
voice: 'Attention! Attention! It is now one o'clock, the hour
of the *tapa*,' and all the guys down on the docks dropped what
they were doing and came up for a drink."

"Yeah," Roberto chuckles, "the siren was one of his specialties. One time he did it on national television. They called
him *el fantástico*. He could make any sound you can think of,
machine sounds, animal noises, cartoon characters . . ."

"Does he still work here?"

"No," says Roberto. "He doesn't work here anymore."
Then he makes a universal gesture, tipping his head to one
side and raising an arm. "Did himself in. A couple of years
ago. The guy had problems . . ."

The world keeps turning. We all must follow our own
Camino. I thank Roberto for the drink and tell him I'll be
back tomorrow to check out the library. Now, before the sun
goes down, it is time to go to the lighthouse.

The lighthouse is an hour or so from the town. The time is
hard to estimate because it's impossible not to stop and look
out at the ocean, or go clambering up the slope to the spine
of the promontory. The land is bare, brambly, littered with
boulders, like a neolithic playground. The lighthouse stands
at the very end. This being Spain, there is a bar in the lighthouse at the end of the world. You stand on the rocks behind
the lighthouse and feel you have really reached a limit, the
end of the road. But it's only a feeling. The road never ends.
Tomorrow you're still walking it, wherever you may be.

Still, there's an urge to turn this comma into a chapter
break, or at least a period, in the book of life. That's why pilgrims burn a piece of their clothing on these rocks, as a sign
or assertion that here something has ended, and a prayer that
from here something new will begin. Today at least, I don't
feel the need for this ritual. Let the story roll on like a road.
No, it's the other ritual I've come for today, the one that has
taken place every day since the ocean was born and will take
place still when none of us are left to watch it: the sun plung-
ing into the sea (in the words of the Roman general Decimus
Junius Brutus) "like a steaming, red-hot iron." Thirty or so
of us have turned up for tonight's show. I recognize one of
them: Monsieur Rickman. We have not seen each other since
our discussion in O Cebreiro. I am sure he believes he has

offended me. Our eyes meet across the distance and I would like to greet him, but that will have to wait.

We sit in silence, ranged out over the rocks, watching the big red ball go down. A cloud bank on the very horizon takes away from the final effect. Still, a satisfying performance. When it is over, the crowd stands, brushes off its pants and heads for the exits. Only Monsieur Rickman goes against the flow, picking his way over the rocks to find me. He stands a moment going over the words in his head. He is wearing a scarf despite the warmth of the day and his toque is pulled down to his eyebrows. He seems to have a cold. He sniffles, and smiles at me with his moist eyes. Then he says what he has to say, slowly, clearly and simply.

"Good luck, good writing, good words, good thoughts . . . and good heart." He takes my hand with touching solemnity.

"I'll do my best," I promise him.

"That will be enough," he replies. "Farewell."

He turns and hastens to the parking lot, where a car is waiting for him, leaving me to consider this final gift of the Camino. What was it he told me in O Cebreiro? *We walk until we meet ourselves. Then we see that the rest was all illusion.*

The ocean douses the sun's last glow. The lighthouse of Finisterre casts a searching eye over the dark sea.

And there is one last memory. That first time, after I heard Luis "el Fantástico" make his air-raid siren call and visited the church of St. Mary of the Sands, I climbed the promontory in the dazzle of the August sun off the waters. I remembered Karl saying that in Finisterre you could watch the whole Camino one more time, like a movie in your head, so I closed my eyes and tried to send my mind back to the narrow pass of Charlemagne where the journey had started five weeks before. But it was hard to be anywhere except where I was, in the now of the sun's heat, the wind's breath, the ocean's low, distant roar.

When I opened my eyes, there was something orange on the rocks above me.

"*Hola, peregrino!*"

"*Hola, peregrina!*"

It was Montse. Her tall hazel staff was in her hand. She sat down with me, and we laughed one more time about the tick, and the journey, and the people we had known. We had never had much success communicating, but that made no difference now. We were two strangers who had shared the same road, and that was enough. I had seen her the first day in Roncesvalles and now here she was in this last place, an orange cotton thread binding beginning to end as tightly as they would ever be bound.

I was happy to stay where I was, but Montse was restless. "Do you think we can go farther down the rocks?" she asked, and without waiting for an answer she was off, springing from boulder to boulder with the agility of a child. When she had gone as far as she could go, she raised her slender arms to the sun and the wind. Then she leaned back, balancing her staff in one hand, and with all her elastic force sent it arcing to the ocean.

"*Gracias!*" she yelled to the void. The call broke, then vanished as cleanly as the staff, snatched away by the wind. "*Gracias!*" she called again. "*Gracias!*" I had no stick to throw, but I stood up and yelled too, as loud as I could, though not as loud or as clear as Montse, who seemed to have had more practice. Then we stood, hoarse and smiling, high above the glittering ocean, and I thought, if the road must end, let it end in this word. *Gracias.*